Detail from the illustrated map of the London Borough of Sutton designed by A. J. Crowe

Five centuries of artists in Sutton ❧

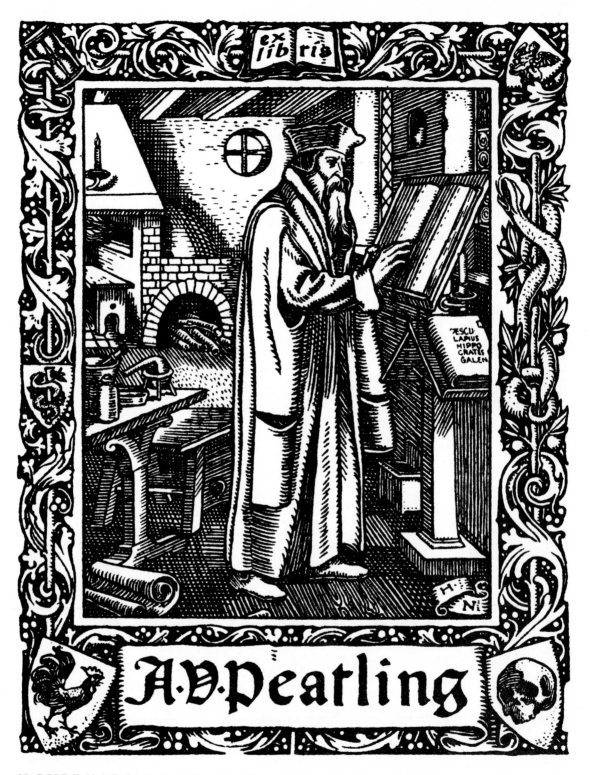

HAROLD E. H. NELSON   Book-Plate (98 × 76 mm) designed for Dr. A. V. Peatling

OPPOSITE: PAULINE NOWLAN   Watercolour 146 × 102 mm
      Portrait of a woman   Private Collection

PAGE 1 (overleaf) MERVYN PEAKE   Indian ink
      Camel   Mervyn Peake Estate
      Reproduced by permission of the Mervyn Peake Estate

FIVE CENTURIES OF ARTISTS IN SUTTON

A Biographical Dictionary of Artists associated with Sutton, London.

Maureen Beasley

❦

Sutton Libraries and Arts Services

Dedication
To my husband, Jimmy, *sine qua non*

Acknowledgements

I should like to express my gratitude to the authorities at Sutton, particularly to Roy Smith, O.B.E., now Director of Leisure Services, and to Martyn Kempson, Borough Librarian, for having the faith in me to undertake the publication of this book, from its inception, and who have provided the continued support and encouragement needed to bring it to completion. I am also indebted to Elizabeth Esteve-Coll, Director of the Victoria and Albert Museum, for her appreciative Foreword to this book.

My special thanks are due to my colleagues June Broughton and Douglas Cluett for their extensive and most willing help derived from their wide knowledge of Sutton's history; to Shirley Edwards to whom the book owes its style and artistry; to Valary Murphy for reading the proofs, and for so much other help; and to George Jenkinson for his fine photographs of pictures in the Local Collection. It would require more space than this to mention all the other individuals who have given help and information; but I should especially like to thank: Patricia Allderidge; Peggy Barnett; Mary Batchelor; Patrick Beasley; Ian Bradley; George Brice; Dawn and Peter Cope; G. F. Crabb; Christopher Dadd, G. T. Dadd and the late Jeanette Robertson Dadd; Gladys Dawson; Jo Evans; John Ford; Stephen Furniss; Peter Geiringer; Millicent Hamilton-Bradbury; John Hind; Peter Horne and the staff of the Music and Arts Library at Sutton; Jennifer Ingham; Linda Jedda; Carole Kendall; the late Mary Lloyd; Beryl Maggs; Sebastian Peake; John Phillips; Frank E. H. Potter; Geoffrey Price; Roy Ray; John Robertson; Audrey Scott; Doris M. Stacey; Auralie Stanton; Winifred Walker; Rita M. Whitney; the late Glenolva Tatton Winter, the late Bill Tatton Winter, Joan Tatton Winter and the late John Tatton Winter.

I should also like to thank the staffs of the following art galleries, auction houses, museums, public libraries and institutions: Abbot Hall Art Gallery, Kendal; Agnews; Art Workers' Guild; Bourne Gallery, Reigate; British Architectural Library, Royal Institute of British Architects; British Museum; Christopher Wood Gallery; Epsom School of Art and Design; Fine Arts Library, Westminster City Library; Herbert Art Gallery, Coventry; London Borough of Croydon Reference Library; National Art Library, Victoria and Albert Museum; Priory Gallery, Cheltenham; Richard Green Gallery; Royal Academy Library; Royal Borough of Kensington and Chelsea Central Reference Library; The Royal Library, Windsor Castle; St Benedict's Studio, Ltd., Wallington; Sotheby's; Sutton College of Liberal Arts; Tate Gallery Library; Whitgift School; Worthing Museum and Art Gallery.

First Published 1989

Sutton Libraries and Arts Services
A department of Sutton Leisure

Central Library, St. Nicholas Way, Sutton, Surrey SM1 1EA
Telephone 01-661 5050
©London Borough of Sutton   Design: Shirley Edwards

ISBN 0 907335 19 5

Printed in Great Britain by John Bentley (Printers) Ltd., Todmorden
A member of the Dunn & Wilson Group

Contents

Foreword

One of the common truisms encountered in art historical circles is that there lies buried in the public library system of this country a great wealth of untapped material on the social and economic background of many important artists and craftsmen, as well as on lesser known figures. There have been isolated attempts to quarry the veins of this rich mine and Local Studies librarians in many authorities have built up impressive indices of local knowledge and association, invaluable to art researchers. However, all too often these files remain in unpublishable form and therefore known to a mere handful of researchers. the London Borough of Sutton is to be congratulated that not only has a member of the library staff, Maureen Beasley, worked long and hard to compile a very comprehensive that not only has a member of the library staff, Maureen Beasley, worked long and hard to compile a very comprehensive list of artists with local associations but that the Director of Leisure Services has taken the decision to publish her findings and so make available a remarkable amount of obscure information which is normally so scattered and diffuse as to be virtually inaccessible to scholars and collectors.

It is to be hoped that the forward looking attitude of the London Borough of Sutton will encourage other art librarians working in local authority areas to organise their research in publishable form and so enrich the collections of primary and secondary research tools available to explore the artistic heritage of this country.

Elizabeth Esteve-Coll

Director, Victoria & Albert Museum

Introduction

My purpose in writing this book is to provide a record of the many artists – some famous, some virtually unknown – and a few of the architects and craftsmen who have lived in, worked in, or had some other connection with what is now the London Borough of Sutton. In this sense it is a book for local people; but I hope it will also serve a wider purpose in being of interest to the increasing number of people throughout the country who study not only the great artists but the countless minor ones as well, particularly from the last century and the first half of this. We have only to note the huge increase in recent times of prices paid for Victorian watercolours, for example, to sense the current enthusiasm. New dictionaries of artists appear regularly, outstanding amongst them in this country being the publications of the Antique Collectors' Club, based at Woodbridge in Suffolk. But it may only be by the work of many researchers like myself, each interested in his or her locality, that we can find out all that people want to know. I should like this book to encourage like-minded researchers to follow my example in studying their local artists, particularly in the boroughs and districts around Sutton. Much is already being done, but there is always more to find out. There would be an added bonus; much of the fascination in art research comes from the discovery of unexpected links between hitherto unconnected artists and societies. Hopefully this can be seen even in this modest work. As other localities are investigated, the interconnecting links should make the work doubly rewarding.

I began my research five years ago, expecting to find perhaps sixty or seventy artists to include here. But the list grew to more than two hundred and, even though more 'Sutton artists' are still coming to light, I felt bound to call a halt or the work would never have been published. Also, I thought it would be appropriate for the book to appear in 1988, the centenary of the foundation of the Surrey Art Circle, now an almost forgotten society but in its heyday the most important art group in Surrey. Sutton can take pride in the fact that the Art Circle was founded here, within a stone's throw of the Central Library, and that five of the eight founder members came from within what is now this borough. The society gained members of national importance and for a considerable period had Sir Alfred Gilbert, the famous sculptor, as President. The Surrey Art Circle continued under this name for forty years before being incorporated with the Southern Society of Artists.

No living artists, so far as I know, (with the exception of Doris Stacey, who no longer practises her art) are entered here, since it would have proved an almost impossible task to decide who to include of the many talented artists now living within the borough's boundaries. Also, I have deliberately given more space to the artists who have, so far, had little published on them. Thus Hans Holbein the Younger, an internationally famous artist, has a much shorter entry than, say, William Tatton Winter, a watercolourist little known outside this country, but with a great significance to the borough, and about whom, so far, little has been written.

For me this has been a rewarding task, except, perhaps, when vital items of information proved totally elusive. I have learned much about the history of Sutton and its surroundings, and discovered something of what it must have been like to have been part of the artistic community of Victorian Sutton. For although some artists were active here in earlier centuries, the great flourishing of art in the borough was during the nineteenth century when, with the coming of the railways, artists were able to move out of London, the centre of the British art world, to more rural areas such as Sutton, Wallington and Carshalton, yet still be within easy reach of the London galleries, art schools and societies.

Through having access to their letters, and reading articles about them in the local newspapers; and also being fortunate enough to meet some of their descendants, I have found that certain artists have become very much alive to me. Nowadays, when I pass Tattenham Corner, I think of the tragic day in 1910 when the promising young architect Lionel Detmar was thrown from a horse and killed; when I visit the National Westminster Bank in Sutton High Street and admire the Art Nouveau stone carvings, I am reminded of Frederick Wheeler, its architect.

As yet there is no public art gallery in Sutton, though there are enough original works of art in the Local Collection to fill one, thanks to the enlightened policy here at Sutton (both now and in the past) of buying works of art of local interest as they appear on the market; and through many generous donations from the public. Works in the collection by the artists featured in this book are listed in the appendix.

Finally, but most importantly, I must draw your attention to my colleagues and friends who gladly came to my aid at a time when writing the book looked a very daunting task, and who contributed entries on artists in whom they have a particular interest or a specialist knowledge. I am most grateful to them all. Their names are appended to their articles. Needless to say, any errors or mistakes in the finished work are mine alone.

M.B.

Abbreviations used in the text

*	Denotes that the artist is represented in Sutton's Local Collection
AA	Associated Artists in Watercolours
AAS	Aberdeen Art Society
AB	Abbey Gallery
AG	Art Gallery
AGN	Agnew & Sons
ALP	Alpine Club Gallery
AMC	Art Masters Certificate
AR	Arlington Gallery
AWG	Art Workers' Guild
b.	Born
B	Royal Society of Artists, Birmingham
BA	Beaux Arts Gallery
BG	Baillie Gallery
BI	British Institution
Bibliog	Bibliography
BM	British Museum
BRU	Bruton Galleries
BWS	British Water-colour Society
c.	Circa
CAR	Carfax & Co Galleries
CAS	Croydon Art Society
CG	Colnaghi & Co Galleries
CHE	Chenil Galleries
CIE	Companion of the Indian Empire
Coll	In the collection of
CON	Connell & Sons Gallery
COO	Cooling & Sons Gallery
d.	Died
D	Dudley Gallery
DOW	Dowdeswell Galleries
Exhib	Exhibition or exhibited
FCIAD	Fellow of the Central Institute of Art and Design
FGS	Fellow of the Geological Society
FIN	Fine Art Society
FRS	Fellow of the Royal Society
FRSA	Fellow of the Royal Society of Arts
FSA	Fellow of the Society of Antiquaries
FZS	Fellow of the Zoological Society
G	Grosvenor Gallery
GCB	(Knight) Grand Cross of the Bath
GI	Glasgow Institute of the Fine Arts
GOU	Goupil Gallery
GRA	Graham Gallery
Hassall's	Art school run by John Hassall, RI (1868–1948)
Heatherley's	Famous London art school, once known as 'A Paris studio in London'
I	International Society of Artists
Illus	Works illustrated
Inst	Institute
ISA	Incorporated Society of Artists
KG	Knight of the Garter
L	Walker Art Gallery, Liverpool
LC	Local Collection
LCC	London County Council
LEI	Leicester Gallery, London
LG	London Group
Lib	Library
LS	London Salon
M	Manchester City Art Gallery
MA	Master of Arts
M InstCE	Member of the Institution of Civil Engineers
M IMechE	Member of the Institution of Mechanical Engineers
MM	Military Medal
Mus	Museum
NEA	New English Art Club
NG	New Gallery
NS	National Society
NWS	New Water Colour Society
OBE	Order of the British Empire
Obit	Obituary
OM	Order of Merit
OWS	Old Water Colour Society
P	Paris Salon
PCAS	President Cathcart Art Society
PL	Public Library
PS	Pastel Society
PSA	Printsellers' Association
RA	Royal Academy
RBA	Royal Society of British Artists
RCA	Royal College of Art
R CamA	Royal Cambrian Academy
RDI	Royal Designer for Industry
RDS	Royal Drawing Society
RE	Royal Society of Painter-Etchers and Engravers
RED	Redfern Gallery
RHA	Royal Hibernian Academy
RI	Royal Institute of Painters in Watercolours
RIBA	Royal Institute of British Architects
RMS	Royal Miniature Society
ROI	Royal Institute of Oil Painters
RP	Royal Society of Portrait Painters
RSA	Royal Scottish Academy
RSMA	Royal Society of Marine Artists
RWA	Royal West of England Academy
RWS	Royal Society of Painters in Water Colours
SAC	Surrey Art Circle
SAM	Society of Art Masters
SAP	Society of Artist Printmakers
SBA	Society of British Artists (later Royal)
SGA	Society of Graphic Art
Slade	The Slade School of Art, London
South Kensington	National Art Training School, later the Royal College
Studio	The Studio Magazine
Sutton's Local Collection	The local collection held by the Heritage Division of Sutton Leisure Services
SWA	Society of Women Artists
TOO	Arthur Tooth & Sons Gallery
V&A	Victoria and Albert Museum
WG	Walker's Galleries, London
WIAC	Women's International Art Club
WWA	West Wickham Art Group

Selective General Bibliography, with abbreviations used in the text

BEN	BÉNÉZIT, E. *Dictionnaire critique et documentaire des Peintres, Sculpteurs, Dessinateurs et Graveurs*. France: Librairie Grund, 1976, 10 vols.
HART (1)	BROOK-HART, D. *British 19th Century Marine Painting*. Antique Collectors' Club, 1974
HART (2)	BROOK-HART, D. *20th Century British Marine Painting*. Antique Collectors' Club, 1981
BRIGHTLING	BRIGHTLING, G. B. *History and Antiquities of Carshalton*. London: Operative Jewish Converts' Institution, 1872
CHERRY	CHERRY, B. and PEVSNER, N. *London 2: South*. Buildings of England, Penguin, 1983
COLVIN	COLVIN, H. M. *A Biographical Dictionary of British Architects 1660–1840*. J. Murray, 1954
COYSH	COYSH, A. W. *Dictionary of Picture Postcards in Britain*. Antique Collectors' Club, 1984
DNB	*Dictionary of National Biography*. 1885–1971. Smith Elder & Co., 1885–1912; O.U.P., 1927–1971
ENGEN (1)	ENGEN, R. K. *Dictionary of Victorian Engravers, Print Publishers and their works*. Chadwyck-Healey, 1979
ENGEN (2)	ENGEN, R. K. *Dictionary of Victorian Wood Engravers*. Chadwyck-Healey, 1985
FISHER	FISHER, S. *A Dictionary of Watercolour Painters 1750–1900*. Foulsham & Co., Ltd., 1972
FOSKETT	FOSKETT, D. *Dictionary of British Miniature Painters*. Antique Collectors' Club, 1972, 2 vols.
GUNNIS	GUNNIS, R. *Dictionary of British Sculptors 1660–1851*. New rev. ed. Abbey Library, N.D.
HALL (1)	HALL, M. *The Artists of Northumbria*. Marshall Hall, 1982
HALL (2)	HALL, M. *The Artists of Cumbria*. Marshall Hall, 1979
HARDIE	HARDIE, M. *Water-colour Painting in Britain*. Batsford, 1966–1968, 3 vols.
HOUFE	HOUFE, S. *Dictionary of British Book Illustrators and Caricaturists 1800–1914*. Antique Collectors' Club, 1978
HUNNISETT	HUNNISETT, B. *A Dictionary of British Steel Engravers*. F. Lewis, 1960
DBA	JOHNSON, J. and GREUTZNER, A. *The Dictionary of British Artists 1880–1940*. Antique Collectors' Club, 1976
JONES	JONES, A. E. *An Illustrated Directory of Old Carshalton*. Published by the author, N.D.
LAMBOURNE	LAMBOURNE, L. AND HAMILTON, J. *British Watercolours in the Victoria and Albert Museum*. Sotheby Parke Bernet, 1980
LISTER	LISTER, R. *Prints and Printmaking*. Methuen, 1984
MACKENZIE	MACKENZIE, I. *British Prints: dictionary and price guide*. Antique Collectors' Club, 1987
MALLALIEU	MALLALIEU, H. L. *Dictionary of British Watercolour Artists up to 1920*. Antique Collectors' Club, 1976, 2 vols.
MITCHELL	MITCHELL, S. *Dictionary of British Equestrian Artists*. Antique Collectors' Club, 1985
PEPPIN	PEPPIN, B. and MICKLETHWAIT, L. *Dictionary of British Book Illustrators: the Twentieth Century*. J. Murray, 1983
PILE	William Pile's directories of Sutton and district 1896–1938
TB	THIEME, Dr U. and BECKER, Dr F. *Allgemeines Lexikon der Bildenden Künstler von der Antike bis zur Gegenwart*. Leipzig: Wilhelm Engelman, 1907–1950; 37 vols.
V	VOLLMER, H. *Allgemeines Lexikon der Bildenden Künstler des xx Jahrhunderts*. Leipzig: E. A. Seeman, 1953–1962, 6 vols.
WATERHOUSE	WATERHOUSE, E. *Dictionary of British 18th Century Painters*. Antique Collectors' Club, 1981
GW	WATERS, G. M. *Dictionary of British Artists Working 1900–1950*. Eastbourne Fine Art, 1975, 2 vols.
WILLIAMS	WILLIAMS, I. *Early English Watercolours*. Kingsmead Reprints, 1970
WOOD	WOOD, C. *Dictionary of Victorian Painters*. 2nd ed. Antique Collectors' Club, 1978

In addition to the above, extensive use has been made of the material, both published and unpublished, in the Local Studies Collection at Sutton Library.

Illustration by THOMAS NOYES LEWIS from *The young Christian's Progress*, by J. A. Douglas, The Faith Press, N.D.

THE ARTISTS

ACKERMANN, Arthur Gerald, R. I. 1876–1960
Sussex House, Cedar Road, Sutton 1905–1915

Arthur Gerald Ackermann, born in Blackheath, London, on 13 February 1876 was the son of Arthur Ackermann, a member of the famous family of fine art dealers and print publishers. Educated at New College, Eastbourne, he studied art at Heatherley's, at Westminster Art School and at the Royal Academy Schools, winning the Creswick Prize and the Landseer Scholarship. In 1893, then aged seventeen, he exhibited his first Royal Academy painting: *A Breezy Morning*. He was a member of the Royal Institute of Painters in Water-Colours (1912) and throughout his life exhibited at most of the major galleries.

For ten years, from 1905 until 1915, he lived in Cedar Road, Sutton, a wide, tree-lined road close to Sutton Station. Cedar Road still has its share of Victorian and Edwardian houses, although most are now converted into flats. In addition, he kept a studio in Chelsea. He joined the Surrey Art Circle (q.v.) when he lived in Sutton, in 1909 exhibiting six titles, including *On the Downs* and *The Old Windmill*.

In the First World War he enlisted in the Artists' Rifles and was represented in the Leicester Galleries' 'Exhibition of Works by a Group of Artists serving with His Majesty's Forces, 1917', a review in the magazine *Colour* (December 1917, p. xix) praising 'Sergt. Ackermann's free, competent use of pure watercolour'. He was a watercolour painter of landscapes; seascapes and town scenes in the style of the Early English Watercolourists, working, as they did, in pencil and coloured washes. He particularly admired the works of Girtin, De Wint, Cox and Cotman.

Ackermann's attractive views of harvesting, haymaking and other rural pursuits in Surrey, Suffolk and Norfolk have risen sharply in price, some now selling for four figures. Because of all the recent changes in the face of the English landscape, people are more than willing to pay high prices for pictures that remind them of the days when fields were filled with hayricks, hens ran freely round the farmyard and ploughs were drawn by horses.

In appearance, Ackermann was slimly built and aesthetic-looking, had a small moustache and preferred a bow-tie to the conventional kind. He lived to be eighty-four, and died at Norwich on 27 December 1960, leaving the bulk of his paintings to his sister.

Exhib: CHE; FIN; GI; GOU; L; LEI; M; RA; RBA; RI; ROI; SAC; TOO; WG
Coll: Australia, Eastbourne AG; Nottingham AG; Southport AG; Wellington AG, New Zealand; Worthing AG
Published: ACKERMANN, G. Sketching in nature in watercolour. *The Artist*, vol. xv, nos 4, 5, 6; vol. xvi, nos 1, 2, 3, 1938

Bibliog: BEN; DBA; FISHER; GW; TB; V; *Who's Who in Art* – several editions; *Who Was Who* 1951–1960; Gaunt, W. Gerald Ackermann. Artists of Note, no. 65. *The Artist*, July 1940

ADAM, Robert, F.R.S., F.S.A. 1728–1792

What a pity it is that the only complete building designed for any site in this borough by Robert Adam – perhaps the greatest decorative architect this country has ever known – was a temporary structure. The building in question, a pavilion in the Corinthian style, was erected at The Oaks, Carshalton. It formed the focus for the magnificent Fête Champêtre held on 9 June 1774 to celebrate the marriage of Lady Betty Hamilton to Lord Edward Stanley, the grandson and heir of the 11th Earl of Derby.

Three hundred members of the aristocracy came to Carshalton that evening, emptying London of the cream of its society; thousands of local people were allowed into the grounds to watch them arrive. They were entertained by a masque, *The Maid of the Oaks*, written by the Master of Ceremonies, General John Burgoyne, who had formerly held the lease of The Oaks. The masque, with additions, was later performed at Drury Lane Theatre.

The guests were wined and dined in the supper rooms of Robert Adam's pavilion and danced in his ballroom. Judging from contemporary engravings – two were published in the Adam brothers' own book of designs – no expense was spared to make this ephemeral structure as fine and elaborate in appearance as one of a more permanent nature. The octagonal stateroom alone measured 123 feet in length.

The whole entertainment is said to have cost the Earl of Derby £5,000, a small fortune in those days. The exact date when the pavilion was dismantled – whether it was immediately after the fête, or some time later – does not seem to have been recorded.

Robert and James Adam are also credited with the castellated additions to *The Oaks Mansion* at Carshalton, demolished in 1957–60. Designs for the rebuilding of the house are amongst their papers.

Bibliog: BEN; COLVIN; DNB; FISHER; LAMBOURNE; MALLALIEU; TB; ADAM, R & J. *The Works in Architecture of Robert and James Adam, Esquires.* London: 1773, 1779, 1822. 3 vols.

ADAMS, John Talbot 1827/8–1909
St Swithin's, Manor Park Road, Sutton 1897–1909

John Thomas Adams, a painter of landscape, flower and genre studies, exhibited as 'John Talbot Adams' for fifty years, yet today his work is little known. When he died in Sutton on 21 February 1909, many paintings were found in his studio; others hung on the walls in the rest of the house. Further paintings were stored at Reeves's Artists' Depository and still more were out at exhibition.

He left neither wife nor child, willing his leasehold house at Sutton to his sister Sarah. Most of his paintings went to his niece's husband and to a local auctioneer. The remainder were sold. If disposed of locally, which is possible, some may still be in this area.

Adams carried out most of his work in oil. His views of Surrey, North Wales and the River Thames were exhibited at the Royal Academy and other galleries. So, too, were his genre paintings, which often had literary quotations for titles. Post-card collectors will be interested to know that Adams painted a series of views of Haslemere for Raphael Tuck & Sons (No. 7103).

St Swithin's, the house in Manor Park Road where he spent his last years, is thought to have been newly built shortly before Adams moved in.

Exhib: BI; BRU; M; RA; RBA; RHA
Bibliog: BEN; COYSH; DBA; TB; WOOD

AIKMAN, William 1868–1959
26 Meadow Road, Sutton 1937–1959
William Aikman, an artist in stained glass and an occasional watercolourist, had a distinguished career that spanned more than two thirds of a century. For a period of over twenty years he lived in Meadow Road, close to the Sutton/Carshalton border.

Aikman was born in Edinburgh in 1868 and first exhibited at the Royal Academy in 1893, showing a total of twenty-eight works up to 1941, mostly designs for church windows. In 1901 he attracted attention by winning a silver medal at the first 'International Studio Exhibition', organised by *The Studio* magazine. Aikman's winning design for a stained glass window, and another design by him, are illustrated in *The Studio*, December 1901. They show how avant-garde his work was for the period – almost Art Deco in concept, and a foretaste of the style which was to become more widely popular during the 1920s and 1930s.

Still actively engaged in stained glass work when he lived at Sutton, in 1941 he exhibited two designs at the RA for windows in a new Presbyterian church. He died at Sutton on 14 January 1959, leaving a daughter, Marian Wallace. His wife, Mary Gray Aikman, had died before him in 1954.

Exhib: G; RA; RSA
Bibliog: BEN; DBA; TB; *Studio*, vol. xxiv, no. 105, December 1901, p. 173 & 175

ALEXANDER, Margaret Exhib: 1913–1928
Warwick House, Denmark Road, Carshalton 1909–1919
Margaret Alexander, one of the four Miss Alexanders living at Warwick House, Carshalton, early this century, may have painted the watercolour *Wrythe Lane, 1915*, signed with the initials 'M.E.A.', now in Sutton's Local Collection. A number of her watercolours, including one entitled *Autumn Sunshine* (sent in from Carshalton) were shown at the Society of Women Artists' exhibitions. She moved to Milford, Surrey, in 1919.

Exhib: AB; D; G; SWA
Bibliog: DBA

*ANDERSON, John Corbet 1827–1907
John C. Anderson, a lithographer of landscapes and sporting personalities, lived not far from Sutton, at Croydon. Born in London on 17 January 1827, the son of William Anderson, a ship's surgeon, he had some early drawing lessons from the tragic artist Benjamin Robert Haydon, who became deranged and took his own life. Anderson's keen interest in cricket is reflected in his numerous portraits of the famous figures of the game like *Wisden*, *Fuller* and *Pilch*, and these are now quite expensive, selling for between £80 and £200 each.

In 1852 he settled in Croydon, where in addition to publishing a number of lithographs of the town, he was renowned for his scholarly writings on the history of Croydon. He visited nearby Carshalton and carried out a coloured lithograph of All Saints' Church, seen from across the ponds (one is in Sutton's Local Collection), showing it as it was in the mid-nineteenth century when the Reverend W. A. B. Cator was the Rector and J. Cressingham and G. Pim the church-wardens.

Anderson died at Croydon on 3 January 1907.

Coll: Croydon PL; Sutton LC
Bibliog: BEN; ENGEN(1); LISTER; MACKENZIE

ANDREAE, Conrad Rudolph 1871–1956
Ettrick Lodge, Langley Park (Albion Road), Sutton 1892–5
The watercolourist Conrad Andreae, who was born in London in 1871, and who married Isabel Mary Macgregor Greer, lived in Sutton during the 1890s when his father Oscar Andreae, a merchant, was the occupant of Ettrick Lodge in the Langley Park area. Also living there at the same time was the artist Conrad Carelli (q.v.) who was possibly related to the Andreaes.

Conrad Andreae was educated first at Osborne House, Margate and then in Germany. He studied art at the Slade, where he was awarded a First Class certificate for 'figure painting', and at L'Academie Julian in Paris. A fine draughtsman, he illustrated a book entitled *Rambles Round French Chateaux*, published by Mills and Boon (N.D.) and he exhibited five watercolours of Brighton at the Royal Academy. He lived in Brighton for much of his life and for a number of years was the Honorary Secretary of the Brighton Arts Club.

His watercolours, carried out in a loose, free style, are somewhat in the manner of Brabazon. An attractive little watercolour by Andreae, entitled *Brighton Seafront*, was exhibited on Nicholas Bowlby's stand at the first 'Annual Watercolour Fair', held in London in January 1986.

Conrad Andreae died in Brighton on 9 December 1956.

Exhib: L; RA; WG; Brighton
Bibliog: DBA; GW; V; *Who's Who in Art*, 1929

ATKINSON, Robert, O.B.E., F.R.I.B.A. 1883–1952
Torwood Lodge, Beeches Avenue, Carshalton 1908–1914
Woodmansterne Corner, Beeches Avenue, Carshalton 1914–1925

Born in Wigton, Cumbria and brought up in Nottingham, Robert Atkinson, the son of a cabinet maker, was apprenticed to a local architect but was dismissed after a trial period with the words 'He was no earthly good!' ringing in his ears. Undeterred, his parents articled him to another architect, their faith being rewarded when Robert won a two-year part-time scholarship to the Nottingham School of Art, where he carried off most of the prizes, twenty-six in total. In 1905 he was awarded the RIBA Tite Prize of £60, the money enabling him to spend nine months in Italy. He followed this with a year in Paris studying Beaux-Arts traditions. Atkinson received an honorable mention in the Soane Medallion Competition (1906) and in the same year won a silver medal from the National Board of Education.

In 1907 he set up a practice in Gray's Inn Road with his old Nottingham friends Horsnell, Gascoign and Nott, for the first three years 'ghosting' designs for other architects. He gradually achieved recognition in his own right for his fine perspective drawings, which were not just impressions of detail and character but were firmly-outlined finished works showing the buildings within their natural surroundings. Another friend, Yerbury, writing of this period, tells how the architect and his three friends made a very reasonable living, especially during the Royal Academy exhibitions, after which they would embark for France

or Italy and return only when their money had run out.

In 1908 Atkinson became the tenant of Torwood Lodge, Beeches Avenue, Carshalton, living there with his German-born wife, whom he had met in Algiers, and his son John. The latter recalls that Torwood Lodge was then the last house in the road and overlooked lavender fields; he remembers how his father used to return home from Carshalton Beeches Station by horse-drawn cab. In 1914 the family moved to a house opposite, called Woodmansterne Corner, designed by Robert Atkinson. They remained there until 1925 when they moved to Sheen.

Appointed Principal of the Architectural School in 1913, Atkinson became its Director in 1920. In this post, which lasted for ten years, he played an important role in revolutionising architectural education, his efforts remembered with respect and admiration.

A close friend was Wallington's 'squire', Sir William Mallinson, who, during the 1930s, was involved in the decision to provide Wallington with a town hall. Who better to design it than his friend Robert Atkinson, the last of the classical architects. The Town Hall (now the Crown Court) built in a traditional manner of brick and stone, with nine bays and a central turret, was completed in 1935. A year earlier, in 1934, Atkinson had exhibited his design, *New Town Hall, Wallington*, at the Royal Academy.

Atkinson, an avid collector of books and antiques had his own fine architectural library and took a keen interest in the building up of the Architectural

CYRIL ARTHUR FAREY Watercolour
Wallington Town Hall, designed in 1934 by ROBERT ATKINSON.

Association Library, even lending – and losing to them – his own books. Atkinson, Mallinson, and Wallington's Borough Surveyor, all keen bibliophiles, used to meet from time to time at Claridges or the Dorchester to discuss plans for a library at Wallington. Eventually, *Wallington Library*, linked to the Town Hall by a formal Italianate garden, was built in 1936. A second storey was added in 1962–3. Its fiftieth anniversary was celebrated in appropriate style by a number of special events held at the library. Although the building work was finally carried out under the aegis of his son John, Robert at that time being engaged on the design of his famous *Barber Institute of the Fine Arts* at Birmingham, Wallington Library bears Robert Atkinson's distinctive signature, the use of urns as a decorative feature. C. H. Reilly, commenting on Atkinson's final home at Sheen, Percy Lodge, mentions 'great urns . . . Fine urns, I notice are almost a trade mark'.

His range as an architect was vast, covering amusement halls, baths, churches, cinemas, colleges, law courts, markets and shops. To name but a few: *The Regent Theatre*, Brighton (1921), since demolished; *St Catherine's Church*, Hammersmith (1921), also now demolished; and *The Gresham Hotel*, Dublin (1926). Refusing to have any truck with the fashionable 'International Style' of the inter-war years, he was viewed askance by the RIBA, but this affected neither his career nor his fine architectural reputation.

When Atkinson died on 26 December 1952, John Betjeman added a footnote to the architect's obituary in *The Times*, praising him as 'an admirable designer and restorer of small houses'.

Janet C. McQueen

Exhib: RA
Bibliog: DBA; V; *Who Was Who 1951–1960*; STAMP, G. *The Great Perspectives.* Treffoil, 1982.
Obit: *The Times*, 29 December 1952

AYLING, Amy Exhib: 1884

2 Cathcart Road (later Clarendon Road), Wallington
c. 1878–1887
In 1884 a flower painting by Amy Ayling was shown at the Society of Women Artists' exhibition, after which nothing more was heard of her in the art world. She lived at Wallington with her retired-farmer father, Dennet Ayling, her mother Jane and her brothers Ernest and Edward; Edward later became the Reverend Edward Ayling.

The family lived next-door-but-one to where the 'Brighton Railway Murderer' Arthur Lefroy lived with his cousins the Claytons. In 1881 the Aylings must have suffered, along with their few neighbours in the road, from the unwelcome consequent publicity which resulted in the name of Cathcart Road being changed to Clarendon Road. Another close neighbour was the artist James G. Bingley (q.v.) from whom Amy possibly had some lessons.

Exhib: SWA
Bibliog: DBA

AYRTON, (Ormrod) Maxwell, F.R.I.B.A. 1873–1960

In 1925, Maxwell Ayrton, in conjunction with his partner Sir John William Simpson and the engineer Sir Owen Williams, designed the *British Empire Exhibition and Stadium* at Wembley. In 1934, nine years later, he designed *St Andrew's Presbyterian Church* in Northey Avenue, Cheam (illus. in *The Studio* March 1934, p. 165).

As a young man, Ayrton had been employed in Sir Edwin Lutyens' office, and Lutyens' influence can be seen in St Andrew's spacious interior, which glows with the golden colours of English oak and birch. Vertical and horizontal panels of plywood, veneered with birch, create an attractive patterned effect on the ceiling, enhanced by reflectors positioned in niches on the walls which direct the light upwards.

As a change from designing art galleries, bridges, churches, football stadiums and viaducts, Ayrton was happy to have the chance to work on a smaller scale when he designed a house for the immortal *Daily Mirror* characters Pip, Squeak and Wilfred, adored by adults and children alike in the 1920s and 1930s. Giving his services free, he created *Mirror Grange*, a delightful and most unusual miniature home. It was completed in 1929 and exhibited in aid of the Chailey Heritage, Sussex, a craft school and hospital.

In 1902 Ayrton married Elsa Marie, the daughter of the artist Sir Ernest Waterlow, R.A. He died at Hampstead in 1960, in his eighty-sixth year.

Exhib: NEA; RA; RSA
Published: AYRTON, M. *Wrought Iron and its Decorative Uses.* Country Life, 1929; *Mirror Grange . . . The Daily Mirror*, 1929. (Ayrton contributed the chapter 'Working in miniature')
Bibliog: DBA; TB; V; *Who Was Who 1951–1960*
Obit: *The Times*, 19 February 1960

BAILY, Edward Hodges, R.A. 1788–1867

Edward Baily was born in Bristol, the son of a ships' carver. He inherited his father's talent and abandoned a commercial career in favour of an artistic one, as a modeller in wax. He went on to become interested in sculpture of a more permanent nature and studied at the Royal Academy.

He was a contemporary of Sir Richard Westmacott (q.v.); together they produced work for the Marble Arch, for the gate at Hyde Park Corner and for other public buildings. They wrote a joint letter in 1831 complaining to the Treasury that their fees for work executed three years previously had not yet been paid.

After a busy career, in which he undoubtedly made a great deal of money, Baily was reduced to penury in old age and had to apply in 1857 to the Royal Academy for financial assistance. There is a memorial by him to the *4th Earl of Carrick* (1846) in the Lumley Chapel, Cheam. Better known examples of his work are to be found in the Houses of Parliament, in St Paul's

Cathedral and in Westminster Abbey.

Jean M. Moore

Exhib: BI; RA
Bibliog: BEN; GUNNIS; TB

BAINBRIDGE, Miss L. F. Exhib: 1908–1910
St Martin's, Stanley Road, Sutton 1890–1896
Ivanhoe, Brighton Road, Sutton 1896–c.1935
Miss L. F. Bainbridge exhibited two still-life paintings at the Society of Women Artists' exhibitions. Her entry in 1910, sent in from Sutton, was an oil entitled *Pomegranates*.

G. A. Bainbridge, who was the householder at Ivanhoe when Miss Bainbridge lived there, may have been her father.

Exhib: SWA
Bibliog: DBA

*BARENGER, James, Jr 1780–1831
James Barenger, nephew of the artist William Woollett, lived at various addresses in Kentish Town and Camden Town. Although he was not quite in the top league of sporting artists, he left an interesting record of the horses and dogs owned by the sporting gentry in the early years of the nineteenth century. From 1815 onwards his paintings, all in oil, were exhibited from 'Mr Tattersall's, Hyde Park Corner, London'.

Particularly interesting to this borough are his paintings relating to The Oaks, the Carshalton property of the 12th Earl of Derby. One of these is *The Earl of Derby's Stag Hounds* (1823), which was later engraved. Two of the huntsmen in the picture are Lord Stanley and the Hon. E. Stanley, the son and grandson of the Earl. Banstead Downs can be seen in the background and Banstead Windmill (on the site of Banstead Hospital) is on the horizon. Barenger also painted *Lord Derby's Fox-Hounds* (1809), sold at Christie's in 1978 for £4,500. His painting entitled *"Darling", a Staghound at Earl of Derby's Park* was exhibited at the Royal Academy in 1818.

Barenger's Earl of Derby, the originator of 'The Oaks Stakes' at Epsom Races, kept his staghounds at The Oaks. Adjoining his land was a field owned by an acquaintance, Durand of Woodcote. The latter was persuaded by the Earl to build a tower on the field, surmounted by a gilt-metal stag, so that the Earl could see the gleaming beast from his window at The Oaks. Both tower and stag were dismantled many years ago (Brightling).

Exhib: RA
Bibliog: BEN; MITCHELL; TB

BARNES, Alfred Richard Innott, F.R.S.A. 1899–1965
75 Tonfield Road, Sutton 1931–
50 Stanley Park Road, Carshalton –1956
Alfred Barnes, an artist in oil, watercolour and pastel, successfully combined careers in art and banking. Born in London on 21 November 1899, the son of Alfred Richard Barnes, he was educated at Archbishop Tenison's School in London. He won a scholarship to Camberwell Art School on the strength of some watercolours of flowers, having first started to paint when he was ten. By the end of his life he had completed hundreds of pictures, mostly flower and figure studies, and had exhibited at venues ranging from local halls to the Royal Academy.

During the First World War he served with the London Scottish Machine Gun Corps; in the Second with the Home Guard. Married, with two daughters, he lived in this borough for many years, studying art under J. Harvey Bloom (q.v.) and teaching at Sutton Art School. In 1946 he made local news – 'Human Head on Lawn' – by modelling a large head of himself in concrete which he placed in the middle of his lawn. Not surprisingly, it attracted startled attention from upper-deck passengers on buses travelling along Stanley Park Road.

Barnes worked at the Wimbledon branch of the Westminster Bank, later becoming manager of the West Wickham branch, and he won prizes at the Westminster Bank Art Club's competitions. With his friend Wally Pharo he helped to found the West Wickham Art Group, a friendly society where raw beginners are encouraged to work alongside professional artists. He was their Chairman for some years and also belonged to the Group of Nine and to the Croydon Art Society.

Many Sutton residents will remember this genial artist who, when he moved to Croydon in 1956, shaved off his famous beard. He died at Farnborough Hospital, Surrey, on 6 June 1965.

Exhib: CAS; COO; LG; P; RA; ROI; WWA; Admiralty Rest Rooms; London District Forces; United Society of Artists
Bibliog: GW; *Who's Who in Art*, 1950

BARNES, Robert Henry Exhib: 1924–1953
11b Bridgefield Road, Cheam, c.1940–
Robert Henry Barnes, a painter of figures and mythological subjects, taught life studies, modelling and painting at Sutton Art School in Throwley Way from September 1934 until August 1940. He was a popular – if sometimes short-tempered – teacher, serving under two principals, Miss Howard-Mercer (q.v.) and William J. L. Gaydon.

Barnes introduced 'painting in oils' as an addition to drawing in the 'costume life class' and donated an annual prize for portrait painting. On one occasion he was asked to judge the 'head-dress' competition at an art school party.

He exhibited ten paintings at the Royal Academy where, in 1935, his paintings *Apollo* and *Ballet Fantasy* were so well received that he was invited to prepare designs for one of Britain's largest luxury liners. In 1936, whilst working on *Poseidon and Aphrodite*, his entry for that year's RA exhibition, he was struck down with a bout of influenza. Unable to finish it in time, he sent off the painting with its background of sea, sky and cliffs merely sketched in. However, the central theme of Poseidon riding upon a sea horse and Aphrodite rising from a shell so impressed the judges that they not only selected the painting for exhibition, but hung it in a prominent position opposite the doorway of Gallery VI.

Eventually, Robert Barnes left the South of England to live in Bridgnorth, Shropshire, from where he submitted his last painting to the RA in 1953.

Exhib: G; RA; RBA
Bibliog: DBA

BATES, Kenneth Raymond, S.G.A. 1927–1985

Born in London in 1927, Ken Bates was educated at Christ's College and studied art at the Medway and the Guildford Schools of Art. He spent his National Service days in the Royal Navy and afterwards attended London University Institute of Education.

He is remembered in this borough as the senior art tutor at the Sutton College of Liberal Arts, and as an art therapist at Queen Mary's Hospital for Children, Carshalton. His hauntingly beautiful oil painting of a nurse holding a sick child, which hangs in Queen Mary's Hospital, is shortly to be used on a Royal Doulton plate commemorating the 80th anniversary of Queen Mary's Hospital.

Noted for his figure studies, Ken Bates carried these out in a variety of mediums, using pencil, chalk, charcoal, pastel, oil and watercolour. His works are to be found in a number of collections, both public and private. Nationally, he served as Vice-President of the Society of Graphic Art and was a member of the British Association of Art Therapists. Locally, he acted as art advisor to the London Borough of Sutton Arts Council.

It was a great shock to his many friends and pupils when he died, suddenly, on 22 March 1985. In January 1986 a memorial exhibition of his work was held in the Europa Gallery of Sutton Central Library.

Exhib: SGA; Europa Gallery, Sutton
Coll: Queen Mary's Hospital, Carshalton; Sutton Picture Loan Collection

BEALE, John Arthur 1890–1977

1 Poulton Avenue, Wrythe Lane, Sutton –1929–
John Arthur Beale, born in London on 13 February 1890, was a commercial artist specialising in black-and-white work, mostly of a humorous nature. His father, Herbert Beale, was a wool-buyer in the textile trade. John Beale married Madeline Bernard by whom he had a son and a daughter.

He studied at the William Morris School, at Walthamstow School of Art, at Hassall's and at the Central School of Arts and Crafts. During the First World War he served with the 17th Battalion Royal Fusiliers, and in the years between the wars was an illustrator for *The Tatler, The Bystander, Passing Show, London Opinion,* the *Humorist* and other magazines.

Beale, who shared a studio in Sutton with William Harold Beards (q.v.), was an early 'do-it-yourself' enthusiast, listing his recreation as 'pottering about with a hammer' (*Who's Who in Art* 1929). He died at Bexhill, Sussex, on 20 March 1977.

Bibliog: *Who's Who in Art,* 1929

BEARDS, William Harold 1895–1974

The Studio, 20 Poulton Avenue, Wrythe Lane, Sutton c.1929–1931
William Harold Beards, born on 10 July 1895 at Sedgley, Staffordshire, studied art at the Wolverhampton School of Art and at the Regent Street Polytechnic. He was a magazine illustrator, portrait painter and humorist, working for *The Bystander, The Tatler, Passing Show, London Opinion* and the *Liverpool Courier*. His hobbies were boating and gardening.

By 1937 he had moved to Thorpe Bay in Essex. He died at Brighton on 2 January 1974, leaving a daughter.

Exhib: B: RP
Bibliog: DBA; V; *Who's Who in Art,* 1929

*BENNETT, Frank Moss 1874–1953

Frank Moss Bennett, an artist of the 'every picture tells a story' category, was born in Liverpool in 1874. Educated at Clifton College, Bristol, he studied art at the Slade, at St John's Wood Art School and at the Royal Academy Schools, winning a gold medal and a travelling scholarship at the RA Schools.

His forte was the historical scene, both real and imaginary, usually set in the sixteenth to nineteenth centuries; but he also painted landscape and genre studies. He was a prolific artist, exhibiting at the RA and other galleries. His work was reproduced by Charles Hauff, by L. Wolff & Co., by Mardon, Son & Hall and by the Medici Society.

Well known to the artists of this area because of his involvement with the Surrey Art Circle (q.v.), Bennett served on the committee from 1902 onwards and exhibited regularly with them, in 1901 showing a group of Venetian views.

For a number of years he lived at Duppas Hill, Croydon, and during this period visited Beddington, where he painted a view of the group of cottages by the River Wandle known as Mount Pleasant, this painting now being in Sutton's Local Collection. An attractive young girl is also present in the picture. The scene has changed little over the years and remains one of the most picturesque in the area.

Frank Moss Bennett was still painting, when he was well into his seventies, the subjects which had made him popular during the 1890s. A recent revival of interest in his style of painting has pushed the prices of his works into the four-figures-and-over bracket. He died in 1953.

Exhib: B; D; L; P; RA; RI; ROI; SAC
Coll: National Portrait Gall., London; Sutton LC
Bibliog: BEN; DBA; GW; MITCHELL; V; WOOD; *Who's Who in Art* – several editions

BERRIDGE, Harold, C.I.E., O.B.E., M.Inst.C.E., M.I.Mech.E. 1872–1949

8 Worcester Gardens, Sutton 1933–1949
In 1933 Harold Berridge, a brilliant architectural engineer, exhibited a work entitled *Waterloo Bridge: design for new structure incorporating Rennie's columns and Entablature* at the Royal Academy.

JAMES G. BINGLEY   Watercolour 235×330mm
On the Road to Bocca d'Arno.   Private collection

JOHN HASSELL   Watercolour 203×159mm
New Parsonage [Cheam Rectory]. 1823.
Sutton's Local Collection

THOMAS C. DIBDIN   Watercolour 349×495mm
Beddington, Surrey [Old Post Office]. 1858.
Sutton's Local Collection

Born in Leicester in 1872, he was educated at the City of London School. He took a Civil Engineering pupilage and eventually became a member of the Institution of Civil Engineers, winning gold medals and other honours for papers on engineering. His career took him to New York, where he was involved with the *Hudson Tunnel* project, and then to India.

He spent twenty-one years in Aden where, during the First World War, he raised and commanded the 45th Aden Lancers. He was mentioned twice in dispatches, winning the C.I.E. and the O.B.E. for bravery under fire. Between the wars he worked as the Assistant to the Administrator of Housing Development Schemes, London County Council. He married twice. Alice, his first wife, died in 1933; in 1934 he married Phyllis Kathleen Doyle. He lived in Sutton from 1933 until 17 June 1949, when he died at Kingslea Nursing Home, Sutton.

Exhib: RA
Bibliog: DBA; *Who Was Who 1941–1950*

BINGLEY, James George 1840–1920
1 Collingwood Villas, Manor Road, Wallington 1875–1878
11 Cathcart Road (now Clarendon Road), Wallington 1878–1883
James George Bingley, born in London in 1840, was a landscape and genre painter in oil and watercolour, frequently using body colour in the latter. Although he visited Italy, painting in the Florence area, most of his work was carried out in Devon, in Cornwall and in the Home Counties. Elizabeth Mary, Bingley's wife, came from Cornwall, and the Bingleys often visited her old home. Their daughter Helen was born at Newlyn in 1875.

The Bingleys moved to Wallington from Godalming in 1875, living first in Manor Road, next door to the Melbourne Hotel, and then in Cathcart Road. The household at Cathcart Road in the 1880s was large. Bingley's widowed mother lived with them, and by then James and Elizabeth had five children. The last three: James, Andrew and Kate were all born in Wallington. A general servant, Sarah Atkinson, looked after them. Next door lived the Tottons (q.v.); a few doors away the Aylings (q.v.); and at no. 4 Arthur Lefroy, the notorious 'Brighton Railway Murderer'.

In 1883 the Bingleys moved to Midhurst in Sussex where James painted many landscapes of the surrounding countryside. Later, they returned to the London area and James Bingley spent his last years at South Norwood, where he died at no. 26 Princess Road on 21 June 1920. A brief obituary in the *Norwood News*, 25 June 1920, informs us that in his later years he 'devoted himself to literary studies'.

Bingley's paintings of rural life in Surrey and Sussex are very popular today when there is a general nostalgia for the simple rustic life of years ago. The Bucentaur Gallery has published a greetings card of one of his watercolours – a charming scene entitled *Ockham Woods*, showing children dressed in pinafores and frilled bonnets, picking bluebells and primroses.

Bingley was a great admirer of the artist Frederick Walker (q.v.). Born in the same year as the unfortunate Walker, who died of tuberculosis, Bingley outlived him by forty-five years. Some of James Bingley's copies of Walker's watercolours are in the Leggatt Collection, now housed in the Department of Prints and Drawings at the British Museum.

Exhib: AGN; D; NWS; RA; RBA; RI; ROI
Bibliog: BEN; DBA; FISHER; GW; MALLALIEU; WOOD

BION, Cyril Walter Madge 1889–1976
Homeleigh, 29 Carew Road, Wallington 1920s
Cyril Bion, born on 31 August 1889, married Mary Dorothy Drayner, and during the 1920s lived in a house called Homeleigh, in Wallington, where the householder at the time was Ambrose L. Drayner. Bion was living at this address when his paintings *A September afternoon* (1924) and *Himalayan Snowfield* (1925) were exhibited at the Royal Academy. In April 1935 he had a one-man show at Walker's Galleries in London, exhibiting nineteen oil paintings and twelve watercolours – views of Northern Ireland, the west highlands of Scotland, and Surrey. They included three watercolours of this area: *Old Cottage, Ewell*; *Woodmansterne*, and *Surrey Cornfields*.

Bion and his family (including his mother-in-law Elizabeth Drayner) lived in Ireland during the 1940s, first in Portrush and then in Belfast, his mother-in-law dying there in 1942. He exhibited twelve paintings at the Royal Hibernian Academy between 1941 and 1949.

Eventually, the Bions returned to England, where Cyril Bion died at North Fleet, Hampshire, on 22 February 1976, survived by his widow and his son and daughter.

Exhib: RA; RHA; WG
Bibliog: BEN; DBA

BLAKE, Rev. James Martindale, F.S.A., M.A. (Oxon). 1863–1934
Christ Church House, Brambledown Road, Wallington 1899–1910
The Reverend James Blake's name does not appear in any art dictionary. Yet he deserves a mention here. He was the artistic and enterprising minister of Christ Church Presbyterian Church, Wallington, who in the best traditions of the Arts and Crafts movement drew the designs and then co-opted ten members of his congregation to help him build a wooden canopy and screen, deeply carved in oak, for the back of the apse in his church.

The news of his efforts reached the editor of *The Studio* magazine, who featured the church in the issue for June 1903. Three of the carved panels are illustrated: *The Burning Bush*, the emblem of the Presbyterian Church, carried out by the Reverend Mr Blake himself; and the *Saint Andrew's Panel* and the *Saint George's Panel*, both carved by a Mrs Coldwells.

The Rev. James Blake, born in 1863, was educated at Oxford University. He was a Chaplain Emeritus of the Church of Scotland and wrote several books, including some religious works, a volume of poems, *Luca della Robbia*, and a travel book, *Joy of Tirol*. In 1897 he married Evelyn Kate Duguid and shortly afterwards became the minister of Christ Church, Wallington.

The Blakes presented a font to the church, a thanksgiving for the birth of their only child, a son who died in infancy. They left Wallington in 1910 when the Reverend Mr Blake was appointed Chaplain of the Scottish Church at Florence. He must have counted himself extremely fortunate to be a resident for over twenty years of a city famous throughout the world for its beauty and art treasures. His last days were spent in Switzerland, where he was able to indulge his love of 'mountain wandering'. He died at Clos de Villard Versoix, near Geneva, on 24 July 1934, leaving his wood carvings to his nephew.

Bibliog: *Who Was Who 1929–1940; Studio,* xxix, no. 123, June 1903, pp. 64–66
Obit: *The Times* 27 July 1934; *Wallington and Carshalton Times,* 2 August 1934

BLOOM, Dorothy (Detta) Harvey Exhib: 1930–1939
15 Talbot Road, Carshalton 1935–c.1939

Detta Harvey Bloom, née Dorothy MacFarlane, married Joscelyn Harvey Bloom (q.v.) in 1929. She painted landscape, still-life and genre studies in oil and watercolour and was also a lino-cut artist. Like her husband, she exhibited at the Royal Society of British Artists' exhibitions where her titles in 1936 were *Near Bruges*, a watercolour, and *Shottisham Mill*, an oil.

She taught at Sutton Art School during the 1930s, when her husband was the Deputy Principal.

Exhib: RBA; RED; ROI
Bibliog: DBA

BLOOM, Joscelyn Harvey, R.B.A. 1895–1978
15 Talbot Road, Carshalton 1935–c.1939

Joscelyn Harvey Bloom, who once lived in Carshalton and taught at Sutton Art School, was the brother of the writer Ursula Bloom. Their father was the popular, charming – but weak where women were concerned – vicar, scholar, writer and more-than-competent watercolourist, James Harvey Bloom. Joscelyn and Ursula were brought up in a large vicarage near Stratford-upon-Avon, their peaceful existence coming to an abrupt end when their father's womanising proved too much for his wife. She left James to his vicarage and lady friend, and went to live in another part of the country, taking her children with her. Ursula Bloom, who died recently, wrote some fascinating books about the family life of the Blooms.

Joscelyn was born in 1895. He was an extremely delicate child who barely survived infancy. But as so often happens with delicate children, he overcame all his various ailments to live to be eighty-three. His mother, with no husband to support her, relied on Ursula to be the breadwinner. Ursula pulled strings to get Joscelyn a job in a bank but he let her down by getting the sack. Later on he took up an apprenticeship in a factory.

An early volunteer in the First World War, Joscelyn served in Egypt with the Royal Field Artillery,

showing bravery – combined with a certain recklessness – under fire. After the war he entered St Martin's School of Art, having discovered that there was one thing he could do really well – paint. At school the only prize he ever won was for collecting the most snails from the headmaster's garden.

He eventually became a successful painter in oil and watercolour and a noted woodcut and linocut artist. Elected a member of the Royal Society of British Artists in 1934, he was on the hanging committee in 1936 when he and his wife were living in Carshalton. The local press loyally described the exhibition as 'one of the best hung in London'. Bloom was also a member of the Art Workers' Guild. He exhibited over fifty works with the RBA, including some views of Epsom Downs and racecourse. In 1938 he exhibited a watercolour entitled *An Old Silk Mill on the Wandle* (RBA).

He married in 1929, when he was thirty-five years old. His wife Dorothy (q.v.), known as 'Detta', was also an artist. On their arrival at Carshalton the Harvey Blooms announced their intention of fostering art appreciation in the area, and to this end organised sketching classes during the summer months. The pair were often seen cycling round the countryside in search of views to paint. During this period they organised visits abroad for the Royal Drawing Society, accompanying the students and giving them daily art instruction. In 1932 the total cost of the fortnight's sketching holiday, per person, was twelve guineas.

Harvey Bloom was a popular member of staff at Sutton Art School, teaching there from 1932–1937. Carefully cultivating an artistic image, he wore a hat with a very large brim; a photograph showing him wearing it appeared in the local press on more than one occasion. He was Miss Howard-Mercer's (q.v.) deputy and gave a series of lectures at the school, open to the general public, on art education (he had made a study of teaching methods abroad) and architecture.

The Harvey Blooms left Carshalton shortly before the start of the Second World War to live at Epsom, where J. Harvey Bloom became the art master at Epsom County School for Boys (now Glyn Grammar School). Douglas Cluett, Heritage Officer of Sutton Leisure Services, remembers being taught by him during the 1940s:

> I remember Harvey Bloom as an eccentric but very kindly man; an excellent teacher to those who wished to be taught. Those who did not, could, as far as he was concerned, amuse themselves as they wished, provided they did not disturb those trying to work.
> However, his attempts at keeping discipline were at the best sporadic and unsuccessful. I remember at least one drawing lesson in the old brickfields at Epsom, with their flooded pits, when some half or more of the class spent its time attempting to make rafts out of drawing boards and sail them on the water. He drove, circa 1945, a little car, a Baby Austin I think, which even for that time was ancient (although few masters arrived at school driving any car at all). Its registration number was BG 100, or something very like it, and many were the attempts to convert the 'G' to a 'C'. The cruising speed of his car was such that every morning he was overtaken by hordes of boys on bicycles who would cheer him as they passed. He was, nevertheless, a dedicated and talented man; and one of

CHARLES J. DE LACY   Oil 610×1067mm
The Pool of London. c. 1900.   Private collection

LEONARD J. FULLER   Oil 1016×1270mm
The Peoples Store [Sutton's first Woolworths].   The Priory Gallery

20

only three teachers whom I remember with feelings of respect and gratitude.

Joscelyn Harvey Bloom's last home was at Saxmundham, Suffolk. He died there on 26 September 1978.

Exhib: AWG; COO; RA; RBA; RDS; RED; RSA; SAP; Canadian National Exhibition, Toronto, 1936; International Exhib. Lithography . . . Chicago, 1935
Bibliog: DBA; BLOOM, U. *Parson Extraordinary*. Hale, 1976; *Sutton Times and Cheam Mail*, 8 May 1936, 11 December 1936, 14 May 1937

*BOOT, William Henry James, V.P.R.B.A., R.I. 1848–1918

The landscape and genre painter W. H. J. Boot was born in Nottingham on 14 June 1848 and studied at Derby School of Art. After travelling in North Africa and Europe he eventually settled in London, and devoted much of his life to painting views of Derbyshire, Devon and Surrey.

He appears to have known this area fairly well, painting views of Beddington, Carshalton and Wallington, which then appeared in the various publications he illustrated. His career took off at the end of the 'golden age' of British book illustration – the 1860s and 1870s. From 1891 until 1910 he was the Art Editor of the *Strand Magazine*, and for roughly the same period served as Vice-President of the Royal Society of British Artists.

One of his sons, James Sydney Boot, was an art editor; another served in the forces in the First World War. W. H. J. Boot died shortly before the end of the war, on 8 September 1918.

Exhib: B; L; RA; RBA; RHA; RI; ROI;
Published: BOOT, W. H. J. *Trees and how to Paint them*. 1883; *Tree Painting in Watercolours*. 1886
Illus: *Art Journal; Boys' Own Paper; Graphic; Illustrated London News; Magazine of Art; Quiver; Strand Magazine*; and others
Bibliog: BEN; DBA; ENGEN(2); FISHER; GW; HOUFE; MALLALIEU; WOOD; *Who Was Who 1916–1928*

BOURNE, James 1773–1854

James Bourne, the youngest son of John and Sarah Bourne of Dalby Hall, Lincolnshire, was born in Dalby and educated at Louth. He travelled to London in 1789, hoping to find work as a drawing master, but failed to find any so went north to Manchester. In 1796 he returned to London and fared better this time when he became drawing master to the Duchess of Sutherland and to Lord Spencer. He began to exhibit at the Royal Academy in 1800 and thereafter used to take summer sketching holidays in the Lake District, the West Country, Kent and Surrey.

On one such visit to Surrey, he painted a large, grey-wash drawing of a wooded hillside scene at Beddington (coll. V&A). Entitled *Beddington, Surrey*, it shows a horse and cart being led up a fenced-off path by the side of a wood. The artist has written his name and address on the back: 'J. Bourne 7 Somerset Street, Portsmouth.' The painting is undated. However, we know from a dated painting entitled *Duppas Hill, Croydon*, now in Croydon Libraries' Local Collection, that he was in this area in 1820, so the Beddington

view may date from then.

Much of James Bourne's work is in monochrome and varies in quality. His daughters painted in a similar style, and there is a collection of paintings by the Bourne family at the Usher Art Gallery, Lincoln, which includes James Bourne's *Cottage at Buckland*.

In 1838 James Bourne entered the church and became the Reverend James Bourne. He died at Sutton Coldfield in 1854.

Exhib: RA
Coll: Birmingham AG; Brighton AG; BM; Croydon PL; Dudley AG; Fitzwilliam Mus., Cambridge; Hertford Mus; Hove PL; Leeds AG; Manchester City AG; Newport AG; Usher AG, Lincoln; V&A; York AG
Published: BOURNE, J. *A Selection of Views in the County of Lincoln*, 1801
Bibliog: BEN; FISHER; HOUFE; LAMBOURNE; MALLALIEU; TB

BRADLEY, Edward Exhib: 1827–1867

Very little is known about this artist except that he lived in Putney for most of his life. He visited Carshalton in the 1840s and painted a view of one of its mills. *Mill at Carshalton* was exhibited at the British Institution in 1843 and again in 1844 (present whereabouts of painting unknown).

Bradley's early works were of dead game; but later on in his career he concentrated more on landscape painting, exhibiting views of the Lake District, Scotland and Italy.

Exhib: BI; RA; SBA
Bibliog: BEN; TB; WOOD

BROWNE, Irene Muriel, R.M.S., S.W.A. 1891–1965
Chestnuts, Mulgrave Road, Sutton pre-1895–1911

Born in Hendon in 1891, Irene Browne, a sculptress in bronze and stoneware, came to live in Sutton when she was a child. She left for London when she was twenty, shortly after becoming established in the art world.

She trained at the Chelsea Polytechnic School of Art and had her first acceptance at the Royal Academy in 1908, when she was still only seventeen. It was a bronze statuette, entitled *Protected*, submitted from Sutton. In 1927 she was elected a member of the Society of Women Artists, and in 1929 she became a member of the Royal Miniature Society. Examples of her work can be found at the Victoria and Albert Museum, at Manchester City Art Gallery, at Hanley Museum and at Aberystwyth Museum.

Her other main interests were the theatre – she was a member of the Theatrical Ladies' Guild – and her cats; she was devoted to her cats, usually owning several. During the 1930s she lived in Sussex, but she eventually returned to London and died in Chelsea on 24 July 1965.

Exhib: GI; I; L; RA; RHA; RMS, SWA
Bibliog: BEN; DBA; GW; V; *Who's Who in Art*, 1929

BURGESS, Henry William 1792–1844

The watercolourist Henry William Burgess, the son of the artist William Burgess and the father of the artist

John Bagnold Burgess, was a drawing master at Charterhouse School. He was obviously acquainted with this area since he painted at least three different views of it. Two were exhibited at the Royal Academy in 1815: *A study of an old willow tree in the grounds of F. Gregg, Esq., Wallington* and *A study of an old beech tree at the Oakes [sic], Surrey, the seat of the Earl of Derby*. The third, *A college at Carshalton*, was shown at the British Institution in 1819; it would have been a view of Bornheim House (a Roman Catholic college), the only college known to have been at Carshalton then. It used to stand where Carshalton Station approach is now, on the west side of North Street. There is an illustration of it, possibly from Burgess's painting, in *Laity's Directory*, 1812 (Jones). The building was pulled down prior to 1847.

Henry William Burgess, who married Sabina Stirling, lived in London for most of his life but toured France and Belgium during the 1820s, sketching churches and cathedrals. In 1832 he was appointed Landscape Painter to King William IV and in this capacity dutifully painted some tree studies of Windsor, trees being his speciality. He died in London in 1844, although his last work, exhibited that year, was submitted to the RA from an address in Dover.

Exhib: BI; RA
Coll: BM; Leeds City AG; V&A
Published: BURGESS, H. W. *Views of the General Character and Appearance of Trees . . . 1827*
Bibliog: BEN; FISHER; LAMBOURNE; LISTER; MALLALIEU; TB

*BURMAN, John 1848–1935
2 Belladonna Villas, Benhill Road, Sutton 1876–c.1880
4 Sunningdale Villas, Robinhood Lane, Sutton
c.1880–c.1897
Coverdale, Harcourt Road, Wallington 1901–1912
Travelling around the world on the frigate H.M.S. *Ariadne* is an oil painting, *Windmill at Tadworth*, by the artist John Burman. The frigate's captain is Ian Henderson, great-grandson of the artist.

John Burman was born in London. He arrived at Sutton in 1876 with his wife Mehetabel, known as 'Metty', and their daughter Mabel, who had been born in London. Their other three children: Ethel, John Albert Edward (Bertie) and Gladys were all born in Sutton. For four years or so, the family lived at no. 2 Belladonna Villas and then moved to Sunningdale Villas, where a general servant, Lizzie Killick, looked after them all.

Burman was a landscape and genre painter in oil and watercolour who occasionally turned his hand to ivory carving. He was friendly with the artist William Tatton Winter (q.v.), with whom he shared a studio; they employed a local boy to keep it clean and tidy. Burman's work, so close in style to his friend's, could at times be mistaken for Tatton Winter's – trees stripped of their leaves making delicate patterns against the sky, misty landscapes showing trees bending in the wind. They went on sketching trips together which sometimes took them to Walton-on-the-Hill and Tadworth; and when Tatton Winter called

to collect Burman he would rush upstairs to see the Burman children, calling out, 'What shall we paint today?'.

Both artists were members of the Surrey Art Circle (q.v.). John Burman exhibited with the society until 1909 (when he resigned), his paintings often hanging alongside Tatton Winter's. His SAC titles included: *A corner of a Surrey Common* (1900), *The haze of early morning* (1901), *Fishing* (1905) and *The Road to Tadworth* (1909). Two of his paintings were exhibited at the Royal Academy, the *Sutton Journal* mentioning them in the issue for 27 May 1886: 'Surrey Painters. In the Academy this year Mr. John Burman has two pictures, one *A Study of Fruit* and the other *Old Fashioned Friends*'.

The family moved away from Sutton in about 1897 to live at Epsom, but in 1901 returned to this area to live at Coverdale, a large Victorian house in Wallington. A family photograph shows John's wife Metty, his daughter Mabel and some friends playing croquet on the lawn. Mabel, an attractive, black-haired, blue-eyed young woman, had just become engaged to tall, handsome Robert Henderson, who played cricket for Beddington and Surrey. Henderson had a long association with St Mary's Church, Beddington; a photograph of him as People's Warden can be seen in *A History of Beddington* (1923) by the Rev. Thomas Bentham, M.A. John Burman painted a watercolour of the exterior of St Mary's Church and this has remained in the family collection.

Bertie, John Burman's son, remained a bachelor, his parents living with him at Norwood during their later years. Burman's daughter Ethel died young; Gladys went to live in Australia.

Mrs Mary Lloyd, who lived in Sutton until she died in 1986, was the daughter of Mabel and Robert Henderson and the granddaughter of John Burman. As a little girl she used to visit the artist at Norwood, where she would sit on a stool in his studio watching him paint. At the end of the afternoon, before tea, he would allow her to clean his brushes. She remembered a 'tall, thin man with penetrating sapphire-blue eyes and a short, pointed white beard, who sported shepherd's plaid trousers'. Whilst he was painting, however, he wore a long smock and took care to protect his small granddaughter from paint splashes by tying a piece of cloth around her. Mrs Lloyd said that painting, music (of which he had a remarkable knowledge), literature and gardening – he specialised in growing carnations – were his only interests; except for blaming the government for anything that went wrong, be it a national disaster or merely a broken fence in the front garden!

He supported his family by selling his paintings and by teaching. He was always reluctant, however, to sell his best works, some of his favourite paintings remaining in his studio up to his death. His wife Metty died before him. When John Burman died on 12 June 1935, he was buried beside her at Bandon Hill Cemetery.

Exhib: RA; RBA; SAC
Bibliog: DBA; WOOD

BURNS, Leonard Balfour 1854–1944
Talfourd Villa, Carshalton Road, Sutton –1882
Meadowcroft, Carshalton Road, Sutton 1882–
The amateur artist Leonard Burns, who was born in London in 1854, was the secretary to a land company by profession. He exhibited at the Royal Academy and with the Society of British Artists. Two of his SBA titles, shown whilst he was living in Sutton, were: *A Thames Backwater* (1880), a watercolour; and *Harvest in the South Downs* (1882), an oil.

Leonard and his young wife Matilda came to live in Sutton shortly before 1880. Their first child, Edgar, who grew up to be a farmer, was born soon after they had moved into Talfourd Villa in Carshalton Road. They later had a daughter, Maud Constance, and another son, Cecil Leonard, who became an architect.

The family left Sutton to live in Streatham, but eventually settled in Sussex, living for many years at Landhurst Cottage, Hartfield. This was where Leonard Burns died, aged ninety, on 26 March 1944.

Exhib: RA; SBA
Bibliog: DBA; WOOD

CACHEMAILLE-DAY, Nugent Francis 1896–1976
Architect of *Sutton Baptist Church, Cheam Road.*
Cachemaille-Day is one of the most interesting church architects of the first half of the twentieth century. He was principally influenced by the continuing Arts and Crafts tradition – he worked with Louis de Soissons designing Welwyn Garden City, and with Goodhart-Rendel, who designed many brick churches, including one in North Cheam. He adopted the attitudes of both these architects about the importance of traditional materials, particularly brick; and honest workmanship. These more traditional views were tempered by the knowledge that the twentieth century had to find its own way of designing churches, looking forward to its own style as well as acknowledging its great Gothic past.

The most important single influence on Cachemaille-Day was Albi Cathedral, a magnificent, towering, thirteenth century building in red brick. He admitted that his most famous building, St Saviour's Church, Eltham, was based on Albi, and Sutton Baptist Church is very like St Saviour's. The Baptist Church was built in 1934 to replace H. D. Searles-Wood's (q.v.) church in the High Street, where Allders now stands. It is a bold design with imposing proportions, built in standard red brick, with decoration above the main doorway in roof tiles laid end-on. The long walls have great concave sweeps, showing how Cachemaille-Day was also heavily influenced by the experiments in building in brick in Amsterdam in the 1920s, where architects like Kramer and de Klerk were responsible for blocks of flats with unexpected sweeps and curves. The windows are a modern, simplified Gothic.

Sutton Baptist Church, designed in 1934 by NUGENT F. CACHEMAILLE-DAY.

The interior is dramatic with sweeping, pointed arches around the building. The walls are left as exposed lime plaster and there is much exposed brickwork. The ceiling is covered with pale blue acoustic panels. The focal point is the panel behind the large stone baptismal font, which features a sculptured panel between two columns of spiralling brick. All the furniture is specially made in oak, with curves that echo the curves of the outside wall. The whole, interior and exterior, is an exciting combination of Arts and Crafts, and Expressionism.

The church received an enthusiastic write-up in the local press, and Cachemaille-Day was reported to be very pleased with the result. He went on to be a prolific church architect, and a prominent member of the profession, setting up his own firm in 1935, after leaving the firm of Welch, Cachemaille-Day and Lander, for whom he designed the Baptist Church.
Cynthia Bradley

Exhib: RA

CARELLI, Conrad Hector Raphael, B.W.S. 1869–1956
c/o Oscar Andreae, Ettrick Lodge, Langley Park (Albion Road), Sutton 1892–5
Holgate, Prince of Wales Road, Carshalton 1896–7
Conrad Carelli, a landscape and architectural painter in watercolour, had an Italian father and an English

Group of pottery and glass designed by
DR CHRISTOPHER DRESSER; the pottery marked
'Linthorpe'; the glass, 'James Couper & Sons'. Private
collection

ROBERT HILLS   Watercolour 222×191mm
The Fords, Beddington. c. 1822.   Sutton's Local Collection

JOHN CONSTABLE   Oil 591×502mm
The Lambert Children. 1825.   Photo courtesy Sotheby's
A portrait of an interesting local family. The Lamberts owned The
Oaks, Carshalton, until 1788, when William Lambert, the
children's grandfather, sold the property to the 12th Earl of Derby.

The Rigi from the Musegg, Lucerne, by
GEORGE JACKSON FLEMWELL.
Watercolour illustration from Flemwell's *Lucerne*,
Blackie & Son, N.D.

24

mother. His father, Gabriel Carelli, the son of Raphael Carelli (artist to the Duke of Devonshire), was a decorative painter who settled in England, married an Englishwoman and took British nationality. Conrad, born in England, was educated privately in Berkshire. In 1889 he studied art at L'Academie Julian, Paris, under Bouguereau and Fleury; and throughout the rest of his life he travelled abroad frequently, visiting Italy, Spain and Palestine.

The Carellis were patronised by the Royal Family, both Queen Victoria and Queen Mary buying their paintings. Queen Victoria was pleasantly surprised to discover how reasonably priced their works were; Conrad only charged her a pound or two each for his studies of Aix-les-Bains.

During the 1890s Conrad Carelli lived in Sutton, at the home of Oscar Andreae, a merchant and the father of Conrad Andreae (q.v.). He then appears to have moved to a house called Holgate in Prince of Wales Road, Carshalton. In Pile's directories of Carshalton for 1896 and 1897 a 'C. Corelli' is listed at that address, but since errors do occur in these directories, this is almost certainly 'Carelli'.

The artist exhibited three paintings at the Royal Academy; his first, a view of Cairo, was hung in 1897. Then, after a gap of more than forty years, two more were shown at the RA in 1941: *Burnsall in Wharfedale*, and *River Wharfe at Burnsall*. He had a one-man show at Walker's Galleries, London, and was represented in several Spring exhibitions at Menton in the South of France. In 1935 he became a member of the British Watercolour Society.

Carelli, who was married, lived to be eighty-seven and spent most of his life in or around London, dying at no. 38 Redcliffe Square, Kensington, on 30 June 1956. He left a bequest to the Langham Sketching Club, of which he had been a member. In 1979 a pencil and watercolour painting by Carelli, *Seville, La Giralda*, was sold at Sotheby's for £200; in March 1986 Christie's estimated price for his watercolour *A View of Jerusalem with the Dome of the Holy Rock* was £400–£600.

Exhib: B; L; RA; RBA; RI; WG; Menton, France
Bibliog: BEN; DBA; GW; WOOD; *Who's Who in Art*, 1950; MILLAR, D. Queen Victoria goes South. *Country Life*, 26 September 1985, pp. 860–862

CARPENTER, George

In 1831 George Carpenter of London, a drawing master, exhibited one work, an untitled sketch, at the British Institution. During the 1870s he taught art at Oakhill Lodge, a boarding and day school near Sutton Green run by Mr Frederick Devonshire. He may have been living in Sutton then. A George Carpenter, aged sixty-nine, is listed in the 1871 census for Sutton.

Exhib: BI
Bibliog: BEN

CAULFEILD, Hon. Rachel 1884–1942

Nonsuch Park, Cheam –1920–
On the nights of the 25 and 26 April 1942 the city of Bath, taken almost completely by surprise, was heavily bombed. Bath had been regarded as 'safe'. Hitler's attack on a cultural target was seen as a retaliation for the British bombing of Lübeck. When Bath counted its losses, 400 people had been killed, 329 houses and shops totally destroyed, and about 700 buildings so badly damaged they had to be demolished.

A major incident during the second night's raid took place at the Regina Hotel. On hearing the siren, some of the guests and staff had taken refuge in the reinforced basement; others had preferred to remain in their rooms. All those sheltering in the basement came out unscathed, but nearly all the thirty or so still in their rooms were killed. One was the Hon. Rachel Caulfeild, a painter of portrait miniatures, a sister of the 8th Viscount Charlemont, and a distant cousin of Sir William Orpen, R.A. – his mother was a Caulfeild. Her body was brought out of the hotel on 1 May 1942.

In Niall Rothnie's book *The Bombing of Bath* (Ashgrove Press, 1983), an eye-witness, one of the rescue squad, tells how the body of Rachel Caulfeild – 'Corfield', according to the witness, but there is no record of anyone of that name being killed in the bombing at Bath – was identified at the hotel by her sister and by an 'Hon. gentleman'. When the blanket covering the body was removed, a string of pearls was seen to be around the artist's neck. In too much of a state of shock themselves to remove the pearls, the relatives asked the man from the rescue squad if he would do so. He in turn asked the undertaker. The 'Hon. gentleman' later returned with gifts of cigarettes for the rescue squad.

Rachel Caulfeild, born in London in 1884, was the younger daughter of the Hon. Marcus P. F. Caulfeild. She knew Cheam well, since she was related to the Farmer family of Nonsuch Park, her mother's sister having married Captain William Gamul Farmer. Also, Rachel's brother, James Edward Caulfeild, 8th Viscount Charlemont, had been educated at Cheam School. Rachel regarded Nonsuch Park, the Gothic style mansion designed in 1806 by Jeffry Wyatt (later Wyatville), as her second home. The mansion, built near the site of Henry VIII's great Palace of Nonsuch, is no longer privately owned. Today its lovely grounds can be enjoyed by all.

In 1920 the Hon. Rachel Caulfeild, giving 'Nonsuch Park' as her address, exhibited a painting entitled *Rear-Admiral P. Nelson Ward, M.V.O.*, at the Royal Academy. The sitter was married to Rachel's sister Dorothy. Rachel exhibited thirteen miniatures at the RA, her first in 1904, her last in 1936. Her sitters included: *Mrs. Farmer* [her aunt] (1906), *Lady Camilla Fortescue* (1914) and *Elizabeth, daughter of Lord and Lady Somers* (1936).

Rachel was a bridesmaid on 30 April 1906 at Cheam's 'wedding of the year', when her cousin Alice Matilda Mary Farmer married Lieut. Col. the Hon. Francis Lionel Lydstone Colborne, Equerry to Princess Beatrice, Queen Victoria's youngest child. The Colbornes were the last private owners of Nonsuch Park; Alice, an only child, had inherited it from her father. House-parties were held frequently, and some of Rachel's sitters were guests there. This may be why, after 1936, the year Alice died and the house was put on the market, Rachel no longer exhibited at the RA. She was left an annuity of £150 by her cousin.

On 4 May 1942, three days after her body had been recovered from the hotel at Bath, the funeral of the Hon. Rachel Caulfeild took place at Boxgrove, West Sussex, where the church of St Mary and St Blaise has a memorial to her brother-in-law, Admiral Nelson Ward, who died in 1937.

Exhib: L; RA; RMS
Bibliog: DBA; FOSKETT
N.B. An exciting discovery was made at Nonsuch Park after Alice Colborne's death. A portrait of a man, by Frans Hals, was found under a leaky roof. It is now in the Burrell Collection at Glasgow.

CAUTY, Horace Henry, R.B.A. 1845–1909
Dorset Villa, 24 Victoria Road, Sutton 1891–1907
Minsmere, 22 Throwley Way, Sutton 1907–1909
Horace Henry Cauty, born in Southwark in 1845, was the son of Horace Robert Cauty (q.v.) and Louisa Cauty. He lived in Sutton for the last twenty years of his life, having earlier lived in the Campden Hill area of Kensington. He married rather late in life and appears to have had no children.

A genre, landscape and historical painter, mostly in oil, he was well versed in the English classics, often using quotations from them as the titles of his pictures. Over a hundred of his paintings were shown at the exhibitions of the Royal Society of British Artists. He was a member of the RBA, serving as Secretary when James McNeill Whistler was President. Cauty was also a curator of the Lower Schools at the Royal Academy. One of his colleagues there, the sculptor Horace Montford, exhibited a portrait bust of him at the RBA in 1892: *Horace H. Cauty, Esq., R.B.A.*

Staying with the Cautys at Kensington in 1881 was Selina Gooding, aged five (described in the census as 'niece'). She was possibly the subject of H. H. Cauty's painting *My first sitting: a shy sitter* (RA 1882). His painting *Coming in on the first of the tide* (RA 1900) is illustrated in *Royal Academy Pictures*, Cassell & Co., 1900.

Cauty died at Minsmere, his house in Sutton, on 6 February 1909, leaving everything he had, which was not very much, to his 'dear wife Laura Anne and her heirs'. His death was totally ignored by the local press. But some years earlier the *Sutton Advertiser*, 18 May 1895, had reviewed one of his paintings:

> Mr. Horace H. Cauty's genre deserves a strong commendation, if only for its ambitious size and aim. It is called *Her Lord and Master* [exhibited RA 1895] and shows a tramp, his wife and his dog. So far from holding his little helpmate "a little dearer than his horse" (as Tennyson had it) he evidently considered her a good deal less than his canine mongrel. How much less than himself only such a poor man's drudge could tell.

The Cautys, father and son, painted hundreds of works, though today their paintings are seldom seen on the market. In October 1979 an oil by the younger Cauty, entitled *The Ace*, showing a tennis match being played on the private court of a large house, was sold

at Sotheby's Belgravia for £1,200.

More recently, his oil on canvas, *Pig and young girl* (illus. in *Arts Review* 1987) was sold for £4,800 at the Devon Fine Art Auction House, Honiton.

Exhib: B; D; L; M; RA; RBA; RHA; RI; ROI
Bibliog: BEN; DBA; GW; TB; WOOD

CAUTY, Horace Robert 1821/2–1895
Dorset Villa, 24 Victoria Road, Sutton 1891–1895
Horace Robert Cauty painted landscapes in oil and watercolour, exhibiting over seventy of them at the exhibitions of the Royal Society of British Artists. Born in Missenden, Berkshire, he lived for many years in Campden Hill, Kensington, a part of London where middle-class families lived alongside a colony of artists – some young and struggling, others who had 'arrived'. Holman Hunt lived in the district; so, too, did Lord Leighton. It was a mixed area of very large houses grading down to 'exceedingly little houses' (LUCAS. E. V. *London*, 1926).

The Cauty establishment, which embraced Horace Robert, his wife Louisa, and their son Horace Henry (q.v.), was modest. They employed one servant, Helen O'Brien, at their first Kensington address; but when they moved to a house in Gordon Place, Kensington, they had a lodger: widower Sidney Trefusis Whiteford, a West Country painter; and were thus able to afford to keep two servants.

In the 1851 census Horace Robert Cauty is described as a 'Private tutor, language in general'; but by 1871 this had changed to 'Visiting tutor and artist'. During the 1870s he started to exhibit at the London galleries where his views of the West Country, Yorkshire and Scotland were all modestly priced at less than twenty guineas each.

Four years before he died, he moved to Sutton, living with his son and daughter-in-law at Dorset Villa in Victoria Road. From that address he submitted three paintings of local scenes to the RBA: *Old Mill, Carshalton* (1892), *An Old Mill on the Wandle, Surrey* (1893) and *Entrance to Carshalton Park, Surrey* (1893). Cauty died at Dorset Villa on 5 May 1895.

Exhib: B; M; RA; RBA; RI
Bibliog: BEN; DBA; TB; WOOD

CHADBURN, George Haworthe, F.R.S.A., F.C.I.A.D., R.B.A. 1870–1950
Trevenna, Cheam Road, Sutton 1889–1899
George Chadburn, a landscape and portrait painter and illustrator, was born in Yorkshire in 1870, the son of Grace (née Tetley), and the Rev. James Chadburn, who succeeded the Reverend Mr Barnes as the Minister of Sutton Congregational Church in 1889. George was educated at Mill Hill School and studied art at St John's Wood Art School, Westminster Art School, the Slade and the Royal Academy Schools. He also spent some time in Paris, where he attended L'Academie Julian under Lefèvre and Fleury, exhibited at the Salon and became a member of the Union Internationale des Beaux-Arts.

The first work he exhibited in this country was a

HORACE HENRY CAUTY   Oil 355×460mm
The Ace. 1885.   Photo courtesy Sotheby's Belgravia

27

ARTHUR HUGHES   Oil 890×495mm
April Love. 1856.   Tate Gallery

FRANK DADD   Watercolour
Portrait of Marjory Dadd. 1910.   Courtesy the Dadd family

MARGARET M. HOWARD
Oil 635×762mm
Adam and Eve in the Garden of Eden.
Sutton's Local Collection

still-life, shown at the 1891 exhibition of the Royal Society of British Artists. In 1902 he was elected a member of the RBA. He was also a member of the Art Workers' Guild, and for a period of five years served on the Technical Education Board of the L.C.C. Central School of Arts and Crafts.

In 1899 he married Mabel Harwood of Boston, Lincolnshire, who was, like himself, an illustrator of children's books. Chadburn exhibited ten works at the Royal Academy, one of which was a portrait of his wife; this was shown in 1909. His landscapes, usually in oil, are in strong colours, Chadburn proving particularly adept at painting river scenes of Norfolk and Suffolk. He signed his work 'Haworthe Chadburn' in big, bold capital letters.

He had two other major interests: horticulture and chess; winning the Dykes Medal for Horticulture in 1934 and 1941, and the Michael Foster Medal for Chess in 1946. He spent his final years in the West Country and died at Budleigh Salterton on 29 January 1950.

Exhib: P; RA; RBA
Bibliog: BEN; DBA; GW; TB; WOOD; *Who Was Who 1941–1950*
Obit: *The Times*, 2 February 1950

CHANTREY BEQUEST

The 'Chantrey Bequest' has been mentioned on a number of occasions in this book; here is a brief explanation of its terms:

Sir Frances Chantrey died in 1841, leaving a bequest for 'the encouragement of British Fine Art in Painting and Sculpture only'. It was to come into effect on the death or second marriage of his widow; and under its terms the President and Council of the Royal Academy were empowered to purchase 'works of Fine Art of the highest merit in painting and sculpture that can be obtained'. The bequest did not become available until 1875 and the first purchases were made in 1877. Most of the collection is housed at the Tate Gallery, though some of the works are usually on loan elsewhere.

CHARLEY, Constance S. Exhib: 1889–1901

Kilmeedy, Ringstead Road, Sutton c.1885–1890
In 1889 Constance Charley of Kilmeedy, Sutton – the name of the householder there was W. R. Charley – exhibited a watercolour entitled *Sheep Haven* at the Society of Women Artists' exhibition, the asking price being four guineas. She later lived in London.

Exhib: SWA
Bibliog: DBA

CHARRINGTON, Mary Louisa 1868–1957

Hawkley Lodge, Worcester Road, Sutton pre-1880–1898
The Rev. Nicholas G. Charrington, his wife Mary, his son Francis and his two daughters Fanny and Mary Louisa, came to Sutton from Hampshire shortly before 1880. Their new home, Hawkley Lodge, was named after the village they had just left.

Mary Louisa, the youngest of the family, was born in Hawkley, Hampshire, in 1868. She was artistic, exhibiting two paintings with the Society of Women Artists, one of which, *A Study in Still-life*, was sent in from Sutton. After the Reverend N. G. Charrington died, the family moved to Leatherhead. Mary Charrington never married, outlived all her family and died in London on 9 December 1957, aged eighty-nine.

Exhib: SWA
Bibliog: DBA

CHESHIRE, William 1837–1915

Stirling Villa, Benhill Wood Road, Sutton c.1869–1915
William Cheshire, a very successful wood engraver whose work, according to Ruskin (q.v.) was 'as good wood cutting as can be', lived in Sutton for over forty years. A popular, much respected citizen, he was an early member of the Surrey Art Circle (q.v.), taking part in their first annual exhibition, held at Sutton Public Hall in 1889.

Born in Lambeth in 1837, the year of Queen Victoria's accession, he was apprenticed at the age of fifteen to Josiah Whymper whose engraving business was then the most thriving in London. Fellow apprentices included Frederick Walker (q.v.), J. W. North and G. J. Pinwell. During this period, the 'golden age' of British book illustration, wood engravers were often paid more for their blocks than were the artists who had drawn the original designs.

At the end of his apprenticeship, Cheshire stayed on with Whymper until he had gained enough experience and made enough money to set up on his own. In 1862, in partnership with a man called Dickenson, he started up his own workshop, engaging a drawing master for his pupils. He later worked alone at various London workshops until the 1870s when he was joined by his nephew, James Reynolds Cheshire. In 1879 they opened an office at 23 Holborn Viaduct, where they remained until 1901, signing their work 'W. J. R. Cheshire sc', or 'W. & J. R. Cheshire'. They supplied engravings for the *Illustrated London News*, the *English Illustrated Magazine* and other periodicals, and provided the blocks for Richard Jefferies's *Summer in Somerset* (1887–8).

William Cheshire knew and admired the work of the Bewicks, like them taking pleasure in observing nature and studying the movements of birds. Charles Whymper, the son of Josiah, was moved to write 'Very beautiful indeed – C. W.' on Cheshire's proof of a blackcock for Whymper's article 'Nature through a field glass', in the *Art Journal*, March 1885.

Well known in Sutton for his charitable deeds, Cheshire would think nothing of walking for miles in the worst sort of weather to answer a distress call. His engraving business was so successful that when he died at Stirling Villa on 18 October 1915, he was able to leave a house to each of his sons and one to his unmarried daughter. The family home at Sutton went to his eldest son; Dowdeswell, in Grosvenor Avenue, Carshalton, was left to his daughter Harriet; and Trescoe, in the same road, went to one of his sons. His other two sons inherited properties at Surbiton.

Exhib: SAC
Bibliog: ENGEN(2); Surrey Artists and their Homes. VI.–Mr. William Cheshire. *Sutton and Epsom Advertiser*, 26 November 1887

CLIFFORD, Harry Percy, R.B.A. (Diploma), R.C.A. 1870–1943

Harry Percy Clifford taught landscape painting and black-and-white work at Sutton Art School in the 1920s, during which time one of his pupils was Frank Worker (q.v.). Born and educated in Rochester, the son of W. H. Clifford, he trained at the Royal College of Art where he won gold and silver medals. He later studied in Paris. Clifford was elected a member of the Royal Society of British Artists in 1898, exhibiting over a hundred works with them.

Specialising in architectural studies, he illustrated several books, including *Lincoln* and *Rochester* in the Bell's Cathedral Series. Some of his finest drawings can be seen in the book *Art in England during the Elizabethan and Stuart Periods*, edited by Charles Holme and published by The Studio in 1908. He lived in the London area for most of his life and died at Putney Hospital on 8 July 1943.

Exhib: B; L; M; P; RA; RBA; RI
Bibliog: BEN; DBA; GW; TB; *Who's Who in Art*, 1929

COMPER, John Ninian (later Sir Ninian) 1864–1960

Born in Aberdeen and articled to the well-known church architect G. F. Bodley, Ninian Comper became a very important figure in the changing world of ecclesiastical design in the last years of the nineteenth century, and came to dominate the scene in the first half of the twentieth. He developed the form of altar known as the English altar which, in accordance with the principles of Percy Dearmer and his followers, reflected the attempts of one part of the Church of England to return to the liturgy and practices of the church in England before the Reformation. This was a reaction against the Italianising influence of the Anglo-Catholic party which had grown out of the Oxford Movement and which sought to copy all things Roman. The 'English' altar was set within four posts (riddells) with curtains or screens on three sides (see Martin Travers (q.v.)).

Bodley had done some work in All Saints' Church, Carshalton, and the rood screen and reredos are his work (from the early 1900s), both being painted later by Comper in the redecoration scheme of 1931. Comper had developed a theory of design in which he tried to avoid the over-zealous copying of earlier historical styles, which in his opinion had become sterile and which he called 'Unity by Exclusion'. After travelling widely as a young man, he came to advocate a form of eclecticism which he entitled 'Unity by Inclusion'. This meant the use of styles, ideas and materials from many different periods and traditions, side by side in one building, brought together in such a way as to produce a pleasing harmony.

Comper was an accomplished architect and liked to be the designer both of the building itself and of its contents, including the vestments and altar linen; but

Interior view of All Saints' Church, Carshalton, showing decoration by J. NINIAN COMPER.

he also undertook restoration work. He must have liked All Saints', with its hotch-potch of building styles from so many different centuries and was happy to add from time to time the vivid polychromatic decorations which can still be seen there. In 1946 he was responsible for the flamboyant organ at the west end of the church and even went so far as to embellish the Georgian pulpit.

Comper was an excellent artist in stained glass. Unfortunately, there are no examples of his work in this sphere in the borough, the nearest being at St Andrew's Church, Croydon, signed with his own special mark, in the tradition of stained glass artists: two strawberries with a leaf and a flower.

It appears, from an undated brochure of the late 1920s or early 1930s, that Comper was engaged to carry out extensive alterations to the church of St Nicholas in Sutton. His design for the chancel can be seen in the brochure. Opinions are divided as to whether to regret or rejoice that it was never carried out.

Sir Ninian died ten years after receiving his knighthood, aged ninety-six and still in practice. His ashes are interred in the north aisle of Westminster

Abbey, below a series of windows which he had designed.

Jean M. Moore

Exhib: RA; RSA
Bibliog: DBA; *Who Was Who 1951–1960; Who's Who in Art* – several editions

CONSTABLE, John, R.A. 1776–1837

Mention must be made, if only briefly, of the visits to this part of Surrey by John Constable, one of the greatest and perhaps the best known landscape painter this country has ever produced. The visits were paid to his aunt and uncle, Mary and James Gubbins, in Epsom. He is known to have stayed with them in 1806, and then yearly from 1809 until 1812 inclusive, but possibly visited them on other occasions as well, although the visits have not been recorded. Oil paintings, watercolours and sketches have survived from the visits, including some delightful drawings of his cousins. There is a small watercolour of *Epsom Common* (coll. Mr and Mrs Tom Girtin), two views of *Epsom Church* (one is in the V&A), a watercolour of *Pitt Place, Epsom* . . . (V&A), an oil painting of *Epsom*, dated June 1809 (Tate AG) and an oil painting entitled *James Gubbins' House at Epsom* c.1806 (private coll.).

His other connection with this area came through his visit to Woodmansterne in 1825. He was there – somewhat reluctantly – to paint in oil *The Lambert Children*. In a letter to his friend Archdeacon Fisher, he wrote, '. . . it is my wife's connection and I thought it prudent to put a good face on it'. The visit took place in the January of that year and he stayed for ten days. The exercise seems to have been a comparatively painless one, since the children – William, George Patrick and Mary – behaved reasonably well. And the resulting portrait of the three children with their donkey is quite charming.

The children had been sent to their grandfather's house, Shortes Place, from India where their father, William, was in the Civil Service; he wished them to have an English education. During the same year (1825), Constable painted a portrait of the children's grandfather, *Mr. Lambert* (William Lambert, J.P. – he sold The Oaks to the 12th Earl of Derby in 1788) who sat for it in London. The two paintings were destined for India, the children's aunt Jane writing to their father that the portraits were 'in oils which must take some time to dry or they spoil before they reach India'. The portrait of William Lambert is privately owned. The painting of the children, which passed down by descent to the Rivaz family, was sold at Sotheby's (Lot 75) on 13 March 1985 for £242,000.

Exhib: RA
Bibliog: BECKETT, R. B. Constable at Epsom. *Apollo*, lxxxi, 1965, p. 191; ROGERS, D. A John Constable rediscovered. *Burlington Magazine*, xcii, Aug. 1950, p. 228; *British Paintings 1500–1850*. Sotheby's, 13 March 1985

CORBOULD, Edward Henry, R.I. 1815–1905

Annandale, Sutton Common Road, Sutton 1880s
In 1851 Queen Victoria was looking for a drawing instructor to the royal children. She had seen and admired the work of the artist Edward Corbould. Indeed, in 1842, the Prince Consort had bought Corbould's watercolour *The Woman taken in Adultery* for the Royal Collection; and in 1848 the artist had painted a watercolour of Britannia which was used on the postage stamps of Barbados, Mauritius and Trinidad. The Queen sent her Equerry, Sir Charles Phipps, to call on the artist to offer him the position of drawing instructor.

Taken by surprise, Corbould accepted immediately. But on thinking it over and realising what it would entail, he changed his mind. He was told firmly by Phipps, however, that since Her Majesty had already been apprised of his acceptance there was absolutely no question of Corbould backing out. So, rather apprehensively, Corbould embarked on an association with the Royal Family which was to last for twenty-one years and which, in fact, proved to be a very happy and rewarding one. He travelled regularly between London and Windsor; used to stay at Osborne House for several days at a time and would occasionally spend up to a month at Balmoral.

Edward Henry Corbould, a third generation artist, was the son of Henry Corbould, an historical painter and draughtsman, and was the grandson of Richard Corbould, a painter of portraits, landscapes and historical scenes. Edward was born on 5 December 1815 at Great Coram Street, centre of London's art

EDWARD H. CORBOULD
Illustration to *The Faerie Queen* by Edmund Spenser, Routledge, 1853.

world, and after early drawing lessons from his father, he studied both at the Royal Academy and under Sir Henry Sass. He was a brilliant pupil, winning gold medals at the Society of Arts for watercolours and sculptures. Watercolour painting gradually became the main focus of his attention, although he also carried out some wood engravings and etchings. He abandoned sculpture at an early age, but left some interesting drawings for proposed sculptures intended for Blackfriars Bridge, which were never carried out.

Corbould was a member of the Royal Institute of Painters in Water-Colours (1838), where he exhibited over two hundred works. He also exhibited regularly at other London galleries including the Royal Academy. His subjects were mainly architectural, historical, biblical and literary; his inspiration frequently coming from the early English poets, or Shakespeare. Countless publications were illustrated by him, including *Sporting Review, Churchman's Magazine* and *Cassell's Magazine*. One of Corbould's most famous paintings, *The Canterbury Pilgrims assembling at the Old Tabard Inn,* became widely known through its 1843 mezzotint by C. E. Wagstaff. Another commercial success, through its engraving by J. J. Chant in 1860, was *Lady Godiva.*

Edward Corbould was one of the most distinguished artists living in Sutton during the Victorian period. He enjoyed a certain aura through his association with the Royal Family and was the obvious choice for President when the Surrey Art Circle (q.v.) was formed in Sutton in 1888. He was a member until his death and designed the Circle's badge. The programme he designed for the Art Circle's first anniversary exhibition was said to be a work of art in itself. Annandale, his home at Sutton during the 1880s, was the first house on the north side of the common, his studio window overlooking Rose Hill.

He married three times. His first wife was Fanny Heath, the daughter of the engraver Charles Heath. She died in 1850, and a year later he married Anne Middleton Wilson who died in 1866. His third wife was Anne Mellis Saunders. Corbould had three sons and four daughters, some of them being named after members of the Royal Family. Whilst he was living in Sutton, he exhibited a portrait of one of his daughters, *The painter's youngest daughter, Editha,* at the RI (1888). Two of his granddaughters, Mrs Eveline Corbould-Ellis and Mrs Weatherley, were artists; the latter painted a portrait miniature of him. Corbould's nephew, the *Punch* artist A. Chantrey Corbould, often stayed at Sutton with his uncle.

Despite his association with royalty and the success he enjoyed in his career, Corbould is said to have remained modest and unassuming. He had a fund of anecdotes about the Royal Family, a favourite being of how the Princess Royal over-zealously drew twenty virgins instead of ten when she was illustrating the parable of the Wise and Foolish Virgins and had to rub out every second one. Annandale was filled with mementos of Corbould's royal pupils. In his will he bequeathed his 'best water colour painting (of recent

years) . . . "The Death of Tursitan the Leader of the Norman Band in Beverley Minster" ' to Queen Victoria, although she did in fact die before him (this painting was exhibited at the RHA in 1886 when the artist was living in Sutton). The Queen always treated him with great kindness; but in 1880, when she was seeking a successor to Richard Redgrave as 'Surveyor of Her Majesty's Pictures', she implied, in a letter to her daughter, that 'poor Corbould' would not do. A large collection of Corbould's paintings and drawings are in the Royal Collection. They include his two watercolour sketches for postage stamps; for in addition to the one already mentioned, he painted a watercolour of Queen Victoria which was engraved by Charles Henry Jeens for the Tasmania (Van Diemans Land) stamp.

Corbould died at Kensington on 16 January 1905, leaving the bulk of his paintings to Victor Albert Edward Corbould, his son by his first wife.

Exhib: G; GI; L; M; RA; RHA; RI; ROI; SAC
Coll: Ashmolean Museum, Oxford; BM; Soane Museum, London; V&A; Royal Collection
Illus: See ENGEN (2), and HOUFE
Bibliog: BEN; DBA; DNB; ENGEN(2); HOUFE; MALLALIEU; TB; WOOD. ROBERTS, J. *Royal Artists.* Grafton Books, 1987; Surrey Artists and their Homes. III.–Mr. E. Corbould, R. I. *Sutton and Epsom Advertiser* 12 November 1887

CORK, Alice b. 1870/1
Grennell House, Grennell Road, Sutton c.1876–c.1905
This artist, born in Hackney, was the daughter and eldest child of Nathaniel Cork, a bank manager, and his wife Isabella. The year 1897 was an auspicious one for the family: Nathaniel was the Chairman of the Sutton and Cheam Conservative Association, and his daughter Alice exhibited a painting entitled *Not to be trifled with* at the Society of Women Artists' exhibition. Since the Corks lived adjacent to the Puckles, Alice Cork and Ethel Puckle (q.v.) may have studied art together.

Exhib: SWA
Bibliog: DBA

*COWIE, Richard Kenneth 1877–1956
58 Salisbury Avenue, Cheam 1941–1956
Richard Cowie, who was employed in a bank, was also an amateur artist, exhibiting one watercolour, *Greenwich* (1940), at the Royal Hibernian Academy and another, *Here stood St. Olave's* (1941), at the Royal Academy.

The Cowies took up residence in Salisbury Avenue, Cheam, during the early years of the Second World War, and Richard Cowie painted two watercolours commemorating the Sutton Civil Defence Staff's valuable contribution to the war effort (Sutton's Local Collection).

A former resident of Cheam who knew the family well (Cowie painted a portrait of her son), says that Cowie and his wife once ran an Austrian Club, first in Blackheath and then in Baker Street, London. Its purpose was to help Austrian students and others to learn English. Cowie's only son, Francis, was tragically killed in a road accident; his daughter Joan now lives in Sussex. Richard Cowie died on 4 October 1956, his wife having died earlier.

Exhib: RA; RHA
Coll: Sutton LC
Bibliog: DBA

CRAIG, Edward Henry Gordon, R.D.I. 1872–1966
Rose Cottage (now 230), London Road, Hackbridge 1898–1899

Edward Gordon Craig had a long and varied life, gaining distinction as an actor, an artist and a stage designer, with an attendant reputation as a womaniser, most notably as the lover of Isadora Duncan. He was the father of many children by various mothers. His enduring importance is as a stage designer, his vision of the theatre being decades ahead of its time in its rejection of 'realism'. He spent about a year, from August 1898 to May 1899, living in a rented house at Hackbridge, at a stage of his life which was, as we shall see, productive and transitional.

Craig, known in the family as 'Teddy', was born in Stevenage, Hertfordshire, on 16 January 1872, the illegitimate son of the famous actress Ellen Terry and the important architect and designer E. W. Godwin. At the time of his birth Ellen Terry was still the wife of the painter G. F. Watts, whom she had married when she was sixteen and he forty-six. Although the marriage was short-lived, Watts did not agree to a divorce until more than ten years later. By then Ellen Terry had eloped with Godwin, temporarily given up her career to be with him and had borne his child. Godwin and Terry never married, separating in 1875, but Craig always maintained that his mother never stopped loving Godwin.

Ellen Terry waited until 1888 to have her son christened. She named him Edward after his father; Henry after her esteemed stage partner, Henry Irving; Gordon after his godmother, Lady Gordon; and Craig from the Scottish island Ailsa Craig, which she had seen in 1883. Keen to have his own name and not to become known just as Ellen Terry's son, at one time Craig called himself Edward Wardell (in 1878 his mother had married an actor Charles Wardell). Craig scarcely remembered his own father, who had taken pains to ensure that his son should have only tasteful toys to play with. Japanese prints adorned the nursery walls, and Teddy was given Walter Crane's children's books to read. He was an attractive, much cosseted boy who grew up in a house full of women. His mother loved him very much and gave him constant support throughout her life. He was familiar with the theatre from an early age, going back-stage and having small walk-on parts from the age of six. However, although he enjoyed acting, he did not take it seriously, preferring to concentrate his energies on stage designing.

He was educated at Southfield Park Preparatory School, which he entered in 1883, then at Bradfield College and finally at Heidelberg, from which he was expelled. He continued his education under private tutors. At about this time – 1889 – his mother rented a holiday home at Hampton Court, called Rose Cottage. Craig later chose this name for his house at Hackbridge, in memory of happy days at Hampton Court.

In 1893 Craig married May Gibson and they set up home at the Audrey Arms, Uxbridge, a house owned by Ellen Terry. Their neighbours were William Nicholson and James Pryde who, under the name of the 'Beggarstaff Brothers', were designing strikingly simple and bold wood-cuts and posters. They influenced Craig, who learned, from watching Nicholson, how to make wood-cuts. He was soon spending most of his time designing and cutting bookplates and illustrations.

During the early 1890s he was drawn more and more to graphic art and spent much of his time with artists, becoming acquainted with Max Beerbohm and William Rothenstein. Craig moved to Bedford Park, an area full of writers and artists (including W. B. Yeats who was to become one of the first people to write and congratulate him on his stage designs). Then, in 1897, he left his wife and four children and went to live at Thames Ditton. In the same year he met Martin Shaw of the Purcell Operatic Society, with whom he was to share an admiration for Purcell and Handel. They later collaborated on *Dido and Aeneas* (1900) and *Acis and Galatea* (1902). Craig enjoyed the experience of working with a colleague whom he admired and who accepted his ideas. It also gave him a chance to work in a rewarding musical context.

In 1898 Craig came to live at Hackbridge, accompanied by his mistress of the time, Jess Dorynne. In his autobiography he is slightly scathing about her, implying that they did not really love each other but were looking for company. For thirty pounds per annum they rented the house that is now no. 230 London Road. Picturesquely covered in ivy, it belonged to Miss Sheppy, who lived next door in Beddington Park Villa. The short terrace of houses directly overlooks Beddington Park, and until about the 1920s there were very few houses in that part of the road, so it would have been a charmingly bucolic place in which to live. Craig decorated the house in typical avant-garde aesthetic style, which must have been quite a shock to his neighbours. He painted the floorboards shiny black and put brown wrapping paper on the walls up to dado level and cream manilla paper above. The woodwork was laurel green, a favourite Aesthetic Movement colour. A house decorated in this way today would still seem pretty avant-garde in Hackbridge, but at the time it was in many ways typical of the original use of often cheap materials.

Craig's main occupation at Hackbridge was wood engraving and designing bookplates. By then he had given up acting, wishing to concentrate more on stage design and the production side of things, but was not yet sure how to go about it. The most significant feature of Craig's stay at Hackbridge was his magazine *The Page*, the first copy appearing early in 1898 with a wrapper in the favoured coarse brown paper. It contained an article about Hamlet, a fable by Tolstoy,

several original wood-cut illustrations and bookplates, and a quotation from Marcus Aurelius. It was printed on one side of the paper only, had a print run of 140 (soon increased to 400) and cost one shilling and two pence per copy. *The Page* was well received in *The Studio, The Artist, The Sphere* and other like publications, and was supported by Craig's friends, who included the artists Max Beerbohm, Burne-Jones and James Pryde, and the actor Henry Irving. When Craig needed more articles he wrote them himself, under a variety of pseudonyms: Edward Arden, Samuel Drayton and James Bath (who had a brother called Oliver). From the second issue to the last, in 1901, *The Page* was published 'at the sign of the Rose', although Craig did in fact move out in May 1899 when his wife came to live at Hackbridge. The magazine did quite well despite the fact that it never actually made any money. The critic J. M. Bulloch concocted a rhyme, published in the *Sketch*:

> At the Sign of the Rose,
> I edit the Page,
> For Belles and for Beaux,
> At the Sign of the Rose,
> And everyone knows
> I'm not on the stage –
> At the Sign of the Rose,
> I edit the Page

At Hackbridge Craig conceived the idea for a *Book of Penny Toys*, his main motivation being to do the book as a present for his own children, whom he now rarely saw as they lived with their mother. He wrote in his autobiography that this separation upset him so much it made him immune from great emotional distress in all future romantic encounters. Since all the plates had to be hand-coloured, the book did not actually appear until over a year after it had been announced in *The Page* (Oct. 1898), giving Mrs Percy Dearmer the time to steal both the idea and the title. Craig's cover had to be re-designed with an amended title: *Gordon Craig's Book of Penny Toys*. The book had a series of bold, simple designs based on Craig's own collection of wooden toys, with a verse and a wood-cut end-piece for each.

It was also whilst he was at Hackbridge that the

pattern of his future life evolved. He became more interested in music, read Goethe and Ibsen and started making sketches for imagined productions. Even at this stage these designs were quite unlike any other contemporary work. Rejecting the clutter of realistic stage sets, Craig aimed for something which would evoke a more emotional response. He used cloths painted in a single glowing colour and stage lighting in a dynamic way that changed the colours of the scene, as the mood of the play changed. England was not, however, ready yet for this sort of thing and Craig had to go to Europe to find the work he wanted in the theatre.

Craig and Jess Dorynne left Hackbridge for Battersea and later lived in Hampstead. Craig staged productions for the Purcell Operatic Society until it folded for lack of funds, even though perceptive critics praised the sense of 'real unreality' he created on the stage. But this kind of work failed to provide him with the income he needed, especially now that he had started another family with Elena Meo, who remained his favourite mistress until her death in 1957. In 1904 Craig went to Germany at the request of Count Kessler, to work at the Lessing Theatre in Berlin. He never took up residence in England again. His fame in Europe grew, helped by the publication of another magazine *The Mask* (1908–1929), which spread his ideas about the theatre. He moved around Europe – to Germany, Italy, Russia and finally the South of France – sometimes with Elena and their children, who came to live in Italy with him in 1917, sometimes alone. His fairly brief affair with Isadora Duncan lasted from 1904 until 1905.

The richness of Craig's work in Europe is outside the scope of this book. But it was at Hackbridge that he finally decided which direction his life was to take; where he concentrated systematically for the first time on getting to know the major works of the theatre, and the mechanics of mounting a production. It was a fertile and contented time in a turbulent life full of emotional and financial troubles.

Cynthia Bradley

Exhib: BG; GI; LEI; RED; RHA
Coll: BM; Courtauld Inst.; V&A; New York; Vienna; Amsterdam; Zurich, etc.
Published: See HOUFE, and PEPPIN
Illus: See HOUFE, and PEPPIN.
Bibliog: BEN; DBA; GW; HOUFE; PEPPIN; TB; V; *Who's Who in Art* – several editions; *Who Was Who 1961–1970*; See also HOUFE, and PEPPIN

DADD, Frank, R.I., R.O.I. 1851–1929

Morwenstow, Springfield Road, Wallington, 1903–1919
In 1903, when Frank Dadd came to live at Wallington, he was an established artist, a member of the Royal Institute of Painters in Water-Colours (1884) and a member of the Royal Institute of Oil Painters (1885). But it was in 1908, when he was living at Wallington,

that his watercolour *Gold Lace has a Charm for the Fair*, now at the Tate Gallery, was bought for £105 by the Chantrey Bequest (q.v.). This charming painting shows three young army officers walking past an inn. One of them is casting an eye over three young ladies, who are directing equally admiring – if somewhat haughty – glances toward the officers. A small girl holding a dog on a lead, and a couple of gossiping servants from the inn complete the picture. This painting, set in Dadd's favourite period, the late eighteenth century, has all the qualities associated with the artist at his best. Like most of his paintings, it tells a story. There is the inevitable dog, no doubt modelled on one of his own; there is a meticulous attention to detail in the dresses and uniforms; there is a touch of humour.

He was born on 28 March 1851 at 54 High Street, Whitechapel, London. His father, Robert Dadd, the eldest of nine children, was a chemist whose brother – and Frank's uncle – was the artist Richard Dadd, who murdered his own father and spent the rest of his life in Bethlem, and then Broadmoor, painting works which are now highly esteemed and extremely expensive. Robert Dadd had to shoulder most of the family problems when his father was killed. An oil portrait showing him in old age, painted by Frank Dadd, is in the family collection.

Frank was the third of six children, three boys and three girls. His mother, Catherine, was the daughter of Thomas Carter, a well known shipbuilder on the Thames; and Frank spent his childhood holidays clambering over the ships in his grandfather's dockyard, acquiring a knowledge of naval architecture which proved very useful later on when he painted river and coastal scenes. An early memory was of being taken to see the great Tooley Street fire. He made a sketch of this – his first attempt at drawing an 'incident'.

Frank Dadd was educated privately. On 23 January 1871 he entered the Royal Academy Schools where he won a silver medal for 'Drawing from Life'. Charles Landseer was the Keeper of the Schools, but it was from Lord Leighton, a Visitor, that Frank learned the importance of good drawing and anatomical accuracy. He sold some of his drawings whilst he was still at the Academy Schools, and was lucky enough to find immediate employment when he left, largely through the good offices of the wood engraver John Greenaway, the father of Kate Greenaway. The Dadds were distant cousins of the Greenaways, their ties becoming even closer when John's other daughter Fanny married Edward Martin Dadd, Frank's brother. John Greenaway introduced Frank to the publishing house of Cassell and to the offices of the *Illustrated London News*.

A 'working artist' in the true sense of the word, Frank Dadd spent six or seven years from 1877 onwards with the *Illustrated London News*, at the same time illustrating stories and poems for *The Quiver*. In 1885 he moved on to *The Graphic*, where he came under constant pressure to meet its deadlines. A large two-page drawing of *The Jubilee Procession outside St. Paul's*, for instance, had to be completed in twenty-four

hours, accurate in all its details. *The Battle of Omdurman*, a four-page drawing, was finished in two days. He was forced to stay up all night, helped by his brother Stephen, to complete the historic *Return of the C.I.V.s*. He found himself cramming into a day and a half the work it should really have taken him a week to complete.

His output was vast. Between 1880 and 1900 he completed an average of one hundred black-and-white drawings per year, illustrated a number of books, and exhibited dozens of paintings at the Royal Academy and other galleries. In 1897 Cecil Rhodes commissioned Frank Dadd to paint *The Gallant Conduct of Lieutenant Fred Crewe*, an incident in the Matabele War; he presented the picture to the town of Durban.

Dadd was an enthusiastic collector of arms and armour, costume, and old furniture, and this might account for the historical accuracy of his work. Charles Ward, an old RA model, sat for him over a period of thirty years, one day disguised as a smuggler or highwayman, the next as a soldier or prizefighter. Jessie, née Hulbert, Frank's wife, can be recognised in an illustration to the story *Her Ambition*, in *The Quiver*, 1878, p. 409.

In 1903 the Dadd family came to live at Wallington, Frank renaming their house in Springfield Road (originally called *Homeleigh*), Morwenstow. They lived there for sixteen years. A photograph of the family, taken shortly before the outbreak of the First World War, shows them playing croquet on the lawn – an idyllically peaceful scene. A year or two later, however, the Dadd family suffered more than most from the horrors of the war. Frank's son, Captain Ralph Hulbert Dadd, never fully recovered from shell shock. Three of Frank's nephews were killed, another badly wounded. They were:
Philip John Dadd (1880–1916), killed on the Western Front. An artist and illustrator, he exhibited at the RA. He was the son of Frank's brother, Edward Martin Dadd, and a nephew of Kate Greenaway.
Stephen Gabriel Dadd, killed whilst serving with the Royal Naval Division in 1915 or 1916. A promising young sculptor, he exhibited four works at the RA.
Edmund Dadd, Captain with the Royal Welsh Fusiliers, killed at Ginchy on 3 September 1916. A friend of Robert Graves and Siegfried Sassoon, he appears in their books.
Julian Dadd, severely wounded in the throat. He was the 'Julian Durley' of Siegfried Sassoon's *Memoirs of an Infantry Officer*.

In 1919 Frank and Jessie Dadd left Wallington to live at West Lawn, Higher Brimley, Teignmouth, Devon, where Frank died ten years later. His daughter Marjory (Mrs Dennis) moved to Croydon. His son Geoffrey and family remained in Wallington until 1927, living in Woodcote Road. His other son, Captain Ralph H. Dadd, a bachelor, lived in Maldon Road, Wallington until 1929.

Frank Dadd sold Morwenstow to Charles Gulliver, the famous music hall and cinema proprietor, and race horse owner. In 1934 Dadd's old home became Collingwood Boys' School. The present Principal, Miss Jennifer Ingham, whose home it was for many

Frank Dadd, his wife Jessie and daughter Marjory, in the garden of their London home. c. 1882.
Photo courtesy the Dadd family

years, says that Frank Dadd's spacious studio, with its gallery modelled on the lines of a minstrels' gallery, remains virtually unchanged. It is now used as the school's assembly hall. Somehow it seems appropriate that the old home of Frank Dadd, illustrator of boys' adventure yarns, should be a boys' school. Wistaria (there when the Dadds occupied the house – Frank Dadd once painted an oil-sketch of it) still blooms in the garden.

Christopher Dadd, Frank Dadd's grandson, twelve years old when his grandfather died, remembers a kindly, but somewhat remote, man who could be rather severe at times. Photographs of the artist show an aesthetic-looking man with a longish nose and a humorous twinkle in his eye. He was an outdoor man, fond of walking in the countryside with his dogs, and he painted many landscape views of favourite places in Devon, in Suffolk and in Ireland.

He enjoyed a happy marriage. Still in the family collection is a Christmas card of a miniature landscape, surrounded with a border of flowers, painted by Frank and sent to Jessie in 1877. He died twenty-three years before her. When Jessie died, her last wish was for her ashes to be scattered at a certain spot near the Portsmouth Road where Frank's had been scattered in 1929.

Frank Dadd was a commercially successful artist who commanded high prices for his paintings. For instance, the asking price for *Horses for the King*, shown at the RI in 1901, was £262.10.0., then a considerable sum for a watercolour. His oil paintings would have been even more. Small wonder, then, that he could afford to buy a house the size of Morwenstow, which had its own studio.

Three military drawings by Frank Dadd are in the Royal Collection, and the following letter from Windsor Castle, dated 6 July 1887, is amongst his papers:

Dear Sir,
Mr. Dadd has been desired by the Queen to paint a picture of the Aldershot Review on the 9th inst.
Will you kindly grant him facilities to carry out Her Majesty's wishes,
Yours very truly
Arthur Biggs
The Quarter Master General

Frank Dadd continued to paint right up to his death on 7 March 1929. On 8 March 1929 the following obituary appeared in the Teignmouth Post:

His work has a pleasing freshness and a delicately sensitive handling of colour value that delight the eye. He continued his work right until the end in the best of health and having no warning of the heart failure that was so suddenly, so swiftly to snatch life away from him. He finished his last picture 'Going Home' only a few days before his death.

A letter to Frank and Jessie, at Christmas 1894, sent from Frank's uncle, John Alfred Dadd, who lived in Milwaukee, serves as a fitting epitaph:

> Frank – you are the veritable Dickens of Painting. I never saw English life scenes so well expressed or portrayed, they strike me so forcibly that on looking at them I seem to be in the Old World again . . .

Exhib: B; D; FIN; GI; L; M; RA; RI; ROI
Coll: BM; Exeter Museum; Royal Collection
Illus: See HOUFE; and PEPPIN
Bibliog: BEN; DBA; ENGEN(1&2); GW; HOUFE; MALLALIEU; PEPPIN; TB; WOOD; *Who's Who in Art*, 1929; *Who Was Who 1929–1940*; *Frank Dadd*. Heywood's Authentic Series of Press Biographies. Heywood & Co., Ltd., 150 Holborn, London, 1902
Obit: *The Times*, 9 March 1929; *The Connoisseur*, May 1929; *Teignmouth Post*, 8 March 1929

DADD, Marjory 1881–1963

Morwenstow, Springfield Road, Wallington 1903–1919
33 Sutton Court Road, Sutton 1958–1963

Marjory Dadd, the first-born child of Jessie and Frank Dadd (q.v.), was their only daughter and the only one of their three children to show any artistic talent. She was born in London in 1881 when the family were living at no. 38 Great Ormond Street. An early photograph shows her in the garden there, sitting on her mother's lap, with Frank Dadd beside them, holding a couple of dogs. Some tender drawings of Marjory as a baby have survived in Frank Dadd's sketchbooks (family collection).

She grew up to be charming and beautiful, tall and slender with reddish-gold hair, and was her father's model on numerous occasions. In 1910 he painted a portrait of her in watercolour, in which she is wearing an elegant gown which had once belonged to her grandmother – a dress of pink silk, trimmed with a fichu of lace threaded through with black velvet, and dating from about 1860. After Marjory's death, this dress and various other items of costume which had belonged to the Dadd family, were presented to the Victoria and Albert Museum, who kept most of the garments but passed the dress on to the Herbert Art Gallery, Coventry.

Marjory Dadd painted miniatures, and exhibited nine of them at the Royal Academy, her first in 1917, her last in 1926. One was of her cousin, *The Late Capt. Edmund H. Dadd, W.C., Royal Welsh Fusiliers* (1917); he was killed at Ginchy in the First World War. Other sitters included: *Captain Ralph Hulbert Dadd, M.G.C.* (1919), *Mrs. Frank Dadd* (1926) and *Peggy, daughter of Sydney Eade, Esq.* (1917).

Several examples of her work are in the family collection, including a number of charcoal drawings, an etched book-plate designed for Arthur Wilson-Green, M.A. and a miniature of her grandmother, *Mrs. Catherine Dadd*, copied from a painting by her great-uncle, Richard Dadd, the unhappy artist who murdered his own father and spent the rest of his life locked away in asylums.

From 1903 until 1919, Marjory lived in Wallington with her parents. After an earlier attachment, of which her father disapproved, she fell in love with Arthur Scotney Dennis and married him in 1913, a year before the outbreak of the First World War. Captain Dennis survived the trenches, and after the war the couple lived in Croydon, later moving to Purley where they remained until 1958. There were no children of the marriage. However, after Frank Dadd's death in 1929, Marjory's widowed mother came to live with them and was cared for by Marjory until she died in 1952 at the great age of ninety-four.

Marjory, the practical, energetic partner of the marriage, did most of the gardening and many of the odd jobs about the house. A photograph showing her in middle age reveals that she kept her good looks and remained slim and elegant. As the years went by she did less and less painting, family commitments leaving her little time for anything else. Also, she no doubt missed the help and encouragement of her father; all her RA paintings were exhibited before he died. Apparently, she did some teaching. Recently, a lady who was introduced to a member of the Dadd family told him that she had been taught art by Marjory Dadd.

After Arthur Dennis's death in 1958, Marjory sold the house at Purley and moved to Sutton, living in Sutton Court Road. She died in a Cheam nursing home on 8 January 1963.

Exhib: RA
Bibliog: DBA

DAVIES, Rita M. Exhib: 1917

Glyndwr, Cornwall Road, Sutton 1917–1928

Rita M. Davies exhibited one work at the Royal Cambrian Academy, sent in from Sutton in 1917. A Dr Davies is listed as the householder at Glyndwr from 1917–1928 (Pile).

Exhib: R CamA
Bibliog: DBA

DE LACY, Charles John 1856–c.1936

Sunnydale, 39 Shirley Avenue, Cheam c.1926–c.1936

Charles John De Lacy, a painter in oil and watercolour of ships, dockyard scenes and naval history, lived in Cheam during the last decade of his life. The house he lived in, Sunnydale, in Shirley Avenue, was then – as it is now – a largish, suburban, detached house set in an attractive tree-lined road on the southern slopes of the village. When the De Lacys moved into the area the house was new. The district still ranks as one of the most attractive in the borough, its land rising gently toward the Banstead Downs. De Lacy, who lived for most of his life in more urban areas, must have found in Cheam a haven of peace during his final years.

He was born in Sunderland in 1856, into a family that already had artistic leanings. His father, Robert De Lacy, was a painter, a photographer and a musician. Charles did not, however, follow his father directly but chose instead to train as an engineer. As such he had service experience in the army and navy, gaining a working knowledge of the sea and ships which later stood him in good stead when he came to paint his large seascapes. His understanding of the way ships perform and his love of the sea and all things naval come through strongly in his paintings.

By 1880 Charles had moved to London, meeting and marrying the nineteen-year-old Alice Harriot Hill. Their first daughter, Constance, was born within a year of their marriage. They settled in Lambeth, where Charles attended the art school, later studying at South Kensington and at the National Gallery. From 1890 onwards he worked as an illustrator on *The Graphic*, the *Illustrated London News*, *Sporting and Dramatic* and other magazines. He also illustrated books. But his real interest lay in painting dramatic panoramas of the important naval events of the Boer War and the First World War.

In 1885 he sent two paintings to the Royal Society of British Artists' exhibition: *The Thames at Greenwich* and *Whitstable Harbour*, and subsequently exhibited thirteen more with the RBA – all river or sea views. In 1889 he had his first acceptance at the Royal Academy and continued to exhibit there until 1918, his most important works being *Troops for Table Bay* (1900), *The sinking of the Lusitania* (1915) and *The storming of Zeebrugge* (1918). Occasionally he would send paintings to Newcastle to be shown at the Bewick Club, and in 1920 he exhibited two works with the Surrey Art Circle (q.v.), *Flanders, 1914 – the canal to Bruges*, and an artist's proof etching of his 'National Picture', *H.M.S. Vindictive storming Zeebrugge Mole, St. George's Day, 1918*.

He became a well known recorder of events, his paintings valued as much for their historical accuracy as for their intrinsic merit. In 1912 the Pool of London Authority exhibited Charles De Lacy's watercolour sketches for the proposed George V Docks. When peace came at the end of the First World War he spent the following years, up to his death, painting views of the River Thames and carrying out commissions for bodies like the Admiralty and Armstrong and Whitworth. Many of his paintings are owned by the Admiralty; others can be seen at the National Maritime Museum at Greenwich.

An interesting work by De Lacy, carried out in his usual energetic style, is still *in situ* at Boyne House, Shirley Avenue, Cheam, next door to where the artist used to live. Entitled *War with Holland*, dated 1928 and on an oak panel, it hangs above the fireplace in the dining room. It was almost certainly commissioned by the then owner, a Mr Dempsey.

Although Charles De Lacy is not in the top league of marine painters, his works are esteemed by collectors for their dramatic, full-blooded, romantic content. His character as an artist is nicely summed up in his own words. Under 'recreation' in *Who's Who in Art* he put 'Busman's holiday – painting something fresh'. By the time of his death it is possible that he was no longer living at Cheam. His wife, Alice De Lacy, died in Sussex in 1934, but as yet the whereabouts or exact date of Charles's death are uncertain.

Gillian Mortimer

Exhib: L; M; RA; RBA; SAC; Newcastle

Coll: The Admiralty; National Maritime Mus., Greenwich.
Illus: COOKE, A. O. *A Book about Ships*. 1914; KINGSTON, W. H. G. *Hurricane Hurry*. Griffith Farran Browne & Co., Ltd. N.D.; MARGERISON, J. S. *Our Wonderful Navy*. Cassell & Co., 1919.
Bibliog: DBA; HALL(1); HART(1); TB; WOOD; *Who's Who in Art*, 1929.

DETMAR, Lionel Gordon, A.R.I.B.A. 1879–1910

Herne Villa, Thickett Road, Sutton 1879–1889
Ashburton Villa, Thickett Road, Sutton 1889–1902
Hazeldene, Benhill Road, Sutton 1902–1910

The tragic, untimely death of the promising architect Lionel Detmar took place on 9 April 1910. It was a Saturday afternoon and he was out riding with his fiancée Maud Hyslop, the daughter of Akroyd Hyslop, J.P., of Hilton Grange, Sutton. Detmar, an inexperienced rider, was on a horse which his father had borrowed from a friend. At the approach to Tattenham Corner, the horse broke into a gallop, and in an attempt to steer it away from some railings Detmar was thrown off. A passer-by managed to catch the horse and Detmar remounted – most unwisely as it turned out. The horse then bolted, heading full-tilt towards Epsom and rid itself of its rider at the top of Ashley Road. Detmar struck the ground with his head and rolled over onto his face. Charles Lloyd of Epsom, who witnessed the accident, undid Detmar's collar and tie and asked a passer-by to fetch some water. But in the meantime a car drew up and Detmar was placed inside. He was driven to two doctors' surgeries, but both doctors being out he was then taken to Epsom Cottage Hospital, where he died from severe head injuries at 6.30 pm the same day. A coroner's inquest decided that the accident had been due to the inexperience of the rider; and the young architect was buried in Benhilton churchyard.

Lionel Detmar, thirty years old when he died, was the only son of a Sutton stockbroker, Thomas George Detmar, and his wife Bertha. Thomas Detmar died six years after Lionel, in 1916, no doubt bitterly regretting the day he had allowed his son to ride a borrowed horse. Lionel Detmar lived in Sutton all his life. He was born at Herne Villa, Thickett Road, in 1879; but by the time of his death the Detmar family were living at Hazeldene in Benhill Road. After an education at Forest's School, Lionel served his articles under Walter Hilton Nash (q.v.) and then spent a short time with John Gibson, F.R.I.B.A. before rejoining Nash as his partner. When Nash retired in 1905, Detmar entered into partnership with Theodore Gregg.

Detmar, a Gold Medallist of the RIBA, became one of its youngest associates in 1901, and in the following year he won an Architectural Association travelling scholarship. A few years later, in 1908, he was one of the three architects chosen to design the British Section at the Franco–British Exhibition, his *Palace of French Applied Art* bearing testimony to his abilities. He was strongly influenced by the architecture of the Renaissance, and during his short career worked on banks and other public buildings, one of which was the *Maida Vale Skating Rink*. Three of his designs, including one entitled *Design for a country town hall*

(1904) were exhibited at the Royal Academy. Up to the time of his death, he had been working on a book, *The Design of Banks, English and Foreign*, which was to have been illustrated with his own drawings. The remaining members of the Detmar family – Lionel's mother and sisters – left Sutton in 1918.

Exhib: RA

Bibliog: DBA; TB; *Building News*, no. 2884, 15 April 1910, p. 511; no. 2885, 22 April 1910, p. 547; *Sutton and Cheam Advertiser* 15 April 1910, p. 5

DEVIS, Arthur c.1711–1787

The eighteenth century artist Arthur Devis painted some beautifully composed conversation pieces in oils, one of which, *Sir Joshua Vanneck and his Family*, signed and dated 1752, is of local interest. It is the only painting, so far as we know, to include a likeness of the Hon. Thomas Walpole (1727–1803), the owner of Carshalton House from 1767 until 1782.

Thomas's first wife was Elizabeth Vanneck, the daughter of Sir Joshua. He married her in 1750, two years before the Devis picture was painted. She is placed next to Thomas in the family group; and the figure on the extreme right of the painting is thought to be Thomas's cousin, Horace Walpole, of Strawberry Hill fame. Four children were borne by Elizabeth before she died in 1760: Thomas (1755–1840), Catherine Margaret (1756–1816), Lambert Theodore (1757–1798) and Elizabeth (1759–1842). The Hon. Thomas Walpole married again. This time his wife was a Frenchwoman, Jeanne Bataile de Montval, whom he had met in France where he had business interests.

Devis's painting, formerly in the collection of Lady Dorothy Nevill, eventually went to America and may still be there. It is illustrated in several books, including *Conversation Pieces* by Sacheverell Sitwell (Batsford, 1936). Sitwell regarded it as one of Devis's most successful portrait groups and he described Elizabeth Vanneck as 'remarkably pretty'.

Bibliog: BEN; TB; WATERHOUSE; SITWELL, S. *Conversation Pieces*. Batsford, 1936

*DIBDIN, Thomas Robert Colman 1810–1893

Although, so far as we know, Thomas C. Dibdin never lived in this borough, he did live nearby during the 1850s, when he had a cottage at Banstead. He was born in Betchworth, Surrey, in October 1810, the son of the dramatist Thomas Dibdin and his wife Ann. His grandfather, Charles Dibdin, was an amateur artist and a writer of sea shanties. Thomas possibly attended school at Ewell. C. S. Willis in *A Short History of Ewell and Nonsuch* (1931) writes: 'The Old House at the corner of Monger's Lane was long occupied by the Monger family who kept an Academy there . . . Among the pupils were the two sons of Thomas J. Dibdin, the actor and dramatist'. Since at least two members of the Monger family were artists, Thomas Colman Dibdin may have received some early art training at Monger's Academy.

After serving an apprenticeship with a chemist, Thomas then worked from the age of seventeen as a clerk in the General Post Office. It may be coincidental, but his watercolour in Sutton's Local Collection is of the old post office, Beddington. Until 1949, when it was pulled down after being badly damaged by a flying bomb in 1944, this picturesque and historic old building stood on the corner of Guy Road and Church Lane. A popular subject with artists, it was also painted by Charles Frederick Allbon, A.R.E., whose watercolour, *Old Post Office, Beddington*, was exhibited at the Society of British Artists' exhibition in 1874.

When he was twenty-two, Dibdin had his first acceptance at the Royal Academy; when he was twenty-eight he abandoned the Post Office for good to devote the rest of his life to painting. Except for the times when he was travelling abroad on the Continent, he always lived in or near London. In 1883 he gave up painting because of failing eyesight, and he died at Sydenham in 1893. He appears to have been self-taught and he specialised in landscape and architectural studies, mostly in watercolour. He is particularly admired for his London views, a splendid example being his oil painting *The Opening of the Great Exhibition of 1851 seen from Beyond the Serpentine*, dated 1 May 1851, which is now in the London Art Gallery. He also worked as a scene painter for the Olympic and City Theatres, and for Sadler's Wells, his penchant for the dramatic prompting him to paint a *Diorama of the Ganges* which was exhibited at the Portland Gallery in Regent Street. It later transferred to Leicester Square, where it closed at the end of the first week, much to the disappointment of Henry Stacy Marks (q.v.), who had been employed as a 'checktaker' at thirty shillings a week.

Dibdin, interested in all things technical and scientific, claimed to have invented chromolithography. His youngest son, William Joseph Dibdin (1850–1925), the Chief Chemist to London County Council, introduced the 'Dibdin Sewage System' to Sutton, where two roads are named after him: Dibdin Close and Dibdin Road. William Dibdin settled at Sutton in 1890, and became Chairman of Sutton Urban District Council from 1898–9. He married Marian Aglio, the daughter of the artist Augustine Aglio junior, and they had three sons and five daughters. Their daughter Marian (q.v.), who married the sculptor Paul Montford, carried on the family tradition by becoming an artist. Marian's son, Adrian, a sculptor like his father, exhibited at the RA and taught at Sutton Art School. Thus, in their various ways, four generations of the Dibdin family contributed to the cultural – and hygienic – quality of life in Sutton.

Thomas Colman Dibdin was a prolific artist who exhibited hundreds of works, the majority of them being shown at the Society of British Artists' exhibitions; they included many views of Surrey. Today his works cost hundreds, sometimes thousands of pounds; so his painting *Beddington, Surrey*, bought for the borough in 1948 for £14, has proved a sound investment as well as being a painting which will continue to give pleasure to Sutton residents for countless years to come.

Exhib: BI; L; M; NWS; RA; RBA; RHA; RI
Coll: Ashmolean Museum, Oxford; BM; Gloucester AG; Hove AG; Leicester AG; Nottingham AG; Sutton LC; Sydenham; Sydney AG, Australia
Published: DIBDIN, T.C. *Progressive Lessons in Water Colour Painting.* 1848; *A Guide to Water Colour Painting.* 1859.
Illus: See HOUFE; and MALLALIEU
Bibliog: BEN; DBA; HOUFE; LAMBOURNE; MALLALIEU; TB; WOOD

DICKINSON, Frank Reginald 1874–1961

Little Holland House, 40 Beeches Avenue, Carshalton 1904–1961

Frank Dickinson was a remarkable man. His house remains as a monument to him; now owned by the London Borough of Sutton and open to the public on a regular basis.

His life began in Paddington, on the first day of 1874, at 3 Bury Terrace 'one of those depressing streets of shabby houses filled almost to suffocation with badly fed and badly clothed human beings, that with devasting thoroughness have destroyed a once pleasant and peaceful countryside around London'. This statement says quite a lot about Frank Dickinson and his approach to life.

His father, Peter Dickinson, was described on Frank's birth certificate as a butler, but it is not known in what house or homes, if any, he served in this capacity. Frank seems to have remembered him only in the role of porter, to which, 'having no ambition or urge to improve or rise above the dead level of faithful servitude . . . [he] descended'. Frank appears to have been impatient of his father, who seems to have been improvident but easy-going; but to have idolized his mother who was the driving force behind the family, in which, with Frank's birth, there were four sons.

The house in Bury Terrace was apparently a cheap lodging-house, and there were moves to two more such lodgings before Frank was five years old. He remembered, in his memoirs, his mother, Isabella ('a lovely name . . . shortened to the ugly sounding one of Bella') puffing Keating's insect powder into corners and crevices. The third move was one for the better, since the family now became landlords rather than tenants; living on the ground floor and in the basement, and letting the rooms above. 'I cannot think my father was responsible for this improvement in our state', wrote Frank: 'It was undoubtedly my mother's more active and thoughtful character that prompted it'.

When he was about four, Frank was sent to an uncle and aunt living in Boulogne, an experience he never forgot. Return was to the new home, where they let rooms to lodgers. The atmosphere at this time was perhaps shabby-genteel, with a parlour and aspidistra kept for Sundays only. At the same time there were less salubrious elements in their life style: the boys' bedroom was in the basement below the kitchen, with a door opening onto a washhouse, 'so that soapsuds and steam pervaded our dismal bedroom; while rats played hide and seek around the room at night'. Traps were set and Frank remembered one rat found in the trap as a head only: 'the rest of his body had been eaten away by his brother rats'.

But the brothers sang part songs; and Peter Dickinson, who must, despite his son's opinion of him, have passed on something of an artistic temperament, 'played the fiddle as a country man should, the simple airs of his youth'. He also attempted to draw; 'though my father had no skill whatever in drawing', said Frank.

The brothers went to school. These were the early days of education for everybody. The school fees for the London School Board elementary schools were 2d per week for each boy.

In January 1881, at the age of seven, Frank received a book as a prize for regular attendance in school. Four years later he won another book prize; this time for good conduct in Sunday School. Both these books he kept all his life, and they undoubtedly influenced him. Both were the lives of sixteenth century artist-craftsmen. One was Palissy, the potter; the other Cellini, the goldsmith.

When Frank was about six, a longed-for sister was born (Frank always idolised and idealised women) and, later, yet another brother.

When not singing, Frank spent his evenings painting and drawing, and his drawing won him another prize at school: a drawing-board, a tee-square, and a 'small box of colours with china dishes'. Seventy years later he was still using these.

Whilst still at school he took a part-time job cleaning knives in a doctor's household, and delivering medicine to patients. There he met a little girl of five who came to clean out the cages in which the doctor's daughter kept white mice and rats. The little girl's name was Florence Marriott. Some eighteen years later, Frank married her.

At thirteen he left school. He joined his elder brothers in delivering milk, working a seven-day week. His beloved drawing-board and paint-box were neglected through lack of time. From milk, Frank returned briefly to the delivery of medicine, this time for a chemist. The job was brief; he was sacked for spending too long studying a painting of the death of Nelson in a shop window opposite.

Frank next went to a more congenial establishment: he became shop boy to a pair of bachelor brothers in a workshop where they made reed organs. They were real craftsmen, and mentally he soaked up the atmosphere whilst physically he made glue and swept up the shavings. But even then, six shillings a week was not a large wage, and he regretfully left to become a clerk in a large store.

He was not happy: 'the clerk produces nothing'. 'Men and women, and girls moved about in dimly lighted passages, smirking or working in an unhealthy atmosphere of sex which crept everywhere'. So, 'with great daring' he answered an advertisement for a young man with a taste for drawing, and found himself working in the drawing office of an engineering firm. Here he was befriended by a man in his thirties with a taste for fine art. This friend is unnamed in Frank's memoirs, but was 'above all a perfect gentleman, and during my six years in the

40

same office I never heard so much as the word damn, or one word of sex or rude jest from him . . .'. He introduced the seventeen-year-old Frank Dickinson to the National Gallery, the Victoria and Albert Museum and the Royal Academy, and to the works of Sir Frederick Leighton and G. F. Watts. Watts especially became of immense importance to Frank, who later named his 'dream house' after the Little Holland House in which Watts stayed as a guest for thirty years. Perhaps a more admirable artist to emulate (who Frank discovered at this time) was Turner, the 'daring' of whose paintings held him, as he said, spellbound. In Frank's Little Holland House, his copies of paintings by both Watts and Turner can be seen today.

Henceforth, Frank says, his whole life was changed; and as well as haunting the great national picture collections he began to read 'the poets, the philosophers, and historians and the classics'. He developed a taste for the great Italian master-painters.

Frank attended local evening classes and won a scholarship of ten pounds for the year's fees and the expense of materials. By now he had been a draughtsman for six years, walking daily five or six miles in each direction between his house in Bayswater and his office in The Borough. Eventually the office and its 'sad routine' wore out his patience, as the walk had worn out so many pairs of boots. Frank got a job at a foundry near Leicester, just after the time that his family moved to a larger house where there was no more sleeping among rats, and Frank briefly had, for the first time, a 'small space for a studio'. He left his unfinished 'Christ Preaching to the Multitude' and moved to a 'simple lodging in a small country village'.

Sorry to leave his office friend (who had been 'like a father' to him), but delighted by the countryside, Frank might have stayed a long time in his new surroundings, except for a 'lodestar' calling him back. This was Florence Marriott, the girl who had looked after the doctor's daughter's white mice and was now a close friend of his sister. The Marriotts had now moved from Bayswater to Reigate. Frank, at about twenty-three, had never been out alone with a girl. After many false starts he wrote her 'a simple friendly letter' and a correspondence began. Visits home to his parents enabled him to go on to Reigate. The time together was brief, for 'the last train from Reigate was at 9 pm', and Frank then had to get the midnight train from St Pancras and walk the five miles from Leicester to his lodgings at two-thirty in the morning – 'two hundred and fifty miles for one brief hour with a simple but sweet girl'.

There was joy when Florence went to Shanklin with Frank's sister for a summer holiday, and Frank stayed nearby and joined them for meals. Back in Leicester, Frank found the distance between there and Reigate too far. He was lucky again, and got a job at the Royal Doulton factory in Lambeth, with art galleries near at hand, and Reigate no longer 250 miles away. Frank bought a bicycle and learnt to ride it.

His life again began to expand by contact with artists and students. He became involved in the politics of idealism, discovering Robert Blatchford's socialist journal *The Clarion*, which followed William Morris (q.v.) and John Ruskin (q.v.) in condemning all forms of mechanical production. Frank joined The Clarion Handicraft Guild, taking, with Walter Crane, an active role in demonstrating and pressing the claims of the work of the hand rather than the work of the machine.

Frank became engaged to Florence but had not the money to marry and live as he wanted. It was not a question of renting a house and buying furniture. 'No! My Masters Morris and Ruskin had put very big and beautiful ideas into my head . . . I wanted a house and home that would meet with their approval'.

The first stage was to start building furniture, with Florence's help, for their future home, which he began to do in the cellar of his parents' house. His designs, he said, were based on the 'prevailing styles seen in the exhibitions of the Arts and Crafts at that time'. His first piece was a coal cabinet, which, apparently unwittingly, he built with a strong echo of the organ stools made in the workshop in which he had once worked.

The problem of the house itself still had to be faced. Frank was earning fifty shillings a week. As he later wrote, this would have secured an ordinary house by rent or purchase. But he wanted 'a house with beautiful things inside it . . . that which an artist and craftsman desires, which the usual builder cannot supply or understand'. Frank joined a Mutual Building Society in Streatham, to which members subscribed a small sum on a regular basis. When the total funds reached three hundred pounds, a ballot enabled one lucky member to use the money to build his house. Frank was fortunate in obtaining his £300 quickly. This was not quite enough for his purpose and he had to borrow another hundred pounds from an elder brother. He had already managed to obtain a plot of land in what was later to be known as Beeches Avenue, Carshalton, 'amidst fields of lavender, herbs and corn'. He had been drawn to Carshalton by the association of John Ruskin with it.

Frank drew up his own plans for the house. He then felt unable to entrust the building of it to a professional builder, so he had to take this into his own hands. With the help of a brother and a hired labourer he started work in October 1902. By March 1904 the house was ready to move into with his bride, and they spent their honeymoon 'cleaning and staining floors, and trying to make the bareness as homely and comfortable as we possibly could'.

This was not so much the end of Frank's work on his ideal home as the beginning. He continued to work on it for at least thirty more years; and some features were never quite finished. His future daughter-in-law, entering the house for the first time, in the 1930s, saw him carving a beam over the front window. He worked in many different media, carving wood and brick; working steel and copper; moulding plaster; painting on paper, canvas, wood and parchment.

Of his paintings, his early watercolours are perhaps his most pleasing; but he also worked in oils, especially on his large allegorical and didactic paintings, such as the triptych *Husbandry* over his

View of the dining room at Little Holland House, Carshalton Beeches, the former home of FRANK R. DICKINSON.

sitting-room fireplace, and *The Death of Ananias*, both of which passed the first hurdle of acceptance by the Royal Academy but were not actually hung. Both can be seen in Little Holland House now.

Frank and Florence had two children. Their son, Gerard, still lives in a house echoing his father's design. Their daughter, christened Isobel, but always called Julie, died in her fifties, after marrying, and bearing three children.

Frank left Royal Doulton (for whom he had been a designer of ceramic bathroom fittings) when the firm moved away from Lambeth. For the rest of his life he described himself as 'artist and designer' and earned his living by a variety of means: selling his paintings (many of them of local scenes); designing interiors and bathrooms; and illustrating publications. He never became rich or famous. All his life he continued to idolise his wife, who survived him by more than twenty years to pass her hundredth birthday and to see the house in which she had lived so long opened to the public in 1974, the centenary of Frank's birth. Before their Silver Wedding in 1929, Frank studied silver-smithing in order to make a present for her, a three-piece silver tea-set, with his own hands. This set, and a coffee pot, are his only major pieces in silver, and amongst his finest work.

In his last years, with failing eyesight and health, Frank sat down to write his autobiography. He called it *Do it Yourself; by Choice or Chance*. He had never ceased to believe in the value of his life's main work; the building of his ideal house; dedicated to his wife and to the principle of the nobility of the work of the artist and craftsman; to the superiority of man over machinery; and to the merits of self-sufficiency, which had caused him to design his garden not only on his artistic principles but as a source of fruit and vegetables and honey from his bees.

His book sets out his reason for designing his house as he did; his wide doors to signify welcome; his stairs leading up from his living room, a landing only a few steps above ground level forming a small platform (used in the amateur dramatics and country dancing he and his wife and friends loved). He died on 10 September 1961.

It was the one-ness of Frank's life, his single-minded devotion to his principles, and the diversity of the means by which he expressed them, including his own recording of his story, that led Roy Smith, then Borough Librarian of Sutton, to press for the preservation of Little Holland House when it was drawn to the attention of the library service (and I went to see it), when it was for sale after Florence, in her nineties, no longer able to look after herself, had left it.

The house is now in the care of Sutton Leisure Services, and open to the public as advertised.

42

Admission is free. Much of Frank's work, including his furniture and many paintings, can be seen inside.

Douglas Cluett

Main Sources: F. R. Dickinson's Autobiography (unpublished), from which material in quotation marks above is taken; personal reminiscences of Gerard Dickinson, and others; Dickinson papers

DIMELOW, Amy Beatrice Caroline 1879–1964

Homecot, 149 Burdon Lane, Cheam c.1923–1964

Amy Dimelow, a sculptor, painter and studio worker, was born in Manchester in 1879, the daughter of J. G. Dimelow and his wife Annie, the family living in the Palatine Road, famous in Manchester for its musical associations. Her own love of music is reflected in one of her principal works, a bust of *Henry Watson, Mus.Doc.*, who gave his name to the Henry Watson Music Library in Manchester Central Library.

She studied at the Manchester School of Art, winning a national silver medal and a Royal free studentship. Working mostly in bronze, although she also modelled some portrait medallions in silver, she exhibited in Manchester, in Liverpool and in London and contributed to the periodicals *Revue du Vrai et du Beau* and *Hippodrome*.

For forty years she lived at Homecot, a house in Burdon Lane, Cheam, next door to Banstead Downs Golf Club. She never married and died in Sutton and Cheam Hospital on 11 February 1964, aged eighty-four.

Exhib: L; M; WIAC
Bibliog: DBA; *Who's Who in Art*, 1929

DOO, George Thomas, R.A. 1800–1886

Hill House, Sutton –1886 (A positive location for this particular 'Hill House' is still uncertain.)

George Thomas Doo, R.A., born in Surrey in 1800, was an extremely important nineteenth century line-and-stipple engraver and oil painter. He was a pupil of the engraver Charles Heath, later studying in Paris. On his return from Paris he established an art school at the Savoy, London, for the 'study from life and antique'. He was 'Engraver-in-ordinary' to both King William IV and Queen Victoria; and he published an impressive list of engravings, many of them portraits. There was an estimated demand of 30,000 copies for his engraving *The Convalescent from Waterloo*, after W. Mulready; but when it finally appeared, published by the Art Union in 1847, it was deemed 'disappointing'. His finest work, according to contemporary opinion, was *The Raising of Lazarus*, after S. del Piombo, published in 1865; this had taken him eight years to complete.

He married twice, both marriages taking place at St Pancras Old Church, London. Caroline Mary Hamilton, whom he married in February 1836, was his first wife; after she died he married Emily Ward in November 1859. Elizabeth and Jane Doo, two of the pupils at the South Metropolitan Schools, Sutton, during the 1860s, may have been related to the artist.

Doo, who was in work almost up to the year of his death, published his last engraving in 1882 and died a widower on 13 November 1886 at Hill House, Sutton. Letters of administration were then granted to his son, Hubert Sydney Barrow Doo, of Stoneleigh House, Epsom.

Exhib: RA
Coll: V&A
Bibliog: BEN; DBA; DNB; ENGEN(1); HUNNISETT; LISTER; MACKENZIE; PSA; TB

*DRAGE, John Henry 1856–1914

John Henry Drage, a watercolourist who painted landscape, animal and genre studies, was born in 1856 in Croydon, Surrey, where for over fifty years his father was the headmaster of Croydon British School. The school was originally in the London Road but later moved to Tamworth Road, which is where the Drage family lived during the last decades of the nineteenth century. John Henry Drage never married but lived in Croydon with his parents until 1902, and then moved to Eastbourne, Sussex, with them. His father, John Drage, died the following year.

Well known to the artists of this area through his association with the Surrey Art Circle (q.v.), John Drage served on the committee until he left the district, his paintings often being mentioned by the local press. His first Royal Academy acceptance, *An exploring party*, was shown in 1882; two other RA titles were *Dartmoor Ponies* (1891) and *Caught napping* (1895). One of his most important works, *Plough Oxen*, was shown at the Royal Institute of Painters in Water-Colours' exhibition in 1892.

Whilst he was living in Eastbourne, Drage painted some rural scenes of Sussex, one of which is now in Michelham Priory, Hailsham, a property owned by the Sussex Archaeological Society, and open to the public. He continued to exhibit until 1905 and died at Eastbourne on New Year's Day, 1914, leaving everything to his sister, Emma Laura Louise Drage, a schoolmistress.

Drage's watercolour, *Carshalton Upper Pond with Horses and Carts in the Ford*, which is now in Sutton's Local Collection, is a particularly pleasing example of his style and has been reproduced on a greetings card. Some drawings of old Croydon, by Drage, can be seen at Croydon Library.

Exhib: L; M; NG; RA; RI; SAC
Coll: Croydon PL; Michelham Priory, Sussex; Sutton LC
Bibliog: BEN; DBA; TB; WOOD

DRAYTON, Frances Sarah 1860–1932

West Hill House, Sutton Common Road, Sutton c.1890–1902

James Henry Drayton, like Mr Bennet in Jane Austen's *Pride and Prejudice*, had five daughters but no sons – no sons to inherit West Hill House and his other properties at Sutton, or to inherit Mill Hall at Horsham, which he also owned. However, three of his daughters married, giving him grandchildren; and he appears to have been particularly attached to his unmarried daughter, Frances Sarah Drayton, an executor of his will. Drayton took pride in the fact that she was an artist; and he hung her paintings on the walls of West Hill House, which was furnished throughout with valuable antiques. Acres of fine gardens surrounded the house, and there were stables and a coach-house.

Frances, born in 1860, lived in Sutton from about 1890 until 1902, the year her father died and West Hill House was sold. She painted landscapes and portraits in oil and watercolour, exhibiting them at various galleries. On visits abroad she made preliminary sketches for paintings which included the titles *Vieille Rue, Caudebec*, a watercolour, and *Italian Scene*, an oil. Two of her other titles were *Maud*, and *On the East Lynn*, both oils.

She died at Bath on 11 July 1932. Her last wish was to be buried in her parents' grave at Roffey Cemetery, Horsham.

Exhib: B; L; ROI; SWA
Bibliog: DBA

DRESSER, Dr Christopher 1834–1904

Wellesley Lodge, Brunswick Road, Sutton 1883–1889

Christopher Dresser, a designer of metalwork, furniture, pottery, glass, textiles and wallpaper, lived in Sutton for six years. He was most successful and distinguished in his own time and remains a highly respected figure, although without the popularity of contemporaries like William Morris (q.v.). He also trained and worked as a botanist, and in 1860 was awarded an honorary Ph.D. by the University of Jena for his publications on botany, after that always calling himself 'Dr' Christopher Dresser. He wrote on the theory of design in the second half of the nineteenth century, an outstanding era for British design, and was very much of his time although too original to be typical.

He was born in 1834 in Glasgow of Yorkshire parents and was interested in design from an early age. In 1847 he went to the School of Design at Somerset House (which later transferred to Marlborough House) where he was a pupil for seven years, winning prizes, medals and scholarships. In 1854, the year he left, he won a prize for his design for garment fabrics, which is interesting, as in his later years his fabric and wallpaper designs are not nearly as exciting as his three-dimensional designs. He was also at this time doing botanical illustrations and diagrams. When he left Marlborough House he married Thirza Perry from Shropshire.

From this time on, Dresser was a working designer and although we do not have any account by Dresser himself of his working life, there are references by other writers to him as a highly distinguished designer and writer. The first indication we have of his place in the design establishment is in 1856, when he contributed one of the plates to Owen Jones's *Grammar of Ornament*, Dresser sharing Jones's views on design, with the addition of his own scientific way of looking at things.

In 1857–8 Dresser wrote a series of articles in the *Art Journal* on 'Botany as adapted to the arts and art manufactures' and published his first major work, *The Principles of Botany*, in 1859. Throughout the 1860s Dresser was lecturing on botany and working as a designer. He designed carpets and advised on design, but it is not known for which manufacturers. An indication of his success is his move in 1869 to Tower Cressy, a large house on Campden Hill, where he stayed until he moved to Sutton in 1883. In 1871 he started a series of articles on the 'Principles of decorative design' in the *Technical Educator*, one of the improving periodicals so typical of the age. During this period he was also doing designs for cast-iron for the Coalbrookdale Company.

In 1873 Dresser went to the International Exhibition at Vienna and in 1874 lectured at the Owen Jones Memorial Exhibition. In 1875 he started doing designs for silver plate for Elkington & Co., and in 1878 for Hukin and Heath. Dresser's metalwork designs are his most remarkable work – they show his scientific attitude to geometry and symmetry, and to form in relation to function. His designs are entirely original, but from a desire to treat the design problem completely from scratch, not from any desire for superficial novelty.

Dresser visited Japan in 1876–7, two years later setting up Dresser & Holme in Farringdon Road, with a colleague from Bradford, to import Japanese wares (Liberty had opened his influential and fashionable shop in 1875). In 1879 he began also to design for the Linthorpe Pottery, near Middlesbrough. Dresser's designs for ceramics are quite different from those for his metalwork, even though he was doing both at the same time. The pottery does not have the stunning simplicity of the metalwork but has great richness of glaze and variety of form. He often based his designs on Japanese or Peruvian shapes, or used incised decoration of flower studies. Some of the shapes are rather awkward, and some distinctly odd, but again the designs show an original approach, based on the plasticity of the clay and the possible richness of colouring from glazes. Linthorpe Pottery was set up by John Harrison, a Yorkshire landowner, after meeting Dresser, and enjoyed a high critical reputation, which did not, however, prevent its economic collapse in 1890. The manager was Henry Tooth, who left Linthorpe in 1882 to set up the Bretby Art Pottery with William Ault. Ault was later to set up his own pottery, with Dresser again as the designer.

In 1880 Dresser was art editor of the *Furniture Gazette* for a year, and art manager of the Art Furniture Alliance, the latter having a shop in New Bond Street selling various wares, several designed by Dresser. In 1882 Dresser published his account of his visit to Japan: *Japan, its Architecture, Art and Art Manufactures*. In his preface he refers to a bad illness he suffered during the preparation of the book and this may in some way be linked to his move to Sutton.

1882/3 does seem to have been a watershed year in Dresser's distinguished career – his involvement with the Linthorpe Pottery, with James Dixon & Co. and with the Art Furniture Alliance ceased and he moved from a prestigious address to the much humbler Wellesley Lodge in Brunswick Road, Sutton (the house no longer stands and there is now a council estate on the site). Perhaps his illness seriously curtailed his activities. However, *Modern Ornamentation* was published in 1886 and presented by Dresser as just some of the designs for furniture, glass, earthenware and metalwork designed by his office. It seems possible that his assistants and pupils were at this time taking the responsibility for much of the designing, as some of the work attributed to Dresser then is highly dubious – for example, there are two claret jugs for Elkington & Co. of 1885 which are uncharacteristically fussy. Also attributed to Dresser at this time are designs for textiles and wallpapers. These are quite delightful but do not have the spark of originality and slight oddness that characterise his other work. So it seems that Dresser's time at Sutton coincides with some sort of crisis, which may not be very complimentary to Sutton, but it does mean that we had a very important person living in the area for a while. The Dressers had thirteen children – five sons and eight daughters; and whilst they were living in Sutton, their son Stanley Lewis Dresser, then aged sixteen, was a pupil for a brief period at Whitgift School, Croydon; he entered in January 1883 and left in December of the same year. In 1889, the year the Dressers left Sutton, this same son died at Winnipeg in Canada, following a short illness. Another son, Frank Perry Dresser, appears to have been the 'black sheep' of the family; his father cut him out of his will.

Dresser left Sutton in 1889 to live in Barnes, and some time in the mid-1890s started to design the famous Clutha range of glass for James Couper & Sons of Glasgow. Again his designs show sensitivity to the qualities of the material – the vases and 'vessels' have very fluid forms and the glass itself has a rich texture, with bubbles and streaks. In the true spirit of Ruskin (q.v.), Dresser had made a virtue of possible imperfections and the end result expresses the way of making an object in glass. Some of the shapes are simple and elegant, with a slight twist in the neck or body, and others are based on Peruvian or Persian forms. The simplest of the vases are somewhat similar to contemporary Art Nouveau glass in France and America, but much more understated. They have a lightness and elegance that shows a quite different side to Dresser's personality from the severity of the metalwork. The common factor is the 'truth to materials'.

Christopher Dresser died abroad on 24 November 1904, at the age of seventy, receiving obituaries in the national press and the design journals. *The Studio* added that Dresser's daughter, Miss Ada Nettleton Dresser, 'who inherits much of her father's talent, and was a great help to him in his latter years' would continue to run the studio at Elm Bank, Barnes. Dresser had been in the forefront of the Victorian movement to educate people into appreciating good design. He was set slightly apart from his contemporaries by his scientific training, which led to a different way of assessing design problems and gave him an intellectual rigour that protected him from the

sentimentality of the Arts and Crafts movement. If his designs still seem unusual to us today, that is a compliment to his originality and unusual approach.

Cynthia Bradley

Exhib: RA
Coll: Birmingham PL; Dorman Museum, Middlesbrough; Glasgow AG; Linnean Society, London; Royal Doulton Tableware Ltd; V&A; Worshipful Company of Goldsmiths; etc.
Bibliog: *Christopher Dresser*. Catalogue of an exhibition arranged by Richard Dennis and John Jesse, October 1972, at the Fine Art Society, London. *Christopher Dresser 1834–1904*. Catalogue of an exhibition at the Camden Arts Centre, 1979, and at the Dorman Museum, 1980, organised by Michael Collins and Zuleika Dobson.
N.B. Both the above catalogues have comprehensive lists of books by Dresser, lists of articles by and about Dresser in periodicals, and lists of the manufacturers for whom Dresser is known to have produced designs

DREW, Herbert J., R.B.A., A.M.S. Exhib: 1910–1930s
During the 1880s, Herbert Drew was the drawing master at the 'Morning School for Young Ladies' run by a Mrs Herbert Green at Sterndale, Wallington, where he no doubt nurtured the talents of some of the artists listed in this book. In an advertisement for the school in the *Sutton Herald*, 4 December 1880, we see that the young ladies were taught 'English, French, Drawing, Dancing and Drilling', this last being conducted by a sergeant-major, no less. Mr Herbert Drew was described as 'Assistant Master, Croydon School of Art'.

Drew attended both the South Kensington and the Westminster Art Schools, and qualified as an art master under the Board of Education. In the early years of his career he tended to concentrate on painting miniatures; but he later took up landscape painting, when he carried out many views of Surrey and Sussex. He exhibited at the Royal Academy and other galleries from 1900 onwards, and joined the Surrey Art Circle (q.v.) of which he was a member until the late 1920s. In 1921 he was elected a member of the Royal Society of British Artists. For most of his life he lived within easy reach of London, but he retired to Worthing in about 1930.

Exhib: Bath; M; RA; RBA; RI; SAC
Bibliog: DBA; GW; *Who's Who*, 1911

EDGERTON, Linda 1890–1983
10 Horse Shoe Green, Sutton 1915–1936
Linda Edgerton, a leading children's book illustrator of her day, also designed well over a hundred children's postcards, published by J. Salmon, Ltd., and by Vivien Mansell & Co. Her work, mostly aimed at very young children, is seen in simple story books

45

like *Boy Blue and his Chum* and *Ten Favourite Fairy Tales*, both published by Raphael Tuck. At least one of her designs was used by Shelley Potteries, Ltd. A child's beaker, attractively decorated with a scene from the nursery rhyme 'Mary, Mary quite contrary', bears her signature; one is illustrated in *Miller's Antiques Price Guide 1986*, bearing an estimated price-tag of £90–£100.

She was born in Staffordshire on 25 March 1890, the daughter of William Edgerton, who died in 1901, aged thirty-seven. In 1915 Linda, her mother, and her sister Dorothy moved to Sutton. Dorothy eventually married a Mr Holland and settled in Mulgrave Road, whilst Linda and her mother lived at no. 10 Horse Shoe Green until 1935.

During the 1930s Linda, by then an established artist, attended Sutton Art School, where in 1931 she was represented in the first-ever exhibition of students' work, winning prizes for 'landscapes' and for 'optional design'. She was praised by the local press for her 'fairy and child studies which are very attractive'.

Her whereabouts after she left Sutton, where most of her work had been carried out, became something of a mystery. Her mother had died in 1935 and the house at Horse Shoe Green had been sold in 1936. In 1979 a researcher who was trying to trace her enlisted the help of the press, and a piece appeared in a Sutton newspaper asking if there was anyone in the district who remembered her. There was no response.

The mystery of what had happened to Linda Edgerton was solved only recently, when it was discovered that her final years had been spent at the Convent of St Katherine, Parmoor, Buckinghamshire, and that she had died at Booker Hospital, High Wycombe, on 24 January 1983.

Bibliog: COYSH

EDWARDS, Mrs L. M. (T.A.) Exhib: 1921–1923
Honeywood, High Street, Carshalton 1914–1939
One of the best-known buildings in Carshalton today is Honeywood, a picturesque house on the edge of the Ponds. Honeywood is a late nineteenth century house with an eighteenth century core and an earlier, perhaps sixteenth or seventeenth century building encapsulated in the northern end.

It was in the last quarter of the nineteenth century that a merchant, John Pattinson Kirk, bought the houses on the western end of the Upper Pond. Confusingly, the house on the site of modern-day Honeywood was called Wandle Cottage; Honeywood then was the name of a house immediately south of it. Pattinson Kirk pulled down Wandle Cottage and transferred the 'Honeywood' name to it.

Nearly a century before Kirk's conversion, a 'John Burke Esq' lived in Wandle Cottage. He and his family have been identified with the subject of a painting formerly attributed to Zoffany (q.v.). In the nineteenth century, William Hale White (the writer 'Mark Rutherford') bought the leasehold of Wandle Cottage but left after a year because of the unhealthy dampness of the place (Maclean, C. M. *Mark Rutherford*, 1955).

John P. Kirk lived at Honeywood until 1913. From then onwards, until the local council took it over on 8 January 1940, Mrs L. M. Edwards, a watercolourist, was its occupant. Her landscapes were shown at the exhibitions of the Royal Institute of Painters in Water-Colours, and the Society of Women Artists, one of her SWA titles being *Close of an October Day, Bruges* (1923).

Due to its romantic setting by the Ponds, Honeywood has been a favourite subject with local artists for many years, William Tatton Winter (q.v.), for one, finding its charms irresistible on more than one occasion. The building is now owned by the London Borough of Sutton; leased, at present, to an association for the disabled.

Exhib: RI; SWA
Bibliog: DBA; JONES

FAIRWEATHER, H. M. Exhib: 1916
Inglenook, 25 Beeches Avenue, Carshalton 1913–1932
H. M. Fairweather, an architect, exhibited one work at the Royal Academy, *House at Ilford*, submitted from Carshalton in 1916.

Exhib: RA
Bibliog: DBA

FARINGTON, Joseph, R. A. 1747–1821
The discovery of the Farington diaries at Wallington, Surrey, in 1921, was one of the most important and exciting events in the British art world this century. The diaries, which had been in the possession of Miss M. L. E. Tyrwhitt of Northwood Lodge, 110 Manor Road, Wallington, came to public notice after her death, when auctioneers were brought in to survey her effects. At Northwood Lodge, where Miss Tyrwhitt had lived from before 1893 until her death, they found the silver plate which had been presented to Farington by the Royal Academy, and also his sketchbooks and a large quantity of drawings. But most important of all, hidden away in the attic were his diaries. These were bought at the auction sale by the *Morning Post* newspaper, who had been prepared to pay up to £1,000 but who were lucky enough to get them for 110 guineas.

The paper began to publish selections from the diaries on 23 January 1922, originally intending to run them for six weeks. However, such was the interest of the public, with letters pouring into the offices of the newspaper, that the *Morning Post* extended the series until October 1923. An edited version, in eight volumes, was published in 1922–8 and there is now a complete version, in sixteen volumes, published by Yale University Press. The owners of the *Morning Post* presented the actual diaries to the Royal Library at Windsor.

The artist Joseph Farington, R.A., the second son of a vicar, was born in Lancashire on 21 November 1747, and there is a certain northern directness about his writings. He studied at the Royal Academy Schools and under Richard Wilson (q.v.), and was a member of the Incorporated Society of Artists (1768–73). Eventually, after a spell in the Lake District, he settled in London, taking up residence at no. 35 Upper Charlotte Street, where after his death the next occupant was John Constable, R.A. (q.v.).

Farington knew most of the leading figures of the day and was very interested in gossip. He picked up some amazing titbits of scandal, and other items of news, from his various friends in society, in the art world – these included Turner, Constable and Harden (q.v.) – and in politics, writing everything down in his diaries. These diaries are now an extremely important source to art historians, and also to social historians, giving, as they do, a further insight into the everyday life of England during the late eighteenth and early nineteenth centuries.

The diaries cover the period 13 July 1793 to 30 December 1821. Farington's first entry takes us on a visit to Horace Walpole (Lord Orford) at Strawberry Hill; his last was written on the day he died, which was a Sunday. His death was both sudden and dramatic; his niece wrote a graphic account of it beneath her uncle's last entry. It appears that Farington was staying in Manchester with his brother at the time. On the day he died, having already attended both the morning and afternoon services at Didsbury Church, he returned there for evensong. Since it 'always rains in Manchester' he arrived at the church equipped with umbrella, galoshes and other paraphernalia. Thus encumbered, at the end of the service he tripped on the stairs leading down from his brother's pew in the gallery and fell headlong onto the hard floor, dying almost instantly.

Although Farington is not a major British artist, his talent by no means matching Turner's or Constable's, he is still a significant figure in the history of the English watercolour. A fine topographical artist and illustrator, working mainly in reed pen, pencil and wash, he spent much of his time travelling throughout this country on sketching trips; and after the French Revolution he visited Paris with Fuseli. A respected and influential figure at the Royal Academy, he was elected a full member in 1785 and took an active part in its politics. His wife, Susan Mary (née Hammond), a relative of the Earl of Orford, died childless in 1800, twenty-one years prior to the death of her husband, who missed her very much.

Farington's diaries were passed down through the family until they reached his great-nephew William Ffarington, who married Cecil Frances Tyrwhitt. In 1885 the William Ffaringtons settled in Wallington, in a newly-built house named Northwood Lodge. Since they had no children, their property eventually passed to Mrs Ffarington's brother, Montague Dymock Tyrwhitt. When he died, his surviving sister, Margaret Louisa Eva Tyrwhitt, inherited Northwood

Lodge and its contents; but she obviously did not appreciate the importance of the Farington diaries, which received no mention in her will. Her property was inherited by various relatives, who arranged for the contents of Northwood Lodge to be sold. This was when, on 9 December 1921, the diaries were bought by the *Morning Post.*

Exhib: ISA; RA
Coll: Ashmolean Museum, Oxford; BM; Cartwright Hall, Bradford; Liverpool AG; Newcastle AG; V&A; Whitworth AG, Manchester
Published: FARINGTON, J. *Views of the Lakes.* 1789; *Views of the Cities and Towns of England and Wales.* 1790
Illus: COMBE, W. *History of the River Thames.* 1794
Bibliog: BEN; HARDIE; MACKENZIE; MALLALIEU; WATERHOUSE; WILLIAMS; *The Farington Diary.* Edited by J. Grieg. Hutchinson, 1922–8. 8 vols; *The Diary of Joseph Farington.* Edited by K. Garlick and A. MacIntyre. Yale University Press, 1978–1984. 16 vols.

FINCH, H. H., A.M.C.
Beaulieu, Egmont Road, Sutton 1912–1924
H. H. Finch, an artist and art master, who lived in London before he came to Sutton, exhibited at the Glasgow Institute of Fine Arts and at the London Salon.

Exhib: GI; LS
Bibliog: DBA

FITZGERALD, Hazlewood Beardsley c.1895–1968
9 Aultone Way, Sutton c.1938–1968
H. B. Fitzgerald, a sculptor in stone and wood and a painter in oil of allegorical subjects, exhibited a statuette, entitled *Youth*, at the Royal Academy in 1925.

He lived in Sutton for about thirty years. Friends who knew him then say that they believe he modelled a portrait bust of Gordon Selfridge (of Selfridges Store), and that he carried out some work on the base of the arch leading to The Mall, London. He died at Sutton on 16 December 1968, after which his widow Norah Cicely Fitzgerald, who survived him by a few years, sold most of his remaining works. In 1979 a large number of these turned up for sale in Humberside.

Exhib: RA
Bibliog: DBA

FLEMWELL, George Jackson 1865–1928
Highfield, Cheam Road, Sutton c.1867–1895
George Jackson Flemwell, artist and author, the eldest son of John and Ann Catherine Flemwell, was born at The Chesnuts, Mitcham in 1865. Shortly afterwards the family moved to Sutton, and from then onwards George led a varied and interesting life, spending the latter part of it in Switzerland. A dubious claim to fame is that he became involved – albeit inadvertently – with the mysterious disappearance of a former Member of Parliament, Victor Grayson.

Flemwell's home in Sutton was a house called

GEORGE J. FLEMWELL   Oil 546×737mm
The Cobbler. 1892.   Photo courtesy Sotheby's

Highfield in Cheam Road, owned by his father John Flemwell, a parish officer and the Captain of Sutton's Voluntary Fire Brigade; it was pulled down some years ago, and the public car park adjoining Sutton Baptist Church is now on the site. George's first drawing lessons were at Miss Rose's Preparatory School in Sutton, which he left to attend Thanet College, Margate. At Margate he was given the opportunity to exercise his artistic talents by painting the scenery for two school plays: *Hamlet*, and *King Lear*.

Margate proved too bracing for the tall, willowy youth. He became seriously ill and was sent to Switzerland to recover, staying with a German amateur artist and his family at Montreux. When the time came for him to return to England he showed a reluctance to leave Switzerland, a reluctance that was justified when his father, with an amazing lack of sensitivity, placed George in the office of his hide and leather factory at Bermondsey. Not only did George find the job uncongenial; he became ill again, the atmosphere of the factory improving neither his health nor his spirits. He returned to Switzerland, staying with the same family as before, and occupied

himself by painting Alpine flowers and by sketching the local Swiss, and the English colony at Montreux.

His gift for caricature soon led to his work being accepted by some of the weekly papers. One of his first efforts: 'Notes on the Derby, by one who was not there' appeared in *Scraps* in 1884. On his return to England – not, happily, to the hide factory – he continued in the same vein, contributing sketches that ranged in size from a few inches to full-page cartoons. Not even the Prime Minister escaped his pen. Gladstone was portrayed as the 'March Hare', the words 'I am not mad' spilling from his lips. Sutton residents were frequently amused to see examples of Flemwell's wit in the windows of the Post Office in the High Street, where posters advertising local events were often embellished with his caricatures. Toward the end of the 1880s he began to take his art more seriously and with an artistic career in view spent four years studying portrait painting under William Powell Frith, R.A., the painter of *Derby Day* (by one who *was* there). In 1889 Flemwell invited Frith to attend a conversazione at Sutton Public Hall to celebrate the first anniversary of the Surrey Art Circle (q.v.). As

Secretary of the Circle, Flemwell was heavily involved with the organisation of the event. A major attraction was a portrait of Frith, painted by George Flemwell.

When his term with Frith ended, Flemwell, on the advice of Sir Lawrence Alma-Tadema, R.A., went to the Antwerp Academy to study under Professor Rosier. Subsequently, he went to Nuremberg and Munich, but eventually settled in Switzerland, visting England only occasionally. His first Royal Academy painting, *Une question embarrassante*, was hung in 1892, sent in from Antwerp; his second, also sent in from Antwerp, was *Patience*, shown in 1893; and his third, and last, painting to be exhibited there was entitled *A Knife-grinder – Ardennes*, submitted from Sutton in 1894.

In Switzerland he devoted most of his time to painting and writing about the Alps and Alpine plants, producing several books and a series of picture postcards. However, he still found the time to paint portraits and to contribute drawings to magazines. In June 1910 an exhibition of his watercolours, entitled 'Alpine Flowers and Gardens', was held at the Baillie Gallery, London. Two years later, in 1912, he married Grace Priddle, the daughter of John Priddle of Muswell Hill.

After the outbreak of the First World War, Flemwell, from his position in Switzerland, was able to pass on details of German espionage to British Intelligence and one rather gets the impression that he enjoyed his involvement in spying. After the war, he arranged a series of art exhibitions at various Swiss centres, in aid of wounded British soldiers and sailors.

Shortly before the war, Victor Grayson, ex-M.P. for Colne Valley, had spent a brief holiday in Switzerland, where he had struck up a friendship with George Flemwell. The friendship was resumed in 1919 when Flemwell invited Grayson, who had been badly wounded in the war, to stay with him in Switzerland. Here, after one or two preliminary sketches, Flemwell finished a watercolour portrait of his friend.

Victor Grayson disappeared, possibly in 1920. But his disappearance was not officially noted until some years later. Maundy Gregory, the secret agent, 'honours tout', acquaintance of Sidney 'Ace of Spies' Reilly, and friend of royalty, has since been suspected of being involved in Grayson's disappearance. Grayson is thought to have obtained some incriminating evidence against Gregory. The 'Victor Grayson Mystery' has been expounded in two books: *Murder by Perfection* by Donald McCormick, and *Victor Grayson, Labour's Lost Leader* by David Clark.

According to McCormick, the last accredited sighting of Victor Grayson was on 28 September 1920 – by George Flemwell. The artist, on a visit to England, was sketching Thames scenes from the bank of the river opposite Ditton Island. Flemwell, who knew Grayson's features well, having drawn them on several occasions, was positive he saw Grayson, with another man, in a boat on the river. He watched them land on Ditton Island and then disappear into a bungalow. Convinced it was his friend, he went over to the island and knocked on the door of the bungalow which, he noted, was called Vanity Fair. A woman

opened it. She indignantly denied knowing anyone called Grayson.

Vanity Fair later turned out to be owned by Maundy Gregory, and the woman answering the door fitted the description of Mrs Edith Rosse, a former actress with whom Gregory had lived. She later died under mysterious circumstances.

The Grayson mystery continues. In David Clark's book some new theories about Grayson's disappearance are aired and Clark reveals that Donald McCormick's information on Flemwell's sighting came from letters written by Flemwell to McCormick's wife's first husband. In 1974 these letters, plus some of Flemwell's paintings, were sent by McCormick to Maples to be auctioned. Most frustratingly, the records of the sale have since been destroyed, so the present location of the letters is virtually untraceable.

On 5 March 1928, eight years after the Ditton Island incident, George Flemwell died at his home in Lugano, Switzerland.

Exhib: BG; L; RA; Switzerland
Published: FLEMWELL, G. *Alpine Flowers and Gardens*. A. & C. Black, 1910; *The Flower Fields of Alpine Switzerland*. Hutchinson, 1911; *Chamonix, Lausanne, Locarno, Lucerne, Villars, Zermatt* in the 'Beautiful Switzerland' series. Blackie & Son, Ltd., N.D.
Bibliog: DBA; GW; MALLALIEU; WOOD; *Who Was Who 1916–1928*; McCORMICK, D. *Murder by Perfection*. John Long, 1970; CLARK, D. *Victor Grayson, Labour's Lost Leader*. Quartet Books, 1985; Surrey Artists and their Homes. IX.–Mr. George Flemwell. *Sutton and Epsom Advertiser*, 17 December 1887

FOSTER, Myles Birket, R.W.S. 1825–1899

Myles Birket Foster, born in 1825 in North Shields, is Surrey's best-loved watercolourist. His delightful scenes of children blackberrying, picking primroses, and playing on the seashore are as popular today as when he first painted them. They have been engraved, reproduced and copied.

When he was sixteen he was apprenticed to the wood engraver Ebenezer Landells, who used to send Foster and Foster's fellow pupil Edmund Evans (later a well known colour printer) out into the countryside to find suitable scenes to engrave for his books. H. M. Cundall, in his biography of Foster, tells how the two young men 'took the train to Croydon, which was then a terminus and walked to Waddon, Beddington Park, Sanderstead and other surrounding villages in search of the picturesque'. Shortly after Foster's death in 1899, Christie's held a sale of his remaining works and the first lot to be sold contained some pencil drawings of Beddington.

In addition to his work as an engraver and illustrator, Birket Foster painted a large number of watercolours, three hundred being exhibited at the Old Watercolour Society alone. A search through the books he illustrated – most of them are works of the poets – could reveal some of his views of Beddington Park and its surroundings.

Foster's success was such that he was able to have a fine house built at Witley in Surrey. He named this house The Hill. It was a popular venue with his friends, who included the artists Helen Allingham and Frederick Walker (q.v.). The latter, treated as one of the family, had his own room at The Hill and took part in some of the amateur dramatic performances staged by the Fosters.

Birket Foster's style has influenced other painters of rural scenes, some of them even adding the artist's monogram to their own work. So it has to be *caveat emptor* where his paintings are concerned.

Exhib: AGN; DOW; FIN; GI; M; NWS; OWS; RA; RE; RWS; SBA; TOO
Coll: See MALLALIEU
Illus: See HOUFE; J. REYNOLDS.
Bibliog: BEN; DBA; DNB; ENGEN (1&2); HARDIE; HOUFE; LISTER; MALLALIEU; TB; WOOD; CUNDALL, H. M. *Birket Foster, R.W.S.* Adam & Charles Black, 1906; LEWIS, F. *Myles Birket Foster.* F. Lewis, 1973; REYNOLDS, J. *Birket Foster.* Batsford, 1984

FRAMPTON, Edward 1848–1929
Beechwood Lodge, Hill Road, Sutton 1883–1916

Two decorative artists of importance who lived in Sutton during the last quarter of the nineteenth century and the beginning of this were the Framptons: Edward Frampton and his son Edward Reginald Frampton (q.v.), whose stained glass windows, frescoes, and sculptures are to be seen in churches throughout this country and overseas.

Edward Frampton senior came from Kent, but was descended from an old Dorset family. He was a boy chorister at the Chapel Royal, Savoy, London; and many years later, in memory of those days, he presented porch windows to the Savoy Schools, Queen Victoria owning the original designs. After an art training at the Langham Sketching Club and at the Royal Academy Schools, he worked for Clayton and Bell, mastering the highly skilled art of painting on glass. He was also a fresco artist, travelling to the Continent to study the great wall paintings of France and Italy.

His first important commission was to design frescoes and windows for *St James' Church*, Bury St Edmunds, working under the architect of the church, Sir George Gilbert Scott. Frampton carried out all the painting work himself, as was to be his custom throughout his life. His greatest challenge came when he was asked to design eleven windows for *St John's Cathedral*, Denver, Colorado, U.S.A., where his brilliantly-painted east window of *The Crucifixion* was one of the largest single windows ever made. Although the bulk of his work was for churches, many of them in the North of England, he accepted the occasional secular commission, as when he painted frescoes of Tennyson's *Idylls of the King* in the home of Thomas Hughes, the author of *Tom Brown's Schooldays*.

A friendship with the Gladstone family – a signed photograph of the Prime Minister always stood on Frampton's sideboard – led to a commission for him to carry out some frescoes of *The Resurrection* in the *Whitley Chapel, Hawarden Church*, near Chester. In this same chapel – at the invitation of the Rev. Stephen Gladstone – Edward placed a memorial window to his

own wife Caroline, whose untimely death had left him a widower with young children to bring up.

The Framptons lived in Sutton from 1883 until 1916, at Beechwood Lodge in Hill Road. The house overlooked a small wood, and Edward had a roof-top studio built on, with windows on all four sides, where he worked on his smaller designs; the larger ones were carried out in his studio in Buckingham Palace Road, London. Although the house was not very large, it contained many treasures. A crimson and white drawing room formed a fitting setting for Frampton's collection of antiques – his early ivories, his pottery and porcelain, his fine Chippendale and Sheraton furniture, his lamps and bronzes from the East. He owned a bust of *Henry Irving* by Onslow Ford – a smaller version of one exhibited at the RA – which had been given to him by the sculptor.

Edward Frampton was below average height; but his fine head, with its crop of thick, prematurely grey hair, tended to compensate for this. Eyes, under heavy brows, were bright and humorous. In 1888 he was a founder member of the Surrey Art Circle (q.v.) and was later made an Honorary Life Member. He knew most of the artists in the district. One of them, William Lewis Hind (q.v.), was his neighbour in Hill Road.

Several examples of Frampton's work can be seen in this area. In 1887 Lady McCulloch of Ewell commissioned Frampton to design a four-light window of the four evangelists for J. Wills's new Presbyterian Church in Stafford Road, Wallington. Then, at St Nicholas Church, Sutton, a short distance from where the artist used to live, there is a stained glass window of *Christ healing the impotent man at the Pool of Bethesda*, commissioned in 1888 by a Sutton widow in memory of her husband, 'W.E.C.', who died in 1887. Also in this church is Frampton's memorial window to Evelyn Frances Turner, who died at Sutton Rectory on 19 September 1895, the window illustrating scenes from the life of St Faith. At Reigate, a few miles from Sutton, Canon Casenove employed Frampton to decorate the chancel of *St Mark's Church* with frescoes.

Edward Frampton must have been gratified when his only son, Edward Reginald (q.v.), decided to become an artist. He took him into his own studio and gave him much help and encouragement. Frampton's daughters proved the ideal models for the angels and saints in his windows and frescoes. In 1916 he left Sutton to live on the south coast, where he died in 1929, outliving his son by six years. To a certain extent his style is derivative. He was strongly influenced by the artists of the fourteenth and fifteenth centuries. A degree of originality, however, is usually present in his work; and he was much admired in America for the way in which his stained glass windows reflected the bright colours of the American skies and landscapes.

Exhib: RA; RBA; ROI; SAC
Bibliog: BEN; DBA; TB; Surrey Artists and their Homes.
1.–Mr. Edward Frampton. *Sutton and Epsom Advertiser*, 29 October 1887

**FRAMPTON, Edward Reginald, R.B.A., R.O.I.
1872–1923**
Beechwood Lodge, Hill Road, Sutton 1883–c.1900
Today the fine, decorative paintings of E. Reginald
Frampton are so highly regarded that they are beyond
the reach of most collectors. In 1986 his painting *A
Maid of Bruges*, which had been exhibited at the Royal

EDWARD R. FRAMPTON   Watercolour 927×394mm
The Gothic Tower.   Photo courtesy Sotheby's

Academy in 1919, was entered for sale at Sotheby's
with an estimated price of £20,000–£30,000.

The only son of Caroline and Edward Frampton
(q.v.), his birth was registered at Croydon in 1872, and
he came to live in Sutton when he was ten, remaining
there for about seventeen years. Reginald and his
sisters were brought up mainly by their father, their
mother having died when they were young. To avoid
confusion with his father, he signed his work 'E.
Reginald Frampton', or simply 'Reginald Frampton'.

His schooldays were spent at Brighton Boys'
Grammar School, where two of his contemporaries
were the artist Aubrey Beardsley and the impressario
Charles B. Cochran, both born, like Frampton, in 1872.
On one occasion Beardsley and Frampton collaborated
on the designs for a school play, Beardsley being
responsible for the programme and costumes, and
Frampton the scenery. On leaving the grammar
school, Reginald Frampton entered Westminster Art
School, completing his training by serving an
apprenticeship in his father's studio.

Edward Frampton senior encouraged his son to join
the Surrey Art Circle (q.v.) which had recently been
formed in Sutton. Father and son exhibited with the
Art Circle for many years, Reginald remaining a
member until 1902. A romantic, lyrical painter, he was
strongly attracted to religious subjects, especially the
lives of the female saints; but he also filled his canvases
with the heroes and heroines of the early romances.
Titles shown at the SAC's exhibitions included: *Elaine*
(1898), *The Adoration of the Magi* (1898), *Cottage Gardens,
Mitcham* (1900), *St. Cecilia* (1901), *The Knight's Tale,
Chaucer* (1902) and *Red Roofs* (1902), some of these titles
later being hung at the RA where, between 1895 and
1923, he exhibited thirty-four works.

He was a member of the Royal Society of British
Artists (1894) but later resigned. He was also a member
of the Royal Institute of Oil Painters (1904), the
Tempera Society (1907) and the Art Workers' Guild
(1910). Frampton spent many enjoyable evenings with
the Langham Sketching Club; he designed the
Langham Sketching Club Mug, and this was exhibited at
the RA in 1896. In 1914 a one-man show of his work
was held at the Fine Art Society, London, and in 1920
he won a silver medal at the Paris Salon for his
painting *The Kiss of Spring*.

The Art Workers' Guild, founded as it was on the
principles of the Arts and Crafts movement, was the
society most suited to Frampton's particular talents.
The artists he admired above all others, William
Morris (q.v.) and Sir Edward Coley Burne-Jones, had
been members of the Guild, and although both had
been dead for over ten years when Frampton joined
the Guild, their influence was still strongly felt.

Frampton's studies of the female form show the
influence of Burne-Jones, particularly in such
paintings as *Navigation* and *St Dorothea* (illus. in the *Art
Journal*, 1907), and he was also influenced by the early
Italian and Flemish painters, and by the Italian artists
of the Renaissance. As a decorative painter during the
last years of the nineteenth century and the beginning
of this – a period which saw the most popular revival
of mural painting this country has ever known –

Reginald Frampton was constantly in demand, responsible for many important schemes, both ecclesiastical and secular. To make certain that his work would endure, he carried out each stage of the work himself, preparing the wall surfaces thoroughly first and sealing them when the work was finished. To prevent chemical deterioration he used a limited palette of azure blue, yellow, light red and rose-orange.

One of his largest murals, a design of angels, was carried out as a memorial to Sir George Mellish in *St Michael's Church*, Rushall, Staffordshire. Equally important work by Frampton was carried out in *All Saints' Church*, Hastings, although today all traces of his presence there have vanished under a coat of creamy-white paint. Possibly someone in the not-too-distant past decided that Frampton's murals were not in keeping with the style of the building and had them painted out. They were illustrated in the *Art Journal* in 1907, shortly after they were painted, so at least we know what they looked like. Who knows – perhaps they will be re-discovered one day.

An example of his church work here in Surrey can be seen in *St Barnabas Church*, Ranmore Common (designed by the architect Sir George Gilbert Scott), where the *Memorial Chapel to Lord Ashcombe* is decorated with Frampton's frescoes, painted in 1918, the colours still remarkably fresh.

His decorative skills are present in his paintings, where a recurring theme is that of a young girl profiled against a stylised landscape. One such work is *Flora of the Fells* (illus. in *Modern Art*, 1919), where a golden-haired Flora, a bunch of spring flowers in her hands, dominates the foreground of the picture, whilst in the background, as a sharp contrast to her fragile beauty, there is a stark view of some mountains and rocks.

In 1898 Reginald Frampton married Ethel Louisa ('Lola') Clark, the daughter of Francis Mallard Clark of the Admiralty. For many years they lived in fashionable Cheyne Row, Chelsea. Reginald was on the staff of the L.C.C.'s Higher Education Art Section, lecturing on art and publishing papers on the subject. His hobbies were sailing and chess.

His death came suddenly and without warning. In the autumn of 1923 he was travelling to Austria, when he stopped off in Paris, staying at the Hotel Studio, Rue de Seine. He was taken ill at the hotel and died on 5 November 1923. His grave is in the Cemetery of St Germain in Paris. The following year, a memorial exhibition of his work was held at the Fine Art Society in London. Five of Frampton's drawings, the gift of Miss Jeanne Bridges, are in the National Collection of Watercolours at the Victoria and Albert Museum.

Exhib: B; BG; FIN; G; GI; L; M; NG; RBA; RI; RMS; ROI; SAC; Japan; U.S.A.
Coll: Bradford AG; V&A; Walker AG, Liverpool
Bibliog: BEN; DBA; GW; HOUFE; TB; V; WOOD; *Who Was Who 1916–1928*; DIRKS, R. Mr. E. Reginald Frampton. *Art Journal*, 1907, pp. 289–96; VALLANCE, A. The paintings of Reginald Frampton, R.O.I. *Studio*, lxxv, no. 309, Dec. 1918, pp. 67–77; *Studio*, xxxvi, no. 154, Jan. 1906, pp. 346–50; lxii, no. 256, Aug. 1914, p. 172
Obit: *The Times*, 8 November 1923

FULLER, Leonard John, R.O.I., R.Cam.A. 1891–1973
Trelawney, 33 St James Road, Sutton 1908–1935
142 Mulgrave Road, Cheam 1935–1938

A seat in Norway Square, St Ives, Cornwall, is dedicated to the memory of Marjorie and Leonard Fuller. Placed there shortly after Marjorie Fuller's death, it was paid for from a fund set up by the pupils and ex-pupils of the St Ives School of Painting, founded by the Fullers on 4 April 1938, and continuing today under Roy Ray. Not only does the seat commemorate the lives of two artists; it also honours a marriage which was described in Leonard Fuller's obituary as 'a devotion to each other through the years that was a symbol of all that is best and uplifting in humanity'.

Leonard John Fuller, the younger son of Mary and John Haire Fuller, was born in Dulwich on 11 October 1891 and was educated at Dulwich College. The Fullers moved to Sutton in 1908 and Leonard continued his education by attending the Clapham School of Art and the Royal Academy Schools, at the latter winning silver and bronze medals and a British Institute Scholarship. At the RA Schools he met and fell in love with Marjorie Mostyn (q.v.), the attractive daughter of the landscape and genre painter Tom Mostyn, R.B.A., R.O.I. Their romance was interrupted by the First World War, when Leonard was sent to France with the 10th Battalion Royal Fusiliers. He later transferred to the Machine Gun Corps and rose to the rank of acting Captain.

Leonard and Marjorie were married in 1917 and for many years they and their only son, John Mostyn Fuller, lived with Leonard's parents in Sutton. From 1922 until 1932 Leonard taught at St John's Wood Art School and from 1927 until 1938 at his old school, Dulwich College. After the war he resumed his studies at the RA Schools, and in 1919 had his first acceptance at the Royal Academy: *Nancy*, an oil portrait of his wife Marjorie, who was known as 'Nancy' to her family and friends. The following year, Leonard exhibited portraits of his father-in-law *Tom Mostyn, Esq.*, and of *Audrey, daughter of Frederick Davey, Esq.*, at the RA. Audrey Davey, now Mrs Audrey Scott, was a lifelong friend of the Fullers. Nine years after Leonard's first portrait of her was shown there, another study by him of Audrey, *Portrait in silver and gold*, was 'hung on the line' at the RA.

Leonard Fuller exhibited thirty-one works at the RA and many others elsewhere. He was a member of the Royal Institute of Oil Painters (1932) and of the Royal Cambrian Academy (1939). Although there are many landscape and genre paintings which bear his signature, he is, perhaps, best known for his portraits, his subjects ranging from sporting personalities such as Jack Hobbs, to public figures like Dr. W. R. Matthews, Dean of St Paul's.

Living first in Sutton and then in Cheam, Marjorie and Leonard Fuller were popular members of the community. They both belonged to the Sutton Amateur Dramatic Society and were regular churchgoers. Leonard, in addition to teaching and practising art, wrote articles on painting technique. His attractive oils of Sutton and Cheam, painted when he was living in the borough, bring to life – far more vividly than many photographs – the unique atmosphere of the inter-war years. His *Moving Pictures* (illus. in *The Tatler*, 13 February 1935, pp. 308–9), for example, is a nostalgic reminder of the crowds queueing cheerfully in the rain outside the old Surrey County Cinema in Sutton High Street to see *Cavalcade*.

Another painting from this period is *By-Pass* (illus. in *The Connoisseur*, February 1940, pp. 268–9), a lively scene of cars, cyclists, hikers, children and dogs, set against a suburban background. Although the location has not yet been positively identified, it is almost certainly within this borough. Fuller's painting *The Peoples Store . . .* – this has recently been on show at the Richard Green Gallery in London – shows the interior of Sutton's first Woolworths. His *Shops across the way*, a view of a group of shops at the top of Sutton High Street, was exhibited at the RA in 1950, but dates from an earlier period when an open-topped 88a bus travelled to Belmont. This painting is now privately owned.

One of his most interesting works, however, is *Sunday* (illus. in *Dictionary of British Artists Working 1900–1950* by G. M. Waters, 1975). In this painting the artist has captured to perfection the 'after-Sunday-lunch' feeling. It shows his own family – mother, father, wife and son – grouped lethargically around the fireplace of the living room in their Sutton home. The costumes and hair styles indicate that it must have been painted towards the end of the 1920s, ten years or so before the Fullers left the district to live in Cornwall.

They already knew the West Country well through vists to Marjorie's father, Tom Mostyn, who lived there. But it was Leonard's old war comrade, the artist Borlase Smart, who persuaded the Fullers to open an art school at St Ives which, at its twenty-first birthday in 1959, was able to boast that over a thousand pupils had passed through its doors.

The Second World War started soon after the Fullers had settled in Cornwall, and a Home Guard unit was formed at St Ives, with Leonard Fuller the Commanding Officer, Borlase Smart his Intelligence Officer and Bernard Leach, England's most famous studio potter, a mere private. The day the unit was issued with a machine gun, Leonard Fuller nearly lost his head. As the gun was being set up, someone accidentally triggered it off, the shots just missing the commanding officer's head.

Painting mostly in oil, Leonard Fuller was a traditionalist, teaching art in that way. However, he was sympathetic towards the modern art movements, even if this was not reciprocated by some of the avant-garde artists who settled in Cornwall after the war. At the RA Schools he had been taught by three Royal Academicians – Sargent, Clausen and Orpen, and his own students often heard of how John Singer Sargent had once stopped by Leonard's desk to enquire where his plumb line was. On hearing that Leonard did not possess one, Sargent said: 'Go and get one, and remember that I never draw a standing figure of that size without one'. Another valuable piece of advice Leonard gave his students was not to over-paint because, he said, it gave a 'tired' look to the canvas.

His own palette was based on titanium or flake white, yellow ochre, light red, Indian red, cadmium red, burnt sienna, raw umber, ivory black, cobalt blue, rose madder, viridian, and pale and middle cadmium yellow.

Very much involved in the social life of St Ives (as he was at Sutton), he was the President of the Rotary Club (1950), served on church committees, and was prominent in the campaign to preserve Cornish churches. From 1942 until 1946 he was the Chairman of the St Ives Society of Artists; and in 1949 he was one of the seventeen members of this society who resigned to form the Penwith Society of Arts; others included Bernard Leach, Barbara Hepworth, Ben Nicholson and Sven Berlin. Leonard Fuller was the first Chairman of this new society. He also belonged to the Newlyn Society of Artists and the Chelsea Arts Club.

On his eightieth birthday he was given a surprise party by his past and present students. He died suddenly, on 24 July 1973, a few months before his eighty-second birthday, an obituary describing him as 'unfailingly charitable, courteous and kind to others, gentle, courageous and much loved'. He is represented in numerous collections.

Exhib: GI; L; M; P; RA; RCA; RHA; ROI; RP; Newlyn; St Ives; Penwith
Coll: Newark Town Hall; Newport AG; Chapter House, St Paul's Cathedral; Plymouth AG; St Ives Guildhall
Published: FULLER, L. For the beginner. *The Artist*, 1962 (a series of illustrated articles)
Bibliog: BEN; DBA; GW; V; *Who Was Who 1971–1980*; *Who's Who in Art* – several editions; BAKER, D. V. *Britain's Art Colony by the Sea*. George Ronald, 1959; CROSS, T. *Painting the Warmth of the Sun*. Lutterworth, 1984

FULLER, William b. 1888
Hawkhurst, 22 The Crescent, Belmont 1921–1935
William Fuller, who was an ornamental sculptor, was born in Dulwich on 20 September 1888, the son of W. Fuller, a bank clerk. He married Grace Evelyn Crowe and lived in Belmont from 1921 onwards.

After studying 'life modelling' at the City and Guilds School, London, where he won a silver medal, Fuller exhibited at London, Liverpool and Paris. In 1924 his bronze statuette, *The Holiday Spirit*, submitted from Belmont, was exhibited at the Royal Academy.

Exhib: GI; L; P; RA
Bibliog: DBA; V; *Who's Who in Art*, 1929

GALLAHER, Mabel Lilian, R.M.S. 1885–1972
Brightside, Christchurch Park, Sutton 1906–1924
Mabel Gallaher, a watercolourist, painted flower and garden studies, and also portraits; many, but not all, were miniatures. She was the daughter of Major George R. Gallaher, and came to live in Sutton when

she was eighteen, the Gallahers occupying a house called Brightside in Christchurch Park. This used to be an area where some of the more affluent citizens of Sutton had their homes during the early years of the present century. However, where once the gracious villas of Mabel Gallaher's day occupied Christchurch Park, modern blocks of flats have now taken over nearly the whole of the area.

Ten of her paintings were hung at the Royal Academy (1909–1921), amongst them two portrait miniatures of her parents, which remained in her possession until her death. Another RA exhibit, shown in 1918, was her portrait of *Sir Ralph Forster, Bt.*, the first and also the last baronet, his only son dying in 1915 from wounds suffered in the First World War. Sir Ralph, who married twice, lived at The Grange in Mulgrave Road, Sutton, and was prominent in local affairs; he was the High Sheriff of Surrey and the Chairman of Sutton Petty Sessional Court.

During the 1930s, Mabel Gallaher, a member of the Royal Miniature Society, exhibited about half a dozen flower studies each year with them. She never married, lived into her eighties and died at Boscombe, Bournemouth, on 12 January 1972. Three of her delicately-painted watercolours of flowers, somewhat in the style of Charles Rennie Mackintosh, are to be found in the Russell-Cotes Art Gallery in Bournemouth, donated by Miss K. L. D. Saunders.

Exhib: GRA; RA; RHA; RI; RMS
Coll: Bournemouth AG
Bibliog: DBA; GW; *Who's Who in Art*, 1929

GILL, Edmund Ward 1820–1894

Linn Villa, Carshalton Road, Sutton 1874–1894

Edmund 'Waterfall' Gill, born in Clerkenwell, London, on 29 November 1820, was the son of W. Gill, a japanner by trade who later took up portrait painting. Edmund, after some early painting lessons from a pupil of John Glover, followed his father at first, and painted portraits. But after a meeting with the great Birmingham landscape painter, David Cox, he decided to devote the rest of his own life to landscape painting.

The Gill family eventually moved away from London to live in Hereford, where in 1841 Edmund's views of the local countryside came to the attention of an eminent barrister, who bought his work and promised to introduce him to Lord Brougham, a notable art patron. That same year, Edmund's friends in Hereford organised a lottery on his behalf, distributing a circular which ended with the words: 'You will be gratified in having the opportunity of cherishing true and youthful genius and moral worth'. The prizes were five paintings by Gill. The proceeds from the lottery enabled him to go first to Wales to sketch and then on to London, where he entered the Royal Academy Schools. By the late 1840s he had become a regular exhibitor at the RA, his numerous paintings of waterfalls earning him the nickname

'Waterfall Gill'. He was even featured in *Punch:*

> *Waterfall and Torrents* by E. Gill
> Edmund Gill went up a Hill
> To paint a pail of water
> Then came down
> And in Town
> His pictures were shown after

Gill was a competitor at the Crystal Palace art competitions, winning silver and bronze medals and cash prizes. He later gave the medals, together with some paintings and other interesting items, to the town of Hereford, in memory of his family.

In 1874 Gill arrived at Sutton, taking up residence in Linn Villa in Carshalton Road, where not a waterfall was in sight, but the Sutton District Waterworks was just up the road. To find his ideal scenery he needed to travel to Wales, or Scotland, or Cornwall, and would then return to Sutton with sketches of rocky coastal scenery, stormy seas and – inevitably – waterfalls. His paintings were greeted with much acclaim, one critic enthusing that Gill displayed 'great talent for representing water in motion', another comparing his skill with the paintbrush to Paganini's virtuoso playing of the violin.

Edmund Gill married late in life. Ann Gill, who came from Gravesend, was his housekeeper before he married her. His brother's widow, Phoebe Gill, lived with them at Linn Villa, and they employed a general servant, Susan Buckle. Next door, at Ivy Bank, was the watercolourist Sophy S. Warren (q.v.)

Gill led a quiet, studious life, reading a lot and spending hours looking at objects through a microscope or telescope. He also dabbled in geology. For some time prior to his death, he had been in poor health; and on 13 May 1894, whilst walking to Hackbridge, he suffered a dizzy spell. After receiving some help, he walked home unaided. But at 10.30 pm that same evening, he fell on the stairs whilst attempting to retire for the night. Friends had to carry him to bed and he died during the early hours of the next morning. He is buried in Carshalton churchyard.

After his death, his widow sold most of his remaining paintings at auction – possibly in Sutton where, in 1888, the auctioneer John Morgan had already sold a small collection of the artist's paintings. Gill was a prolific artist, whose paintings are to be seen in many stately homes, as well as in public galleries. Henry Wallis (q.v.) was one who admired his work and acquired one of his paintings.

Exhib: BI; L; M; RA; RBA; RHA; ROI; TOO
Coll: Bath AG; Hereford AG; Newcastle AG; V&A
Bibliog: BEN; DBA; MALLALIEU; TB; WOOD; *Sutton and Epsom Advertiser*, 31 March 1888 and 26 May 1894; *Art Journal* 1874, p. 41 ff.

*GILPIN, William 1724–1804

Headmaster of Cheam School, Surrey 1752–1777

William Gilpin was a competent watercolourist, a distinguished art critic and respected essayist. His influence on the development of late eighteenth and early nineteenth century art was considerable, and he played an important role in the movement away from

EDMUND W. GILL   Oil 292×241mm
A Waterfall. 1890.   Photo courtesy Sotheby's

classicism into romanticism. For more than a quarter of a century Gilpin was associated with Cheam School, first as an assistant master and then from 1752 as headmaster, acquiring a reputation as a humane and enlightened teacher. A man of high-minded principle, he was held in affection by his family, his friends and his pupils. William Gilpin was far more than the headmaster of a school for the privileged few; his prolific writings won him a reputation – spreading far beyond Cheam – as the master of the 'picturesque'.

Gilpin was born in 1724 in the appropriately romantic setting of Scaleby Castle in Cumberland. His father, a professional soldier and talented painter in watercolour, taught his son the rudiments of painting, and passed on to him an appreciation of nature that was to influence his artistic philosophy throughout his long life.

William was sent to school at St Bees on the Cumberland coast. From there he proceeded to Queen's College, Oxford, where his artistic interests took up a great deal of his time. He spent many hours in the study of paintings, and to widen his own artistic experience sought out the only engraver in Oxford and became a passable etcher. He formed a collection of prints and engravings and by the age of twenty was fully capable of producing a carefully considered analysis of them.

After Oxford he returned briefly to his native Cumberland and, having taken holy orders – as essential as a present-day teaching diploma for the eighteenth century schoolmaster – he moved to Cheam School. The exact date of his arrival is not clear, but by 1751 he was certainly established at Cheam as an 'usher' or assistant master. Cheam School left modern suburban Cheam in 1934, but the site of the school in Gilpin's day is quite clearly defined. It stood at what is now a modern block of flats slightly to the east of Cheam Village. Eighteenth century Cheam was a quiet Surrey village, pleasant enough but almost certainly lacking the dramatic qualities which Gilpin sought out with so much vigour – the 'picturesque'.

Having married his first cousin Margaret in 1752, Gilpin, now Headmaster, devoted himself to the development of Cheam School, even to the extent of giving up his etching and painting. By careful management and discreet advertisement, he was able to build up the reputation of the school. From a mere twenty boys in 1759 he increased the numbers to thirty-one in 1762 and by 1766 over sixty boys attended the school.

There is little doubt that William Gilpin was an outstanding teacher. The curriculum followed at Cheam was, by eighteenth century standards, progressive, and thoroughly enlightened, and included such subjects as gardening, geography and, of course, drawing. It is not surprising that the school became something of a model to which other private schools might aspire. William's younger brother Sawry Gilpin, an animal painter of great distinction, spent some time at Cheam as an occasional drawing master. Thomas Grimston, a pupil, wrote to his father in September 1761: 'I have finished one drawing book and have drawn three pictures in the next one of

H. WALTON   Oil 254×203mm
Portrait of William Gilpin. 1781.   National Portrait Gallery, London

which one is Cheam Church from Nature and two others from pictures of Mr. Sawry Gilpin's doing'.

For all his success as a teacher, it is doubtful whether Gilpin's reputation would have endured had he not promoted the theory of the picturesque. As an artist he rarely rose above the level of the gifted amateur. His watercolour landscapes are pleasing enough to the eye, but in many ways are intended as illustrations of his artistic theories rather than works of art in their own right. Gilpin's theory of the picturesque is based on the assumption that landscape painting should illustrate nature at its wildest and most dramatic. The rough and rugged scene was always preferable to the smooth and ordered picture. Ruins were better than complete buildings and brooding storm clouds superior to the clear sky.

Gilpin was no armchair critic. From 1760 onwards he devoted as much of his spare time as possible to touring the British Isles. These excursions formed the raw material for a series of six books, with illustrations based on his own sketches. The first appeared in 1782: *Observations on the River Wye . . .*; the last, the *Eastern Tour*, appeared posthumously in 1809.

Gilpin's reputation as a writer and traveller was remarkable. His books were very popular and went to several editions. The manuscript of his tour of the

Lakes was shown to King George III and Queen Charlotte by Lord Dartmouth who had three sons at Cheam School. What the King thought of the book is unrecorded, but Gilpin, not unreasonably, was worried lest the manuscript might simply be accepted as an addition to the Royal Collection.

Most of the tours were illustrated with Gilpin's own line and wash drawings, engraved in the new method of aquatint. Inevitably, Gilpin's dedication to 'The Picturesque' invited a certain amount of derision. He is almost certainly the central figure in William Combe's *Dr. Syntax* books which first appeared in 1806, with a series of brilliant illustrations by Rowlandson (q.v.). The cult of the ruin has long since gone out of fashion but Gilpin did succeed in bringing a fresh approach to landscape painting in England.

In 1777 Gilpin decided to retire from the headmastership of Cheam School, which passed into the hands of his son. He took a living at Boldre in Hampshire where he continued to take a lively interest in the education of the local children. Shortly before his death, he authorised Christie's to sell his drawings and watercolours. They raised a substantial sum with which Gilpin was able to set up a trust fund for the maintenance of the local school.

After a short illness, he died in April 1804 in his seventy-ninth year. His coffin was borne by four of his poor parishioners, and the teachers and children joined in the funeral procession. It was a fitting end for a man who had devoted so much of his time to the education of the poor.

A memorial tablet in the Lumley Chapel, Cheam, reminds us that not all William Gilpin's days at Cheam were happy ones. It records the sad death of a child: 'To the tender memory of an only daughter W. and M. Gilpin inscribed this. She was born Feb 5 1762 and dyed Oct 7 1767'.

Peter Jackson

Coll: BM; Fitzwilliam Museum, Cambridge; Leeds City AG; Leicester AG; Newport AG; Sutton LC; Ulster Museum; V&A
Illus: See HOUFE
Bibliog: BEN; HALL(2); LAMBOURNE; MALLALIEU; TB; WATERHOUSE; BARBIER, C.P. *William Gilpin . . .* Clarendon Press, 1963; PEEL, E. *Cheam School from 1645.* Thornhill Press, 1974; REDGRAVE, S. *A Dictionary of Artists of the English School.* 1878. Kingsmead Reprints, 1970; RUSSELL, R. *Guide to British Topographical Prints.* David and Charles, 1979

*GOLDTHWAIT, Harold 1869–1932
Meadowside, Duke of Edinburgh Road, Carshalton 1893–1897
Painting mainly in oil, Harold Goldthwait was a landscape and genre artist, exhibiting rural views of Southern England at the Royal Academy and other galleries. During the 1890s he lived in a house called Meadowside, at Carshalton, where the householder was Oliver Charles Goldthwait (Pile). By 1898, Harold had moved to Norwood Hill in Surrey, and he later lived in Sussex.

In 1903 he joined the Surrey Art Circle (q.v.) and remained a member until 1909. He served on the committee and exhibited several paintings each year at

their exhibitions; these included views of the South Downs and the Isle of Wight. His paintings occasionally turn up in the salerooms: in 1979 a rural landscape by Goldthwait was sold at auction for £270 and in 1981 a pair of similar, but smaller, scenes made £150.

Sophy Goldthwait, Harold's wife, herself an artist, exhibited a painting at the Walker Art Gallery, Liverpool, in 1915. Harold Goldthwait died at Hampstead on 21 July 1932.

Exhib: GOU; L; LS; RA; RHA; ROI; SAC
Bibliog: DBA; WOOD

*GRIFFITHS, Tom 1887–1986
Mill Lane, Carshalton 1887–
Victoria Road, Sutton 1920–1984
Tom Griffiths was born in a house in Mill Lane, Carshalton, on 5 February 1887. At the time, his father was one of Carshalton's two mounted policemen. As he liked to point out, Tom's home all his life was within three-quarters of a mile of the River Wandle.

After leaving school at the age of fourteen, and spending a year as a 'printer's devil' at the Hackbridge printing works of William Pile (then publisher of Pile's local directories and the *Sutton Herald*) Tom Griffiths went to work for Rickett Cockerell the coal merchants (at first in Wallington) and stayed for sixty years.

After he retired in 1961, aged seventy-four, he resumed the hobby of painting, abandoned for many years. He had made watercolour sketches whilst serving in India in the First World War but had not painted since. He never received any art training.

With the death of his wife in 1965, Tom devoted much time to painting watercolour pictures of the district as he remembered it in his youth, recreating a lost world of lavender fields and still-rural villages. He seldom sold his paintings, except for charity, preferring to give them to those who admired and appreciated them.

As well as painting Tom loved gardening, growing many plants and trees in the garden at his home in Victoria Road, Sutton, where he lived from 1920 until a couple of years before his death. At the age of seventy-eight he was growing his own tobacco for the pipe he smoked, and giving gardening lessons several days a week to the patients of Henderson Hospital. He was Treasurer of the Sutton and District Horticultural Society, and his wife was a founder member of the Sutton Floral Group. He was a member of the congregation of St Barnabas Church, Sutton.

Although he was still riding his bicycle at the age of ninety, his eyesight was failing and he could no longer paint. In March 1984, with pneumonia, he had to enter Carshalton War Memorial Hospital. He recovered, but had become almost totally blind, and, at the age of ninety-seven, was unable to return home to look after himself, even with the willing help of the friends and neighbours to whom his door had always been open. He died on 12 July 1986, just under seven months short of his hundredth birthday. To the end, though frail, he remained able to talk to visitors, especially about his beloved Carshalton.

In his youth Tom had met William Tatton Winter (q.v.) and had acquired two of his paintings: one of a goose-girl in Banstead, and one of the 'Blue House' on Mitcham Common. The influence of these paintings, looked at for more than half a century, was very evident in Tom's work. It was typical of his generosity that, once showing Tatton Winter's daughter round the places in Carshalton associated with her father, he had offered her both paintings as a gift, much as they meant to him.

Tom's paintings were exhibited locally several times, the last in his lifetime being in the Europa Gallery, Sutton Central Library, in May 1979. A number of them, with his two Tatton Winter's, were presented to the local art collection of Sutton Leisure Services by Mrs Josephine Tanner, to whom he had left them; complementing some given to the Collection by the artist in his lifetime.

Douglas Cluett

Sources: Local press (1965+); conversations and taped interviews with Tom Griffiths; Mrs Josephine Tanner; personal knowledge

GROOM, Charles William 1853–1917
8 Ross Road, Wallington 1882–1889
Crowhurst, Park Hill, Carshalton 1889–1914
30 Taylor Road, Wallington 1914–1917
Known for his atmospheric views of sunsets, autumn mists and sun-drenched days, the oil painter Charles Groom lived in this borough for over thirty years, in 1888 serving on the Executive Committee at Wallington. An early member of the Surrey Art Circle (q.v.), he exhibited with them until 1910, showing, in total, more than thirty works. A close friend and fellow member was William Tatton Winter (q.v.), whose advice he often sought on art matters.

Groom, born in London in 1853, lived in Bognor, Sussex, before settling in this area, where his first address was no. 8 Ross Road, Wallington. In 1889 he moved to Park Hill, Carshalton, and lived in a house called Crowhurst, until the outbreak of the First World War, when he and his wife Annie moved back to Wallington. Groom's last years were spent at no. 30 Taylor Road, where he died on 9 March 1917.

He exhibited five titles at the Royal Academy, all submitted from Carshalton. They included: *The cottage by the moor* (1892), *Drear December* (1892) and *The Withered sward* (1895). His painting *Kentish Common*, shown at the Royal Institute of Oil Painters' exhibition in 1893, was described by the local press as 'a dextrous reminiscence of a wooded heath'.

Exhib: B; G; L; NG; RA; RBA; ROI; SAC
Bibliog: BEN; DBA; WOOD

GUY, Edna Waverley, R.S.M.A. 1897–1969
Born at Sutton in 1897
The watercolourist Edna Waverley Guy, born at Sutton in 1897, was married to Lieut. Col. Norman Greenwood Guy, who was killed in action in 1942 whilst commanding the 13th Battalion 14th Force Rifles. His name can be found on the Rangoon War Memorial. They had two sons.

She studied art in South Africa under J. H. Amschewitz, R.B.A., and in Paris at L'Academie Julian under O. D. V. Guillonnet. In England, she attended the Slade, and also studied at the Spenlove School of Art under R. G. Eves, R.A. As an army wife she travelled the world, visiting India, Kashmir, Australia and other exotic places; painting, on her travels, many impressionistic watercolours which were exhibited at the local galleries. When, in 1942, her husband was killed, she was in Bombay, but by the end of the year had returned to England and was living at Hastings in Sussex. In 1944 the war brought another tragedy when her young sailor son, Gordon Greenwood Guy, was killed in action aboard H.M.S. *Quorn*.

After the war, Edna lived in Cheyne Walk, Chelsea, close to the Thames, which features in so many of her paintings. She exhibited at the Royal Academy and other galleries and achieved the distinction of being elected a member of the Royal Society of Marine Artists, whose membership is strictly limited. Titles exhibited with the RSMA included: *Chugging through the Fog*, *The Thames from Festival Hall* and *Sunset Glow, Battersea*. Her atmospheric scenes of the London river inspired one critic to write: 'Edna Guy gives us the pictorial content of the Thames that could make sailors of us all' (*The Artist*, Dec. 1956).

She died at her London home on 16 February 1969.

Exhib: NS; P; RA; RI; RSMA; RWS; SWA; Australia; South Africa; India
Bibliog: GW; HART(2); *Who's Who in Art* – several editions

*HARDEN, John 1772–1847
John Harden, thought to have been self-taught, was a fine amateur artist, producing many delightfully fresh-looking watercolours. Well-known in the art world, he counted Constable (q.v.), Havell and Farington (q.v.) amongst his friends. He was never short of money, so was able to travel abroad at will and to entertain his friends in style.

Born in Ireland, he first visited England in 1795. He made a return visit in 1797 and came again in 1798, when he toured the Lake District with fellow artist Dennis Brownell Murphy. In 1799 he came yet again, this time accompanied by William Cuming, P.R.H.A., and visited the South of England and the Isle of Wight.

He married twice, meeting his second wife 'Jessy' (Janet), a talented artist herself, on board ship during the crossing from England to Ireland. She was Scottish, the daughter of Robert Allan, the proprietor of the *Caledonian Mercury*. Harden spent some time in

Edinburgh assisting his father-in-law on the paper and later settled in the Lake District where he lived, at various addresses, until his death in 1847. He is buried in St Anne's churchyard, Ambleside. Hundreds of charming watercolours and drawings by Harden, carefully preserved by his descendants, are now in the Abbot Hall Art Gallery, Kendal, a number of them recording the family's everyday life at Brathay Hall, near Ambleside. The Hall, situated at the head of Lake Windermere, is today used as a study centre.

John Harden visited Carshalton, Surrey, at least twice. In 1835 and again in 1842 he painted views of the ponds. Although the original watercolours have long since disappeared, autotypes of them are in Sutton's Local Collection. Rather disappointingly, a search through Harden's sketches in the Abbot Hall Art Gallery has failed to reveal any drawings of Carshalton.

Coll: Ambleside; BM; Burton-on-Trent AG; Carlisle AG; Kendal; National AG, Scotland; National Lib., Scotland; Tullie House Museum, Scotland
Bibliog: HALL(2); MALLALIEU; WILLIAMS; FOSKETT, D. *John Harden of Brathay Hall*. Kendal: Abbot Hall Art Gallery, 1974

*HASSELL, John 1767–1825
John Hassell, friend and biographer of the artist George Morland, was a watercolourist, an etcher and a drawing master. He left, through his watercolours, a valuable record of the buildings and countryside of England in the eighteenth and early nineteenth centuries. Since they were carried out before the age of photography, his watercolours are much prized by local historians, especially in Surrey, where during the last five years of his life Hassell painted at least eight hundred views. After his death, his son Edward Hassell (1811–1852) continued the daunting task of trying to record every interesting building in the county.

Travelling extensively throughout the South of England, John Hassell visited Beddington in 1817, 1823 and 1824; Carshalton in 1817 and 1823; and Cheam in 1823 and 1824. There are no known paintings of Sutton. Five watercolours of Cheam are in the Local Collection at Sutton; his views of Beddington and Carshalton are to be found in the Minet Library, Lambeth, and the Guildhall Library, London. The Minet Library also has two views of Beddington Church by Edward Hassell – one showing the exterior, the other the altar.

John Hassell published several books, which he illustrated himself. Of particular local interest, since it has a description of a trip down the River Wandle, is *Picturesque Rides and Walks within Thirty Miles of the British Metropolis* (1817–18). He was a competent line-engraver, passing on his skills in his manual *Graphic Delineations*, published by his widow after his death.

Although Hassell's paintings are prized more for their topographical content than their intrinsic merit – Iolo Williams dismisses them as 'rather dull, matter-of-fact little sketches of buildings . . .' (*English Watercolours . . .*, 1970) – he deserves admiration for

the dedicated way in which he set about recording so much of Surrey.

Exhib: RA
Coll: Guildford Museum; Guildhall Library; Lambeth PL; Manchester City AG; Sutton LC; Wimbledon PL
Published: Comprehensive list of works by Hassell in BATLEY and MOSS
Bibliog: BEN; HOUFE; LISTER; MACKENZIE; MALLALIEU; TB; WILLIAMS; BATLEY, J. C. and MOSS, G. P. *A Catalogue of Pictures of Surrey and Elsewhere by John Hassell (1767–1825) and his son Edward (1811–1852)*. Offprint from *Surrey Archaeological Collections*, vol. 75, 1984

HAWES, Edward Burn, M.A. 1871–1936
Tanglewood, Grove Road, Sutton 1913–1936
Born at Richmond in Surrey, Edward Burn Hawes, the brother of the Rev. John Cyril Hawes (q.v.), was a solicitor who painted in his spare time. He exhibited four paintings at the Walker Art Gallery, Liverpool.

He lived in Sutton for over twenty years, also owning properties in Cheam, Tangmere and Putney. Hawes was a keen amateur sailor, with a boat named the *Miss Brittany*. He died in 1936, leaving a widow, Dorothy Marion Hawes.

Exhib: L
Bibliog: DBA

HAWES, John Cyril 1876–1956
Tanglewood, Grove Road, Sutton –1923–
John Cyril Hawes, a church architect, converted to the Catholic faith and became a priest. Born in Richmond, Surrey, on 7 September 1876, the son of a solicitor, he was educated at King's School, Canterbury, and later studied art at the Central School of Arts and Crafts.

In 1898, at the age of twenty-two, he designed the *White Tower* at Bognor Regis and also designed three or more houses there. During the same year he had his first acceptance at the Royal Academy: *Design for a Westmorland church*. Another building from this period was his *St Christopher's Church* at Gunnerton, Northumberland.

Thereafter he spent most of his time abroad. He lived in Australia for twenty-four years, where his address in 1929 was The Presbytery, Mullewa. In 1939 he settled in the Bahamas where he died in 1956. On visits to England he would stay with his brother Edward (q.v.) at Sutton; and in 1923 he exhibited two designs for Australian cathedrals (one in Perth, the other in Geraldton) at the RA, sending them in from his brother's address.

Exhib: RA
Bibliog: DBA; V; *Who's Who in Art*, 1929

HEAD, Timothy J. Exhib: 1895
Arundel House, Worcester Park –1895–
Timothy Head exhibited a painting entitled *'Tween Gloaming and the Mirk* at the Royal Academy in 1895.

Exhib: RA
Bibliog: DBA

59

HIGHAM, Bernard 1871–1945

Stratton House, Woodcote Avenue, Wallington 1912–
Dower House, Park Hill Road, Wallington –1945

Bernard Higham, born in Lewisham in 1871, was a landscape painter and illustrator who lived in Wallington for over thirty years. In 1912 he took up residence at Stratton House in Woodcote Avenue and he died at the Dower House in Park Hill Road on 10 November 1945.

He exhibited two paintings at the Royal Academy: *To a higher plane* (1917) and *La vie cosmique* (1919). The latter, a nude study, was singled out for praise by the local press and was described as 'one of the most attractive drawings on the screen in the South Rooms . . . the work of a really accomplished watercolourist'.

Known mainly for his illustrative work, Higham contributed to the *Idler*, the *English Illustrated Magazine* and other periodicals. His figure studies were admired for their grace of line and colour harmony.

Bernard Higham's wife, Marguerite, bore him a son, Geoffrey, who followed his father to become an artist.

Exhib: RA
Bibliog: BEN; DBA; HOUFE

*HILLS, Robert, O.W.S. 1769–1844

Watercolours, drawings, etchings – occasionally oil paintings – by Robert Hills turn up fairly frequently in the salerooms. This is hardly surprising, since he was a prolific artist, exhibiting six hundred paintings with the Old Water Colour Society, of which he was a founder member, and many other works elsewhere.

Hills was born in Islington on 26 June 1769. After early drawing lessons from John Gresse, he entered the Royal Academy Schools in 1788. Apart from a trip abroad in 1815, when he visited the site of the Battle of Waterloo, he carried out all his work in this country.

He was an impressive animal painter, but was also such a skilled landscape artist that even his animal paintings have backgrounds of recognisable places. His early watercolours – and it is generally agreed that these are his best – are in the outlined colour-wash style of the Early English School. Later on he developed a stippled, pointillistic style which sometimes gave a blurred effect to his work.

On a sketching trip to Surrey during the 1820s, he stopped off at Beddington to make some rapid watercolour impressions of the area around the Fords. One of these sketches is now in Sutton's Local Collection, whilst others from the same series appeared in exhibitions in London in 1985 – one at Agnew's, two at Spink's. They obviously all came from the same sketchbook, and were possibly studies for his finished watercolour, *Lane Scene at Beddington*, exhibited at the OWS in 1823.

During the last few years, Hills's watercolours have risen sharply in price, with works similar to the one at Sutton, bought at Sotheby's a few years ago for £50, occasionally costing the buyer in excess of £1,000.

Exhib: OWS; RA; SBA
Coll: Ashmolean Museum, Oxford; Blackburn AG; BM; Fitzwilliam Museum, Cambridge; Leeds AG; Sutton LC; Ulster Museum; V&A; Warrington AG

Published: HILLS, R. *Etchings of Quadrupeds.* 1798–1815; *Sketches in Flanders and Holland.* 1816
Bibliog: BEN; HARDIE; HOUFE; LAMBOURNE; MACKENZIE; MALLALIEU; WILLIAMS; WOOD; HARDIE, M. Robert Hills (1769–1844). *Old Watercolour Society's Club,* vol. 25, 1947; HERRMAN, L. Robert Hills at Waterloo . . . *Connoisseur,* vol. 150, no. 605, July 1962

*HIND, William Lewis 1830–1901

The School House, Mill Lane, Carshalton 1830–
5 & 6 Benhill Street, Sutton 1862–1871
Acacia Villa, Hill Road, Sutton 1871–1901

Members of the Hind family have lived in this borough for at least a hundred and fifty years, the present generation being represented in the firm of Dixon, Hind & Co., Estate Agents and Surveyors.

William Lewis Hind, artist, poet, photographer, signwriter, businessman, publisher, auctioneer and estate agent, was born on 15 April 1830 at The School House in Mill Lane, Carshalton. His father, Samuel James John Hind, was the schoolmaster but had originally been a printer until an unfortunate accident had forced him to abandon this trade. One of William's uncles was an artist; it was he who inspired William's lifelong interest in the arts.

Hoping to follow his father into the teaching profession, William won a scholarship to St Mark's Training College at Battersea and graduated as a 2nd Class Queen's Scholar. Shortly afterwards, he was appointed head of a school in Baldwin's Gardens, Gray's Inn Road, but his voice was not strong enough to withstand the rigours of teaching and he had to resign. He then worked in a bank and followed this by working for a solicitor in Lincoln's Inn.

Early in 1862 he moved to Sutton and opened a shop in Benhill Street, going into business as a publisher and dealer in works of art. Occasionally, he sold one of his own works in the shop. He later moved his business to the High Street and advertised in the *Sutton Journal,* offering paintings, prints, portraits 'highly finished in colours', 'drawings made and copied' and similar goods and services. Unfortunately, his business folded as a direct result of the Franco-Prussian War, when he was no longer able to obtain the photographs from Paris and Berlin needed for his book illustrations.

He then became the Assistant Overseer and Collector of Rates for Sutton, and held this post for seven years, leaving to work for John Morgan, the local estate agent and auctioneer. After seven years of learning the business, he set up on his own as an estate agent and moved into the house next door to Sutton Public Hall. This was Acacia Villa, his home for the last thirty years of his life.

In the 1860s he took up the new craze: photography. Some of his efforts in this direction have survived – artistically composed, very pleasing examples of the art. His photographs of Sutton are some of the earliest known of the village (as it then was) and two can be seen in books published by Sutton Libraries and Arts Services. One is in *All Our Yesterdays* (1977); the other forms the cover of *No Small Change . . .* by Frank Burgess (1983).

Hind, active in local affairs, was a member of the Sutton School Board and was a regular worshipper at St Nicholas Church, where he had his own pew from the time when the church was rebuilt in 1864. Reputed to be a kindly, good-natured man, he was also strongly patriotic and joined the Volunteer Force, where he was an efficient marksman in the St George's Rifles, winning cups and other prizes. A few years before his death, he published a volume of his own poems, each poem with a heroic or patriotic title: 'Do and Dare', 'Britons, hold your own', and others in a similar vein.

His wife Maria (née Nuthall) was well-educated; she had attended Cheltenham College. They were married on 13 August 1853. The Hinds were a typically large Victorian family; nine of their children – four boys and five girls – survived their parents. William Lewis Hind died at Acacia Villa on 19 January 1901, three days before the death of Queen Victoria. His 'dearly beloved and gentle wife', whose memorial card is in Sutton's Local Collection, had died the previous year. Hind's funeral was well attended, with friends from the arts mingling with local dignitaries. Edward Frampton (q.v.), his neighbour in Hill Road, was a mourner by the graveside.

Published: HIND, W. L. *Poems*. Privately printed. c.1895
Obit: *Sutton and Epsom Advertiser*, 26 January 1901, p. 3

HOLBEIN, Hans the Younger 1497–1543

During his visits to England, Hans Holbein the Younger, Court Painter to King Henry VIII, carried out numerous portraits of the English nobility, amongst them a drawing and an oil portrait of Sir Nicholas Carew, K.G. of Beddington (c.1490–1539), who was beheaded on Tower Hill on the morning of 3 March 1539.

The drawing, in black and coloured chalks, is now at Basle, where the Holbein family used to live. It was made prior to 1528 on Holbein's first visit to this country. The oil portrait, which is on a wooden panel, dates from the 1530s and is thought to have been painted during the artist's second visit to England. Identical in pose to the drawing, it shows Sir Nicholas clad in armour, a lance in his right hand, a sword in the left. A cartouche, inscribed at a later date, reads: 'Sir Nicholas Carewe Master of the Horse to Henry y 8'. The painting is thought to have been given to the Earl of Arundel of Nonsuch Palace by Queen Elizabeth I, and is now in the collection of the Duke of Buccleuch at Drumlanrig Castle, a former Duchess of Buccleuch having bought it for ten guineas at the Lumley Castle sale in 1785 – surely a bargain, even then. It is listed in the Lumley inventory of 1590.

Controversy exists over whether Holbein himself painted the oil. Even in the nineteenth century doubts were expressed as to its authenticity. One art critic, 'M.P.J.', reviewing the 'Old and Modern Masters' exhibition at the RA in 1880, wrote: 'Sir Nicholas Carew, "Henry VIII's Master of the Horse", is surely not by Holbein but probably by some Flemish Master' (*Magazine of Art*, 1880, p. 200).

In the oil portrait, Sir Nicholas, with his hooded eyes and rather melancholy gaze, appears almost aware of his impending doom. Having been held in high esteem by King Henry VIII, his fall from grace was particularly painful. In happier days the monarch had showered him with gifts, had valued his friendship and had visited him at Beddington on more than one occasion. Rumour had it that Sir Nicholas lost his head through an argument with the King during a game of bowls. However, Henry's excuse for having Nicholas executed was that his former friend had committed High Treason, a common enough offence in those days.

The drawing of Sir Nicholas – without question by Holbein – shows a younger, more carefree nobleman at the peak of his career. He had a beautiful, high-spirited wife, Elizabeth, Lady Carew, who, after her husband's death, suffered the humiliation of being turned out of the family home. She also had her jewels confiscated, some of which had once been given to her by the King. Lady Carew was eventually buried by the side of her husband at St Botolph's Church, Aldgate.

Holbein would almost certainly have carried out a drawing or painting of Lady Carew, to match her husband's. If one has survived, it is possibly hanging in some stately home as 'a portrait of an unknown lady'. It was once thought that Holbein's drawing of Lady Guildford (now at Basle) was of Lady Carew (née Bryan), and it is entered as such in the *Catalogue of Engraved British Portraits in the British Museum* (British Museum, 1908. 6 vols.).

Beddington Manor (now Carew Manor School), the ancestral home of the Carews, has survived the years well, its Great Hall still intact despite all the alterations that have taken place around it.

Bibliog: BEN; TB; GANZ, P. *The Paintings of Hans Holbein*. Phaidon, 1950; ROBERTS, J. *Holbein*. Oresco Books, 1979; MICHELL, R. *The Carews of Beddington*. Sutton Libraries and Arts Services, 1981; ROWLANDS, J. *The Paintings of Hans Holbein the Younger*. Phaidon, 1985

HOLLOWAY, Charles Edward, N.E.A.C., R.I. 1838–1897

Illustrated: SMEE, Alfred. *My Garden*. Bell and Daldy, 1872

Born in Christchurch, Hampshire (now Dorset), in 1838, Charles Holloway lived in London for most of his life, studying art at Leigh's Academy where a fellow pupil and close friend was Frederick Walker (q.v.). Later, Holloway joined William Morris (q.v.) and worked on designs for stained glass, but left Morris in 1866 to concentrate on landscape painting.

During the 1870s he was commissioned by Alfred Smee, creator of the famous garden at The Grange, Wallington, to carry out some drawings for Smee's book *My Garden*, and he spent some time in the district sketching views of the River Wandle and Beddington. The resulting attractive vignettes were engraved for the book by Harrison. Charles Holloway may have been related to the Holloway family who settled in Wallington during the nineteenth century and who came from the part of Hampshire where Charles

Holloway was born.

Charles Holloway was an engraver, a watercolourist and a lithographer. He painted some impressionistic studies of Venice in the style of his close friend James McNeill Whistler, but was known mainly for his River Thames and Fenland views which were exhibited at the Royal Academy and other galleries.

At one time he was a member of the New English Art Club but resigned out of loyalty to his friend when Whistler fell out with the club, the latter repaying this loyalty by showing a true and genuine concern during Holloway's last illness; he sat with him often throughout the final days and painted a portrait of his dying friend, calling it *The Philosopher*. A memorial exhibition of Holloway's work took place at the Goupil Gallery, London, in 1897.

Exhib: B; FIN; G; GI; L; M; NEA; RA; RBA; RE; RI; ROI
Bibliog: BEN; DBA; ENGEN(1); HARDIE; LISTER; MACKENZIE; MALLALIEU; TB; WOOD
Obit: *Art Journal*, 1897, p. 127

HOWARD, Henry James 1876–1960
St Katherine's, 36 (later 49) Mulgrave Road, Sutton 1918–1960

Henry James Howard was born in London on 23 February 1876, the son of a Civil Servant. After an education at the City of London School, he too entered the Civil Service but devoted much of his spare time to painting and printmaking, interests which he passed on to his daughter, Margaret Maitland Howard (q.v.).

An etching by H. J. Howard, *Vieille maison, Abbeville*, was exhibited at the Royal Academy in 1929. Other works by him were shown at the Society of Graphic Art's exhibitions in London, and he also exhibited abroad. He illustrated a book entitled *Shakespeare's Homeland* (author and date unknown).

In 1918 he settled in Sutton, living at St Katherine's, a house in Mulgrave Road, until he died there on 6 November 1960. Throughout his years of retirement from the Civil Service he continued with his artistic activities and also pursued his other major interests – gardening and stamp collecting.

Exhib: RA; ROI; SGA; British Empire Society; Canada
Bibliog: DBA; V; *Who's Who in Art*, 1934

*HOWARD, Margaret Maitland, F.Z.S. 1898–1983
St Katherine's, 36 (later 49) Mulgrave Road, Sutton 1918–
Flat 3, Ashwood House, 69 Grange Road, Sutton –1981

Margaret Maitland Howard, the daughter of Henry James Howard (q.v.) and Margaretha Magdelena Howard, came to live in Sutton when she was twenty and stayed for the rest of her life. Her father had bought St Katherine's, a large house in Mulgrave Road next door to where the landscape painter Sidney Richard Percy (q.v.) had lived half a century earlier.

Born on 31 July 1898 at Friern Barnet, Hertfordshire, she was educated privately, displaying an early talent for painting that led to her attending the then recently established Byam Shaw and Vicat Cole School of Painting. Subsequently, she entered the Royal Academy Schools where she proved to be an exceptionally gifted pupil, winning no less than five silver medals and a British Institute Scholarship.

She worked mainly in oil, watercolour and pastel, but was also a black-and-white artist, illustrating several children's books including Ian Cornwall's *The Making of Man*, which won the Carnegie Medal in 1960 for the best children's book. Ten of her paintings were exhibited at the Royal Academy, her first in 1923, her last in 1940, some being illustrated in the annual publication: *Royal Academy Illustrated*. They nearly all had religious or mythological themes and showed the influence of Raphael and Botticelli, with *The Return of Persephone* (RA 1924) being regarded as one of her major works. She also painted portraits, including miniatures, and won the prize for portrait painting at the National Eisteddfod, Swansea, in 1926. The bombing of Sutton in the Second World War is recalled in her painting *Our Hero, Soldier and Sailor too; Bill Pollock, George Medallist of the Sutton Rescue Squad*, shown at the Royal Society of Portrait Painter's exhibition of 1941.

Complementary to her career in art was her love for and knowledge of archaeology, and this led to her assisting Professor Zeuner at the Institute of Archaeology and illustrating his book *Dating the Past*, which ran to several editions. She was also the Official Artist to the Department of Environmental Archaeology at London University. Sir Max Mallowan and his wife Agatha Christie (the famous creator of Hercule Poirot) invited her to join their expedition to Iraq to excavate the Balawat Gates. Later, at the British Museum, she took part in the restoration of the gates. Her writings on archaeology included papers on *Dried Cats* and *Nimrod Ivory Tablets*.

After her father died she moved to a flat in Grange Road, remaining there until she became too ill to live alone, when she entered a nursing home. She died on 31 August 1983. She was a wealthy woman who left most of her money to animal charities, her faithful companion throughout her latter years having been her Jack Russell terrier, Whisky. She left the Royal Academy a table which had once belonged to William Parrott, R.A.; other items went to the Victoria and Albert Museum, the Institute of Archaeology and the Natural History Museum.

Here at Sutton, her lasting memorial is her gift to the borough of a collection of Victorian and Edwardian toys and costume. Some of them have already been displayed in the borough's libraries. She was well known to the staff at Sutton Library and in her final years, when too frail to visit the library, she kept in touch through the visits of a member of the library staff, who was also a personal friend.

Exhib: COO; L; NEA; RA; ROI; RP; SWA; Panton Club; Bournemouth
Illus: CORNWALL, I. *Bones for the Archaeologist*. Phoenix House, 1956; *Making of Man*. Phoenix House, 1960; *World of Ancient Man*. Phoenix House, 1964; *Hunter's Half Moon*. J. Baker, 1967; *Prehistoric Animals and their Hunters*, Faber, 1968; ZEUNER, F.E. *Dating the Past*. Methuen, 1958
Bibliog: DBA; GW; V; *Who's Who in Art* – several editions

HOWARD-MERCER, Cicely Honor Augusta 1898–1939
60 Sutton Court, Brighton Road, Sutton 1930s
In 1935, at the annual prizegiving of the Sutton and Cheam Art School, Canon Courtenay Gale, Chairman of the Governors, described Miss Howard-Mercer as one of the most inspiring influences the town of Sutton had ever known.

Cicely Honor Augusta Howard-Mercer , born in 1898, trained at Hammersmith Art School. In 1931 she took over the running of Sutton Art School, which at that time had only thirty pupils attending twice-weekly classes at the Institute in Throwley Way. When she retired in 1938, the art school, with three hundred pupils, twelve members of staff and fifty classes per week, had taken over the whole of the Institute. She was the new broom who, within her limited budget and the inadequate accommodation at Throwley Way, swept away some of the old traditions and injected new life and tremendous enthusiasm into the school. There was an immediate face-lift consisting of an all-round clean-up, new lighting schemes, poster displays and an exhibition of material lent by the Victoria and Albert Museum.

The first-ever exhibition of students' work – which was to become an annual event – was opened by Sir Edward J. Holland, High Sheriff of Surrey, on 19 October 1931. In 1934 Sutton Art School was officially recognised by the Board of Education and the following year Miss Howard-Mercer, who until then had been employed on a part-time basis, was appointed full-time head at a salary of £400 per annum, increasing by £10 per year to £500. The school started to take full-time pupils and was open every weekday.

During her first year, Miss Howard-Mercer inaugurated a sketching club which met monthly for criticism of members' work and went out into the country on Saturday afternoons for practical sketching sessions. She also introduced art and handicraft competitions for local schoolchildren and ran a series of lectures at the school, open to the general public. In 1932 she accompanied eleven students to the Holmbury St Mary's area of Surrey where – according to the local press – they 'sketched, painted, walked, swam, sunbathed, ate acid drops and potato crisps during a midnight thunderstorm, and scattered their paintbrushes over the Surrey Hills'.

Art school dances, reported as 'absolutely first rate' and 'a howling success' were regular events, with Miss Howard-Mercer helping to organise them and the students designing the posters. At one of these parties, in March 1934, the students provided the cabaret: Elva Blacker rendered 'My Prayer', Olive Spink sang and Marjory Gold played the piano.

Many new subjects were introduced to the curriculum during Miss Howard-Mercer's time, particularly in the fields of fashion design, fabric printing, bookbinding and calligraphy. Her students were encouraged to experiment. No opportunities were ever wasted. For instance, in 1932, when some caged monkeys were outside the cinema in the High Street advertising a film, she sent her students along to

sketch them. Mice were introduced as models – until two escaped and ran up the sleeve of one of the girls. Goats, ducks – even a pony – found their way to the school, and the local press joked that the students were advertising for 'elephants and gnus'.

Miss Howard-Mercer's duties at the school left her little time for her own work. However, in 1937, her oil painting *Freedom of body, mind and soul*, an allegorical panel for a Bermondsey Hostel, was hung at the Royal Academy. She paid dearly for all her hard work at the school. In 1937 her students heard to their dismay that she was too ill to attend the art school dance. In 1938, ill health caused her to resign and she died shortly afterwards, in 1939. Some of her friends expressed the opinion that she had killed herself through overwork, but she had, in fact, died of cancer.

Her monument is the school as it is today. Now known as the Sutton College of Liberal Arts, it is housed in a specially designed building in the same complex as the public library.

Exhib: RA
Bibliog: DBA; Sutton College of Liberal Arts Archives

HUGHES, Amy b. 1858
Wandle Bank, 135 Hackbridge Road (now 284 London Road), Wallington 1876–
Amy Hughes, the artistic daughter of Tryphena and Arthur Hughes (q.v.), was born in London in 1858, when her family were living at no. 6 Upper Belgrave Place. That year, appropriately enough, the title of her father's Royal Academy picture was *The Nativity*.

When the Hughes family came to live at Wallington, Amy was just eighteen years old. She was still unmarried, aged twenty-three, at the time of the 1881 census, when her occupation was entered as 'Art student'. Her marriage must have taken place between 1882 and 1887, since in 1881 and 1882 her paintings were exhibited under the name 'Amy Hughes', but in 1887, when one of her paintings was shown at the Society of Women Artists' exhibition, she exhibited as 'Amy Chester'.

The date of her death is uncertain; but by 1915, the year her father died, she was already dead, Arthur Hughes leaving bequests to 'my grandchildren the children of my deceased daughter Amy Chester'.

Exhib: G; ROI; SWA
Bibliog: DBA

HUGHES, Arthur 1832–1915
Wandle Bank, 135 Hackbridge Road (now 284 London Road), Wallington 1876–1891
Arthur Hughes, an associate of the Pre-Raphaelites, lived at Wandle Bank, a house in Wallington, for fifteen years; his 'nice old cottage in the country' he called it. Earlier, he had lived in the London area, but had long wished to settle in the country – away from the smoke and grime.

Of Welsh descent, he was born in London in January 1832, the youngest son of Edward Hughes. He was educated at the Archbishop Tenison School in

London, where his artistic talents proved so remarkable that he was allowed to enter the Government School of Design at Somerset House at the age of fourteen. The following year he became a student at the Royal Academy Schools, where in 1849 he won a silver medal for antique drawing; and in the same year exhibited his first RA painting: *Musidora*.

It was at the RA Schools that he first met members of the Pre-Raphaelite Brotherhood and read their short-lived magazine *The Germ*, which so impressed him he adopted their ideals. Under their influence, particularly Millais's, he painted his best known works: *Ophelia* (1852), *April Love* (1856), *The Long Engagement* (1859) and *Home from Sea* (1863). He gained the approval of Ruskin (q.v.), who attempted to buy *April Love* but was outbid by William Morris (q.v.). Ruskin described Hughes as one 'whose genius is, beyond a doubt, of the highest order', and one 'whose sense of beauty is quite exquisite'. In 1857 Hughes, invited by Rossetti, was one of the artists employed on the Oxford Union frescoes, contributing the panel *The Death of Arthur*. The work was carried out amidst riotous behaviour and much laughter and was enjoyed enormously by all concerned; but the venture was not a complete success since some of the paint later flaked off. Until quite recently, the frescoes had been considered beyond repair, but this opinion has now been reversed and restoration work is underway.

Hughes's most admired paintings are his 'Pre-Raphaelite' ones, which today are very expensive, *The Lady of Shalott*, an oil on canvas, signed and dated 1873, selling for £42,000 at Christie's in October 1981. Yet in 1973, a group of his landscapes, painted in a more traditional style, realised only £100–£400 each at Sotheby's. Some art historians have implied that after about 1860, when Hughes first moved away from London to live in the country, he did little worth mentioning. This is far from the truth. Gradually his wide range as an artist is becoming more appreciated, the 1971 'Arthur Hughes Pre-Raphaelite Painter' exhibition, held first at the National Museum of Wales and then at Leighton House, London, having done much to promote his work. He has become even more widely known since his paintings were shown in the major 'Pre-Raphaelite Exhibition' at the Tate Gallery in 1984.

Hughes's hauntingly beautiful, brilliantly-coloured paintings like *April Love* and *Home from Sea* command an immediate emotional response. Who can fail to be moved by the grief of the young sailor, not much more than a boy, in *Home from Sea*; just returned from a voyage – perhaps his first – to discover that his mother has died in his absence. When the painting made its first appearance (at Russell Place in 1857) it was called *A Mother's Grave* and had, it seems, only the figure of the boy by the grave. When it was shown at the RA in 1863, not only did it have a new title, but the boy's sister, modelled by the artist's wife Tryphena, was by his side. Many years later, Arthur Hughes wrote to his friend William Hale White: 'At the time I painted it my wife was young enough to sit for the sister; and I think it was like' (Tate AG archive).

Arthur Hughes was a portrait painter of exceptional merit. As an illustrator, also, he was in a class of his own, illustrating over thirty books and carrying out hundreds of other drawings. Forrest Reid devoted six pages to Hughes in his *Illustrators of the Sixties* (1928), writing that he had 'a spark of genius, and a personal charm so persuasive that it goes far to make up for a somewhat wobbly technique'. Hughes's most famous illustrations are those for George Macdonald's fairy tales, and are seen at their best in the magazine in which they first appeared, *Good Words for the Young* (1869–1873), where Macdonald's *At the Back of the North Wind* and *The Princess and the Goblin* were serialised before coming out in book form. Hughes's remarkable lyrical qualities enabled him to do full justice to Christina Rossetti's verses when he illustrated her *Sing Song* (1872) and *Speaking Likenesses* (1873).

His personal life was spent in domestic contentment. In 1850 he met and fell in love with Tryphena Foord, although he did not marry her until 1855, when Ford Maddox Brown wrote to Holman Hunt that Arthur was married to 'a little lady very meek and mute . . . He's immensely fond'. To more raffish friends, like Rossetti and Holman Hunt, he must have seemed a model of propriety. Violet Hunt rather unfairly called him 'dull Hughes' (*The Wife of Rossetti*, 1932). Hughes, a handsome young man with Welsh features, was the model for Millais's *The Proscribed Royalist* (1853); and his self-portrait, donated in 1935 by his daughter Emily, can be seen in the National Portrait Gallery.

His amiable personality brought him many friends. There were, of course, the Pre-Raphaelites; but he also formed friendships amongst other artists. One good friend was the watercolourist Albert Goodwin (an executor of Hughes's will) whom Hughes first met when the former was a youth of sixteen sketching from nature; he invited him to his studio and gave him some lessons. Another friend and pupil was Sydney Prior Hall who collaborated with Hughes on the illustrations for *Tom Brown's Schooldays* by Thomas Hughes (1878) – no relation. Arthur Hughes's nephew, whose childhood portrait he painted, was the artist Edward Robert Hughes, who studied under his uncle and Holman Hunt. The wealthy Newcastle factory owner, James Leathart, was both patron and friend; he bought Hughes's paintings and also commissioned him to paint portraits of the Leathart family.

In 1876, when Arthur was forty-four and Tryphena forty-five, they came to live in Wallington, at Wandle Bank, which is now a Grade 2 listed building and the oldest house in Wallington. Wandle Bank, as its name implies, is near the bank of the River Wandle and dates back to the early eighteenth century, but is on the site of a much older building. During the period of the Hughes family's occupancy, the old-world garden stretched as far as the river; but since their day, Riverside Close has been built in-between.

In anticipation of a longish stay at Wallington, Hughes had a studio built onto Wandle Bank; he exhibited at the RA every year but one whilst he was living there. The family soon became part of the local scene and their neighbours must have become

Wandle Bank (now 284 London Road, Wallington), home of ARTHUR HUGHES from 1876 until 1891.

accustomed to seeing distinguished visitors from the worlds of art and literature arriving at the house. One was the poet William Allingham, the husband of the popular watercolourist Helen Allingham; the former mentioned Wandle Bank in his *Diaries* (1907) and *Letters* (1911). Arthur had earlier contributed seven illustrations to W. Allingham's *The Music Master* (1855).

Through sharing a jobbing gardener, Arthur met William Hale White, the writer 'Mark Rutherford', who lived not far away at Carshalton. They became lifelong friends, sharing interests which included art, poetry and nature. Both men appreciated the comic side of life and used to send each other nonsense verses. In 1887 Arthur Hughes carried out a drawing of his friend, which has been reproduced as the frontispiece to Catherine Macdonald Maclean's 1955 biography of Hale White. From the 1881 census we see that the Hughes family employed a general servant, Amelia Osborn, and that in 1881 there was a young art student staying at Wandle Bank: John W. Taylor.

Tryphena and Arthur had five children, of which

three, like their father, were exhibiting artists: Amy (q.v.), Arthur Foord (q.v.) and Godfrey (q.v.); and no doubt the other two, Agnes and Emily, would have had some form of art instruction from their father. Agnes Hughes married Jack Hale White – to the satisfaction of both sets of parents – the young couple's first meeting taking place in a local lane. Jack White was taking his invalid mother for an outing in her wheelchair when he saw two beautiful young women coming down the lane towards them, one being Agnes. As in all the best romantic novels, it was love at first sight and Jack and Agnes were married on 30 September 1891. Earlier that year, Arthur Hughes and his family had left Wallington to live at Kew Green in Surrey. Two of their friends, a Miss Fearon and a Mr Robinson Moss had then moved into Wandle Bank.

During the 1890s, Arthur Hughes visited Cornwall, where he painted a large number of landscapes, mainly for his own pleasure. Eighty of these were exhibited at the Fine Art Society, London, in 1900. He was awarded a Civil List Pension by King George V and in gratitude gave him an oil painting, entitled

65

HORACE M. LIVENS   Watercolour
Bridge over a River.   Windsor Castle, Royal Library
© 1988 Her Majesty The Queen

W. TATTON WINTER   Watercolour
Windmill scene.   Windsor Castle, Royal Library
© 1988 Her Majesty The Queen

These were two of the miniatures painted for Queen Mary's Dolls' House (designed by Sir Edwin Lutyens in 1924). The Dolls' House is now at Windsor Castle.

FRIEDRICH W. KEYL   Oil 559×940mm
View of The Culvers, Carshalton, with portraits of Mr. and Mrs. Sam Gurney, 1851.   Photo courtesy Richard Green. Private Collection

66

Wonderland, a sugary-sweet confection of a child in a garden. Queen Mary later gave it away to a friend and it was eventually sold at auction a year or two ago. It has recently been on exhibition at the Christopher Wood Gallery in London. Hughes, who died on 22 December 1915 at Eastside House, Kew Green, and is buried in Richmond Cemetery, continued to paint almost to the end of his life. In 1921 a large number of his remaining works were sold at Christie's.

Exhib: B; D; FIN; G; GI; L; M; N; NG; RA; RI; ROI
Coll: Aberdeen AG; Beverley AG; Birmingham AG; Bournemouth AG; Bristol AG; Carlisle AG; Fitzwilliam Museum, Cambridge; Lady Lever AG; Liverpool; Lincoln AG; Melbourne AG, Australia; Preston AG; Tate AG; Toledo Museum, U.S.A.; Toronto AG, Canada; Walker AG, Liverpool; William Morris AG, Walthamstow
Illus: See HOUFE; and ENGEN(2)
Bibliog: BEN; DBA; DNB; ENGEN(2); GW; HOUFE; LAMBOURNE; MALLALIEU; PEPPIN; TB; WOOD; MACLEAN, C. M. *Mark Rutherford; a biography of William Hale White*. Macdonald, 1955

HUGHES, Arthur Foord 1856–1934
Wandle Bank, 135 Hackbridge Road (now 284 London Road), Wallington 1876–1890
Arthur Foord Hughes, the eldest child of Tryphena and Arthur Hughes (q.v.), was born in London in 1856, a year after his parents' marriage. After early drawing lessons from his father, he studied art at Heatherley's, at the Slade and at the Royal Academy Schools. He was nineteen when the Hughes family settled in Wallington; two years later, at the age of twenty-one, he experienced his first RA acceptance, a genre study entitled *The fireside*. He also exhibited two paintings with the Society of British Artists whilst he was living at Wandle Bank: *The stream by the sea* (1880) and *Goodbye!* (1882).

From 1891 until 1912, however, he submitted his work to the RA from Thurloe Square Studios, South Kensington, so he must have either moved there by then or merely been using it as a London base. In 1914, when he exhibited his last painting at the RA, he was living at Eastside House, Kew Green, the house his parents had moved to on leaving Wallington. At least two art dictionaries have – mistakenly – entered his year of death as '1914'.

A. F. Hughes was a member of the Arts Club from 1899–1904. He was a painter of landscape and genre studies in oil and watercolour; and a number of his fresh-looking watercolours are to be seen in Hove Art Gallery, including *Dicker Windmill*, *The Barbican House at Sandwich* and *Ringmer Windmill*. He specialised in windmill scenes, in 1930 illustrating a book by G. M. Fowell entitled *Windmills in Sussex*. He also designed headpieces for the *English Illustrated Magazine* (1886–7).

Arthur Foord Hughes, known affectionately in the family as 'Artie', died in a Hastings nursing home on 20 July 1934, having spent his last years at 130 Harold Road, Hastings. Apparently, poor Arthur had been living in reduced circumstances. He left hardly any money, dying intestate, and his widow Lizzie Foord Hughes followed him to the grave within the year.

Letters of administration were granted to her sister, Ada Florence Bond of Twickenham, Middlesex.

In 1979, one of his original watercolours for *Windmills in Sussex* was offered for sale by the Ewhurst Gallery, near Basingstoke; in the same year, his painting *Sharpening a scythe* was sold at Sotheby's Belgravia for £170.

Exhib: AGN; G; L; NG; RA; RBA; RI; ROI
Coll: Haworth AG, Accrington; Hove AG; Maidstone AG
Bibliog: DBA; ENGEN(2); GW; HOUFE; MALLALIEU

HUGHES, Godfrey 1865–
Wandle Bank, 135 Hackbridge Road (now 284 London Road), Wallington 1876–1891
Godfrey Hughes, a genre painter, was the younger son of Arthur Hughes (q.v.). He was born in Wandsworth in 1865 and was only eleven years old when the family came to live in Wallington. It was many years later, after the Hughes family had moved to Kew Green, that Godfrey exhibited four paintings at the Royal Academy: *The Shrimper's home* (1905), *Unappreciated efforts* (1910), *Saved* (1914) and *A stitch in time* (1914).

Exhib: NG; RA; ROI
Bibliog: DBA

HUNN, Thomas Henry 1857–1928
13 Pellatt Road, Sutton –1879–
Binfield, Bute Road, Beddington 1913–1928
Thomas Hunn, a painter of landscape scenes in watercolour, was born in Hackney in 1857. He spent most of his life in Surrey and Sussex, first coming to this area in the 1870s, when he lived in Sutton for a brief period before moving on to Godalming. In 1880 he exhibited two local views at the Royal Academy: *At Cheam Hall Farm, Surrey* and *The School Farm, Carshalton, Surrey*.

His watercolours are similar in style to Helen Allingham's, but he used stronger colours. He is particularly admired for his paintings of Surrey gardens, nine of which were exhibited at the RA, including: *Lady Weston's Walk, Sutton Park, Guildford* (1900), *Cottage garden, Clandon, Guildford* (1900) and *Tangley Manor, Surrey* (1901).

At the age of fifty-six Thomas Hunn, with his wife Rosina Jane and his unmarried sister, Mabel Rose, returned to this area, living in Bute Road, Beddington, close to Beddington Park. They all died within two years of each other – Rosina Jane first in December 1926, followed by Mabel Rose in August 1927, and finally Thomas himself, aged seventy-one, on 25 March 1928. However the artist did not die in the borough but in Tonbridge, where his daughter Mrs Cecil Simms lived. His other daughter, Mrs Ethelwald Grover, lived in Wallington.

The artist's watercolours appear fairly frequently in the salerooms and private galleries. In 1986, £432 was paid at Christie's for his attractive springtime study entitled *Iris by the Maori House at Clandon Park, Surrey*.

Exhib: D; M; NG; NWS; RA; RBA; RI
Bibliog: BEN; DBA; FISHER; MALLALIEU; TB; WOOD

THOMAS H. HUNN   Watercolour 279×419mm
Crimson Rambler at Clandon.   Christopher Wood Gallery
Photo courtesy Sotheby's

JACKSON, Emily Frances 1850–1933
Beechwood Lodge, North Street, Carshalton 1859–1933
When Emily Frances Jackson died on 3 June 1933, after having lived in Carshalton for seventy-four years, her obituary in the local paper described her as a 'sweet dispositioned old lady . . . greatly respected in the neighbourhood'. Curiously, there was no mention of the fact that in her younger days she had been a talented flower painter, exhibiting over seventy works at galleries in London and in the provinces.

She was born in Bromley, Kent, in 1850, the daughter of Henry Jackson, a solicitor, and his wife Susannah Emily. She had a sister Constance, and three brothers. In 1859 her father bought Beechwood Lodge, a centuries-old house at Carshalton, and Emily lived there for the rest of her life. Beechwood Lodge stood at the corner of North Street and West Street, Henry Jackson adding to his property in 1863 by buying the meadow adjoining the Waterhouse (Brightling). A fine garden with plenty of trees surrounded the house, and there was also an orchard. The Jacksons knew Alfred Smee, creator of the famous garden at The Grange, Wallington. He invited Mrs Jackson to contribute two drawings to his book *My Garden* (1872): *Cedar Cones* (fig. 959) and *Ansell's Snuff Mill* (plate 7).

Emily Frances inherited her mother's talent, exhibiting at the Royal Academy and other galleries. She did not have far to go to find her subject matter, painting, nearly always in watercolour, the flowers in the Jacksons' garden: the roses, daffodils, camelias, azalias, jonquils, stocks and violets. Rarely did she paint anything else, except in 1890 when she exhibited a title *Little Miss Muffet* at the Society of Women Artists' exhibition.

Most of her paintings were priced within the five to ten guinea range. Today they are scarce, seldom appearing in the salerooms. Many may still be in private hands. In her will she left two paintings to Croydon Hospital 'for use in the Sisters' Sitting Room': *Roses in a Blue Jar*, and her copy of Turner's *Venice*.

She outlived her parents, her brothers and her sister, and was the last Jackson to live at Beechwood Lodge. In fact she was the last owner, for after her death the property was put up for sale; the sale catalogue – a copy is in Sutton's Local Studies Collection – describes it as 'ripe for immediate development'. The house was pulled down and the Beechwood Court block of flats was put up on the site.

No known photograph of Beechwood Lodge exists, but there is a good description of it in the sale catalogue. Built of brick, it stood three storeys high. Enclosing the gardens was a high brick wall, and there was a flint-cobbled courtyard at the side of the house, entered through a pair of carriage gates. Of the six rooms on the ground floor, one was an elegant drawing room with a marble fireplace, french windows and a verandah. Seven bedrooms were distributed throughout the first and second floors. The kitchen and cellar were in the semi-basement. Henry Jackson kept his wine in the cellar and once had a well-publicised row with the gas company when leaking gas ruined £80 worth of his wine. He sued, but lost the case when it was ruled that the gas had come from his own installation and not the main (Jones).

The bulk of Emily Jackson's money went to charities to do with the welfare of ex-servicemen, but she also left generous bequests to her friends and employees. Her gardener, Frank Holder, who had been with her for forty-five years, and her maid, Miss Wayland, who had served for forty, were left well provided-for.

Exhib: B; D; G; L; M; RA; RBA; RI; SWA
Bibliog: BEN; DBA; TB; WOOD

JACKSON, Sir Thomas Graham, R.A., F.S.A. 1835–1924
In 1869 Thomas Graham Jackson, a well-known and extremely distinguished architect, designed Cheam's *Parochial Rooms* in Malden Road, the land having been donated by Spencer Wilde, owner of Cheam House. Earlier, Wilde had commissioned Jackson to design an extension to *Cheam House*. The building known as the Parochial Rooms continues to serve as an important venue for public and private functions at Cheam, but Cheam House was pulled down many years ago, in 1922.

Born in Hampstead in 1835, Jackson was educated at Brighton College and then entered Wadham College, Oxford, where he had some drawing lessons from William Turner of Oxford. A small collection of Jackson's charming wash drawings from this period can be seen at the Fitzwilliam Museum, Cambridge; and some of his books are illustrated with his own watercolours. He rose to fame as a church and college architect, training under Sir George Gilbert Scott before setting up in practice on his own. He designed buildings for public schools and for Oxford and Cambridge colleges.

Many honours and awards came his way. He was elected a member of the Royal Academy in 1896 and received a knighthood in 1913. In 1887 he settled in Wimbledon, buying Eagle House in the High Street. He restored this early seventeenth century building to its former glory, keeping as far as possible the original features, though he had to rebuild the back central wing. Eagle House, with Thomas Jackson's initials above the door, remains one of Wimbledon's most interesting buildings.

Jackson was the author of several books. In addition to architecture he had numerous interests which included boating, gardening and music. He died on 7 November 1924.

Exhib: D; RA
Published: JACKSON, T. G. *Reason in Architecture*. John Murray, 1906; *A Holiday in Umbria*. John Murray, 1917; *Recollections of T.G.J.* O.U.P., 1950
Bibliog: BEN; DBA; DNB; GW; HOUFE; LAMBOURNE; MALLALIEU; TB; WOOD; *Who Was Who 1916–1928*

E. WINIFRED MADDER   Watercolour 165×248mm
Strawberry Cottage, North Street, Carshalton. 1912.
Sutton's Local Collection.

THOMAS MAISEY (after)   Engraving 165×241mm
Cheam School. c. 1835.   Sutton's Local Collection

JAMES C. MIDDLETON   Watercolour 254×356mm
Dockyard scene. c. 1950.   Private collection

*JARVIS, Henry Charles 1867–1955

Henry Charles Jarvis, who painted watercolours in a delicate, impressionistic style, trained at Goldsmiths' College, London under Fred Marriott and Percy Buckman. In addition to his painting *Cheam from near Banstead*, now in Sutton's Local Collection, he painted at least two other views of this area: *A September morning on the Wandle by Beddington Park* (1929) and *On the Wandle, Beddington Park, Surrey* (1950), both exhibited at the Royal Academy.

Jarvis, who was married and had two sons, died at Sevenoaks, Kent on 7 April 1955.

Exhib: AB; D; RA; RI; Sevenoaks
Coll: Northampton AG; Sutton LC
Bibliog: DBA; GW; WOOD; *Who's Who in Art*, 1950

KEYL, Friedrich Wilhelm 1823–1871

Born on 17 September 1823 at Frankfurt-am-Main, Friedrich Keyl, a pupil of Eugene Verboeckhoven, came to London in 1845, to remain there for the rest of his life. A pupil and close friend of Sir Edwin Landseer, R.A., he recorded his conversations with Landseer in a journal, which is now at Windsor Castle. Landseer's influence is apparent in the work of his pupil, a particularly good example being Keyl's oil painting of the Gurneys, to be described later. A sporting artist like Landseer, Keyl was a regular visitor to London Zoo, having found that drawing the animals improved his anatomical knowledge.

During the 1850s he visited Carshalton and painted: *View of the Culver[s], Carshalton with portraits of Mr. and Mrs. Sam Gurney*, exhibited at the Royal Academy in 1851. It was shown again as recently as 1980, at Richard Green's annual 'Exhibition of Sporting Pictures', when it was bought by a private collector. In this painting the Gurneys, a handsome young couple, are seen chatting to their gamekeeper. Their home The Culvers, although well in the background, is clearly delineated. It is harvest time and a haymaking wagon and farmworkers are present in the scene. Mrs Gurney, née Ellen Reynolds, the daughter of William Reynolds of Carshalton, is dressed in black and appears to be in mourning.

The fortunes of Samuel Gurney, M.P. (1816–1882), a prominent Quaker and a nephew of Elizabeth Fry, were founded on the family merchant bank of Overend, Gurney and Co. He owned all but two of the large houses and estates on the Wandle in the Hackbridge area, living with his family at The Culvers. The Keyl painting shows him when he was at the height of his prosperity which, unfortunately for him, did not last. Fifteen years later, in 1866, the bank failed, and The Culvers and all his other Wandle properties were put up for sale.

But before this happened, the Gurneys, no doubt delighted with their portraits, commissioned Keyl to

paint another picture, this time *Spanish oxen, the property of Samuel Gurney, Esq., M.P.*, which was exhibited at the RA in 1857. Gurney, a collector of rare breeds of cattle and exotic birds, made an aviary on an island of his estate at Carshalton, where he introduced the first black swans to Europe, sent over from Australia by some relatives. He was also a campaigner for 'total abstinence' and had a 'teetotal ballad' composed in his honour, commemorating his gift of 'the first public drinking fountain'. A copy of the attractive lithographed music cover of 'Oh come with me to the Fountain of Love', composed by Henry Walker, can be seen at Harvey's Wine Museum in Bristol.

Keyl exhibited two other paintings of local interest at the RA: *Walton Heath* (1856) and *Companions, The property of James Nicholson, Esq., of Woodhatch, Reigate* (1859). He was also an engraver and illustrator, contributing to *Beaton's Annual* (1866), Mrs. Gatty's *Parables from Nature* (1867) and other publications.

Keyl's wife, Susan Constance, bore him eight children. One of them was named Edwin after Landseer, another, Albert after the Prince Consort. Landseer introduced Keyl to Queen Victoria and Prince Albert who commissioned Keyl to paint studies of the royal dogs and other royal animals; a number of his paintings are in the Royal Collection. The Keyl family lived in the St John's Wood area of London, then thickly populated with artists.

Keyl was still quite young – only in his forties – when he died on 5 December 1871. He is buried in Kensal Green Cemetery.

Exhib: BI; RA
Coll: BM; Royal Collection
Bibliog: BEN; DNB; ENGEN(2); HOUFE; MITCHELL; TB; WOOD

KILBURNE, George Goodwin, junior, R.B.A. 1863–1938

Chasemore, Park Hill, Carshalton c.1912–1915

George Goodwin Kilburne, junior was born in 1863, the son of the artist George Goodwin Kilburne, senior. Their paintings are so alike it is often difficult to tell them apart. Indeed, many art dealers and critics fail to do so. For about three years, George junior lived at Chasemore, Carshalton, a house owned at the time by E. J. Thompson.

An artist in oil and watercolour, the younger Kilburne specialised in historical, genre and sporting subjects. His mother, his father's first wife, was the daughter of the engraver Robert Dalziel and a niece of the famous 'Brothers Dalziel', who must have engraved at least half the illustrated books of the nineteenth century – or so it seems.

Before coming to Carshalton, George lived with his father at Haverstock Hill and then at various addresses in London, Sussex and Kent. After he left Carshalton he lived in Sussex, where at one period his address was The Forge at Waldron.

The Kilburnes, father and son, were prolific and very popular artists. George junior was elected a member of the Royal Society of British Artists but later resigned. He was possibly the Kilburne who designed a series of picture postcards – portraits of literary men – for Raphael Tuck.

His later years must have been rather lonely. His wife died before him; his son, Roy Goodwin Kilburne, was in Nepal; and his daughter, Maud, married to a military gentleman, John Wordsworth Bingham, spent much of her life travelling abroad with him. Kilburne's last days were spent at the Charterhouse in London, where he died on 23 March 1938.

Exhib: L; M; RA; RBA; RI; ROI
Bibliog: BEN; COYSH; DBA; MITCHELL; WOOD

KNIGHT, Alfred Ernest 1861–1934

Silverdale, Marshalls Road, Sutton 1910–1912
Kingsley, Brunswick Road, Sutton 1912–1921
Kingsley, 19 Bridges Lane, Beddington 1921–1934

Alfred Ernest Knight, author, artist and illustrator, was born in Camberwell in 1861. His father was the Victorian portrait and genre painter William Henry Knight (1823–1863), who exhibited at the Royal Academy and other galleries during the 1840s and 1850s, and whose sentimental scenes of children snowballing, playing see-saw and watching Punch and Judy are very popular today, selling for hundreds, sometimes thousands of pounds. William Knight died when Alfred was barely two, so Alfred Knight scarcely knew his father.

On leaving school, Alfred worked in an office, but finding the work uncongenial he 'drifted into art'. Considering his background, this is hardly surprising. Although he was self-taught, he no doubt received some help and encouragement from family friends like the marine and landscape painter Henry Dawson, a close friend of his father.

Alfred Ernest Knight, however, became better known as a writer than as an artist. He was the author of at least twenty-five books, covering a wide range of subjects from historical biography to religion. Some were novels – he published his first before he was twenty – some were volumes of verse. He illustrated many of them himself and designed some of their covers. A competent scientific draughtsman and botanical illustrator, he provided the illustrations for, as well as being the joint author of, Edward Step's *The Living Plant* (retitled *Popular Botany* when it came out in an enlarged edition).

Knight remained a bachelor until he was forty-two. Then, in 1903, he married Edith Maria Nesbit Ross and they had a son and a daughter. The family's first home in the borough was Silverdale in Marshalls Road, Sutton; their next was Kingsley in Brunswick Road. In 1921 they bought an old flint cottage – originally two but converted into one – in Bridges Lane, Beddington, and once again called their home Kingsley. Here, amidst the village atmosphere of Beddington, Alfred Knight lived out the rest of his life. He was fond of the countryside and discovered many pleasant walks in Beddington Park and by the River Wandle.

At one time he was interested in the religious sect known as the Exclusive Brethren, publishing some writings on them. But he later became disillusioned with their strict doctrines. He was the editor of *The Antiquarian Quarterly*, and his interest in local history led him to assist the Rev. Thomas Bentham with the latter's *History of Beddington* (1923). Knight provided an illustration for the book, a 'beautiful pen-and-ink drawing' (Bentham) showing the Roman lead coffin in St Mary's Church.

Although Knight is known to have carried out many paintings and drawings, he rarely exhibited his work, an exception being when his oil painting, *Fruit*, was shown at the Society of British Artists' exhibition of 1879; this was when he was living in Hackney. He died at Kingsley on 24 February 1934 and is buried in Bandon Hill Cemetery. A modern block of flats now stands on the site of his cottage.

Exhib: SBA
Published: See Knight's entry in *Who Was Who 1929–1940*
Bibliog: WOOD; *Who Was Who 1929–1940*
N.B. Original research on this artist was carried out by Miss Auralie Stanton, who received some of her information from the late Mr Orton of Bridges Lane, Beddington.

LAKE, Mabel H. Exhib: 1907–1909

Alaska, York Road, Sutton 1904–1908

Mabel Lake, a painter of portrait miniatures, exhibited two works at the Royal Academy: *Mabel* (1907) and *Hilda W. Lake* (1909). She married C. P. Blatchley and left Sutton to live at Golders Green in London.

Exhib: RA
Bibliog: DBA

LAMBERT, John William 1790–1864

Beddington 1790–
Carshalton –1822–

During the first half of the nineteenth century, John William Lambert, a landscape, sporting and genre artist painting in oil and watercolour, carried out a number of views of Beddington and Carshalton. Baptised at St Mary's Church, Beddington on 29 August 1790, he was one of the eight children – four boys and four girls – of Allen and Elizabeth Lambert. His father may have been the *Mr. A. Lambert*, a Carshalton miller, whose oil portrait, painted in about 1800 by an A. H. Monies, has recently been purchased for Sutton's Local Collection. Charles Lambert, the snuff manufacturer of Beddington Snuff Mills, who appears in Pigot's *Directory* of 1823 and in Robson's *Commercial Directory* of 1839, was possibly his brother.

We know nothing of John Lambert's early years – where he attended school or studied art, or if his artistic talent was inherited. We do know, however, that in 1822, whilst he was living in Carshalton, his painting *View at Carshalton, Surrey; a sketch* was hung at the Royal Academy, one of the nine works he exhibited there between 1822 and 1843. Another local

'Edmund in the Blues'. Illustration by ALFRED E. KNIGHT for his book: *Twice Born*, Sunday School Union, N.D.

Above
HORACE A. MUMMERY   Watercolour 140×191mm
Wood Green.   Private collection

Left
ALFRED J. HOWELL MOORE   Watercolour 343×267mm
The Scottish girl. c. 1900.   Private collection

Below
MARJORIE F. MOSTYN   Oil 356×457mm
Launching the Lifeboat at St Ives. c. 1940.
Private collection

74

scene shown by him at the RA was *Sheep shearing at Beddington Park, Surrey* (1837). In 1825 he exhibited *Beddington Church* (a view of the church where he was baptised) at the Society of British Artists' exhibition.

Three children were born to John Lambert and his wife Mary Ann: a daughter Mary Anne, named after her mother, and two sons, John Frederick and Henry Stone. Lambert's wife, the daughter of John Smith, a Norfolk millowner, was a woman of property, having inherited the bulk of her father's estate. When she died, on 24 May 1860, she left a carefully-considered will, in which only the small sum of £50 went to her son Henry. But she hastened to add that this was not through any lack of affection on her part but 'by reason of his having had more money from his father than any other of my children'. After his wife's death, John Lambert, by then living at Crown Hill, Croydon, was cared for by his daughter until his own death on 22 March 1864.

John Lambert had inherited nine leasehold cottages at Wallington, Surrey, from his uncle, Captain Charles Stone. These were passed on to his children, along with his paintings, silver and other items. His daughter Mary Anne, his chief beneficiary, inherited Lambert's painting *The Lace Maker* (exhibited at the SBA in 1851) whilst he bequeathed to his son Henry his portraits of *Captain Stone* and *Mrs Stone*. One of his nephews, Allen John Lambert, an executor of his will, was also invited to select a painting from the estate.

Exhib: BI; RA; SBA
Bibliog: MITCHELL; WOOD

*LEONI, Giacomo c.1686–1746

Giacomo Leoni, a Venetian by birth, and the self-styled Architect to the Elector Palatine, came to England to supervise the publication of Palladio's *Four Books on Architecture* (1715–20). He stayed for the rest of his life. With hindsight he may have regretted coming to this country at all, since towards the end of his life he found himself living in straitened circumstances, and he died intestate, aged sixty, in 1746. Having held no public office in England, he had been obliged to support himself in this country on his earnings as an architect.

He was involved in Thomas Scawen's grandiose scheme to build a large mansion – Leoni called it a 'palace' – complete with orangery and outbuildings, in Carshalton Park, Surrey (1723). Designed in the Baroque style, based on Palladian sources and on a scale comparable to Blenheim, it was the largest commission Leoni ever obtained.

Leoni's building was meant to replace the old manor house, Mascalls, left to Thomas Scawen by his uncle, Sir William Scawen, the previous owner; but it scarcely progressed beyond the drawing board. A large quantity of materials were bought and building work commenced; but the whole project was abandoned when Thomas Scawen found himself without sufficient funds to finance an enterprise which would have cost several million pounds in today's money.

Nothing certain remains of Leoni's work at Carshalton. His eleven plates of plans, engraved by Picart, which are in the appendix to Leoni's translation of Alberti's *Architecture*, act as a reminder that a great house was once planned for Carshalton.

Leoni's name is also given to the stone bridge in The Grove Park, Carshalton, and his name is associated with the bridge in Talbot Road, but it is highly unlikely that he had anything to do with either of them. However, there is a handsome, nine-bay stuccoed building in The Square, Carshalton, with a four-column Tuscan portico, which is possibly based on a plan by Leoni for a larger building. This was converted to offices in 1980–81. His best-known building in this area is Clandon Park (1713–29) near Guildford, now owned by the National Trust.

Published: LEONI, G. *The Architecture of A. Palladio . . .,* 1716–20; *The Architecture of Leon Battista Alberti,* 1726
Bibliog: BEARD, G. Leoni's English Houses. *Country Life Annual,* 1968, pp. 85–7; HUDSON, T. A Venetian Architect in England. *Country Life,* vol. 157, 3 April 1975, pp. 830–833; COLLINS, P. New light on Leoni. *Architectural Review,* vol. 127, 1960, pp. 225–6

LEWIS, Thomas Noyes 1863–1946

Oaklands, Benhill Road, Sutton 1912–1927
St Francis Holt, 4 Queen's Road, Belmont 1927–1946

Thomas (Tom) Noyes Lewis, born in Barnet, Hertfordshire, in 1863, eventually settled in Sutton, where he spent the last thirty years of his life. He was possibly the Noyes Lewis who exhibited with the Bushey Society of Artists in 1909 and 1910.

Influenced by William Morris and the Arts and Crafts movement, he was a landscape and genre painter, mostly in oil, and was also a black-and-white artist. His interest in medievalism is reflected in his illustrations to *The Young Christian's Progress,* a book for children, which has an abundance of knights in armour engaged in knightly duties, like rescuing fair maidens and slaying dragons.

His work was exhibited at the Royal Academy and other galleries, one of his RA paintings, *After long vigil, dawn* (1904), being inherited by his son 'Noynie'. Tom Noyes Lewis left a rather unusual will in the form of a letter, beginning: 'To my two dearly loved boys God bless them both . . . Well chaps here is my will–'. Nearly all his possessions, including his favourite Chippendale armchair and the Noyes Lewis silver tankard, went to his sons; and he suggested, rather diffidently, that all unwanted pictures should be put on a bonfire and burnt. William Gaydon, then the Principal of Sutton Art School, inherited the artist's collection of books and painting materials.

Tom Noyes Lewis, a widower, died at his Belmont home, St Francis Holt, on 16 June 1946.

Exhib: RA; ROI
Illus: BIGGS, Rev. D. R. D. *Gospel Vestments.* Faith Press, N.D.; DOUGLAS, Rev. J. A. *The Young Christian's Progress.* Faith Press, N.D.
Bibliog: DBA; WOOD

LILEY, Henry George 1848–1923

Wallington Bridge, Wallington –1871–

Henry G. Liley, born at Chelsea in 1848, was a nineteenth century decorative architect whose drawings for ballrooms, dining rooms and ceilings were exhibited at the Royal Academy between 1878 and 1891.

He was a boarder in a house at Wallington Bridge during the 1870s, and this possibly indicates that he was in the district to carry out some decorative scheme for one of the large houses in the area. Canon Bridges, who was then refurbishing Beddington House (see Marks, H. S. (q.v.)) may have employed him.

Henry Liley died on 14 January 1923, at his home in Hawkhurst, Kent.

Exhib: RA
Bibliog: DBA

LIMPUS, Lady Florence Mary (née Travers) 1863–1954

Church Farm, Cheam 1863–1888

Florence Mary Travers, the third daughter of Otho William Travers, gentleman farmer of Cheam, was a talented amateur artist in watercolour. Born and brought up in Cheam, in 1888 she married Lieut. Arthur Henry Limpus (later Admiral Sir Arthur Henry Limpus, K.C.M.G., C.B.). Thereafter she spent much of her life abroad, living in China, Turkey, Malta, Italy and other countries where her husband held important posts. They had one child, a daughter Lorna Florence Limpus. ·

Florence's older sister, Norah Travers (q.v.), was an exhibiting artist, and the two sisters often sketched together, sometimes producing watercolours of identical views. Florence continued to paint after her marriage, signing her work 'F. Limpus'. There are two known views with this signature: a photograph of one of them is in Sutton's Local Collection and the other is illustrated in *My Sketch Book* by Frank Worker (q.v.).

Sir Arthur Limpus, whose family home was Cartref Verwood in Dorset, died at Val d'Olivo, Alassio, Italy, in 1931. Lady Limpus remained in Italy for some years after his death, but she eventually returned to England and died, aged ninety, at Boscombe, Hampshire, on 28 March 1954.

Bibliog: *Kelly's Handbook to the Titled, Landed and Official Classes 1934*

*LIVENS, Horace Mann, R.B.A., I.S. 1862–1936

Bryn Llan, 10 Alfred Road, Sutton 1902–1912

Horace Mann Livens, a friend of Van Gogh, was a landscape, genre, flower and poultry painter, working in watercolour, oil and pastel, his portraits and drawings of children often being done in pastel. His oil paintings were painted in short, vigorous brush strokes, the paint lying thickly on the canvas. He also carried out numerous dry-point engravings.

Livens was born in Croydon on 16 December 1862. The family possibly had some connection with the American educational reformer Horace Mann, since

HORACE M. LIVENS   Drypoint 140×305mm
Study of Fowls.   Private collection

Horace bore this name and their house at Croydon was named Mannsfield. After an education at Bishops Stortford Grammar School, Horace joined his father George Livens, a colonial broker, in his office in Mincing Lane, London. His evenings, however, were spent at Croydon Art School where Walter Wallis, the principal, advised him to take up art full-time. So in 1885 he went to Antwerp to study at the Academy, where a fellow pupil was Vincent Van Gogh, nine years his senior.

The two men became friends, sharing the same views on art. When Van Gogh was ill, Livens took him to his own studio and nursed him back to health. After Van Gogh left the Academy he wrote to Livens from Paris, inviting him to share his studio. But this was not to be. Livens did go to Paris, in about 1890, but by then Van Gogh was painting in the South of France. From Van Gogh's letter we learn that Livens's landlady in Antwerp was a Mrs Roosmalen who helped her student lodgers by selling their work for them. Livens drew a sketch of Van Gogh, one of the earliest known, when they were both students at the Academy.

In 1894 Livens married Gertrude Evangeline Brock and they set up home in Croydon, where their two children were born. In 1902 the family moved to no. 10 Alfred Road, Sutton, and remained there until 1912. The house is still there, recently modernised. Livens's ten years at Sutton were some of his most productive and most successful ones. He was by then a member of the Royal Society of British Artists and a founder member, along with Whistler and other famous names, of the International Society. In 1905 he became a founder member of the Society of Twenty-Five Artists.

Exhibiting regularly at the London galleries, and with a one-man show at the Goupil Gallery in 1911, his work was commended in the art magazines of the day and his paintings were frequently illustrated in *The Studio*. Affectionately known as 'the Old Fowler' on account of his numerous studies of poultry, he acknowledged this by calling one of his paintings *The Old Fowler*.

Unfortunately, success in his career was not matched in his marriage. His personal life took on the pattern of a Greek Tragedy or a play by Eugene

O'Neill, though no doubt there were some happy times. Tender studies of Gertrude sewing and engaged in other domestic duties have survived. But as the years went by she became increasingly eccentric and obsessively houseproud, banning Livens from doing his painting in the house. He was obliged to use his chicken-house as a studio. Fortunately, he was exceedingly fond of his hens – indeed, of all feathered creatures. A self-mocking, pen-and-ink drawing by Livens, entitled *The Fowl Doctor*, shows him in his garden at Sutton feeding medicine to one of his hens.

His children, Leo and Evangeline, were musical prodigies, but Gertrude is said to have put felt dampers on the piano keys to deaden the sound. Sadly, the children, like their mother, were emotionally unstable and during the 1920s were confined in Napsbury Asylum. This must have been a truly depressing time for Livens, whose sensitively drawn pastel and charcoal sketches of his children, most of them carried out at Sutton, reveal his fondness for them. On visits to Napsbury he sketched some of the children there: his poignant drawing *Patients at Napsbury* was shown in the 1978 touring exhibition of Livens's work.

The final act of the tragedy commenced during the 1920s when this gentle, religious man – his brother was a Nonconformist minister – was affected with paralysis. The day came when he could no longer hold a paintbrush. He exhibited his last work in 1930 and died at Harrow on 5 October 1936. An obituary in the *Morning Post* described him as an artist whose work 'may not be known to the present generation'.

After his death, a large number of paintings by Livens, stored in London, were destroyed in the Blitz. In 1957 others were lost in a fire at his widow's home. Until fairly recently he had remained a neglected artist; considering his fine international reputation in the early years of this century, this is hard to reconcile. With a boldness of style that cuts out superfluous detail, his best work can be compared with Sickert's. His fowl and child studies have been mentioned already. In addition, he painted still-life studies in the manner of William Nicholson and Vallon, and flower studies which Wedmore considered the equal of Latour's. The artists he admired and who influenced him most were Manet, Courbet, Whistler and Van Gogh. During the 1880s he saw and admired his friend Arthur Morrison's collection of Japanese prints. Struck by their boldness of line and colour, he aimed for a similar effect in his own work.

Many of his paintings and most of his dry-points, were carried out at Sutton. His one-man show at the Goupil Gallery in 1911 included three watercolours of local interest: *My Garden in Winter*, *The Water Mill* and *Croydon Art Students*. At his second Goupil exhibition, in 1914, two of his watercolours were *Carshalton* and *Cheam*. Many studies of his house and family were carried out at Sutton, including the dry-points: *Corner of My House* and *Self-Portrait in the Kitchen*, both dated 1909.

When Queen Mary invited him to paint a miniature for her famous Dolls' House, it was no easy task for Livens who could have filled the allotted space with one sweep of his brush. But he coped admirably and the result can be seen on page 66. His best known book illustrations are in E. V. Lucas's 'London' titles, which ran to many editions. The British Museum has a collection of his etchings, donated by Campbell Dodgson, its one-time Keeper of Prints and Drawings.

When Livens died, he left generous bequests of paintings, drawings and etchings to numerous relatives, and also to Arthur Morrison, whose Japanese prints he had so admired. His last request was to be buried near his mother's grave at Elmers End Cemetery.

Exhib: ALP; BA; BG; BI; CG; CHE; G; GI; GOU; IS; L; M; NEA; P; RA; RBA; RHA; RI; ROI; RP; RSA; RWS; Fairfield Halls, Croydon, 1965; New Grafton Gallery, London, 1969; Touring exhibition, 1978
Coll: Bradford AG; Brighton AG; BM; Leicester AG; County Hall, London; Sutton LC; Tate AG; V&A; Nat. Mus. Wales; Walsall AG; Nat. AG, Canada
Illus: LUCAS, E. V. *A Wanderer in London*. Methuen, 1906; *London Revisited*. Methuen, 1916; and other illustrations in various publications
Bibliog: BEN; DBA; GW; LAMBOURNE; LISTER; TB; WOOD; *Who's Who in Art*, 1929; *Who Was Who 1929–1940*; WEDMORE, F. *Some of the Moderns*. Virtue & Co., 1909; The watercolours of Horace Mann Livens. *Studio*, vol. lxxiv, no. 306, Sept. 1918, pp. 103–110; DENVIR, B. Some rediscoveries. *Art and Artists*, vol. 13, no. 3, iss. 148, pp. 4–9; GROSE, I. *'The Old Fowler'; The Life and Work of Horace Mann Livens (1862–1936)*. Belgrave Gallery, London, 1978; *The Dry-Points of Horace Mann Livens*. Belgrave Gallery, London, 1979

LOCKE, Edward, F.G.S. b. 1845

Southfields, Sutton Common, Sutton 1854–c.1870
Ellerslie, Brunswick Road, Sutton pre-1881–c.1890
Baynards, Oakhill Road, Sutton c.1890–c.1896

Edward Locke, artist, architect, antiquary and geologist was the son of Anthony Locke, a London merchant and builder. Born in 1845 at Weaver's Hall in Basinghall Street, London, he spent his early years at this ancient house which, even though it was in the middle of the City of London, had an old garden where the children played and where Anthony Locke grew potatoes, peas and strawberries.

When Edward was seven the family moved to Sutton. Two years later, Anthony Locke built himself a house called Southfields, on Sutton Common, which, after the Lockes, had a succession of distinguished owners including the architect W. Hilton Nash (q.v.) and General Blake.

Edward's grandfather, William Huggins, was Marine Painter to King William IV; he painted scenes of the *Battle of Trafalgar* in Hampton Court Palace. An uncle was the marine painter Edward Duncan. Although he never knew his grandfather – William Huggins died the year Edward was born – he inherited some of his paintings and also his artistic talent.

Anthony Locke, intending his son to become a merchant, placed him in Boyd's Cloth Warehouse in Friday Street, giving him a warehouse of his own when he was eighteen. But Edward hated the work. Bored, he would roam the streets of London,

FRANK H. POTTER   Oil 530×430mm
Portrait of Belinda.   Private collection

ROBERT ROBINSON   Oil
Detail from a capriccio in the Painted Parlour at
Carshalton House (now St Philomena's School).
pre-1706.

PERCY C. PACE   Oil 292×394mm
Low tide, Mistley.   Private collection

sketching doorways, windows, old coaching inns and anything else that took his eye. Although his father disapproved, his mother, Caroline, proved sympathetic; she persuaded Anthony Locke to article Edward to Edmund Woodthorpe, District Surveyor to the City of London.

Woodthorpe was then engaged in restoring old London churches and he let his pupil try his hand with one or two. When Edward reached the foundations of *St Giles*, Cripplegate, he was shocked to discover hundreds of human skeletons piled one on top of the other to a depth of thirty feet, the remains of plague victims. Many years later, he had a similar experience when he was supervising the construction of the *King's Arms*, being built on the site of the old Bishopsgate churchyard. Here, under the foundations, he found three thousand or so skeletons.

During his apprenticeship, Edward sent drawings to the Royal Academy Schools and was accepted as a pupil, winning a silver medal there. In 1869 he was awarded an RIBA prize for an essay on the application to modern architecture of moulded, shaped and coloured bricks and terracotta; his manuscript is in the RIBA Library.

On receiving his articles he set up in practice with A. E. Taylor, and they designed buildings in Central London, Tottenham, Finchley, Hornsey, Hackney, Cheam, Brighton and Wales. These included the *Saracen's Head* at Holborn Viaduct and the *Duchess of Newcastle's Mansion* in Berkeley Square. In conjunction with Sir Horace Jones, the City Architect, Locke was responsible for the front of *Leadenhall Market* in Gracechurch Street. One of Locke's best known works, however, was his restoration of *Fawkham Manor House* and *Church* in Kent, where he had some exciting finds: Norman windows hidden under plasterwork and a fifteenth century porch covered over with matchboarding.

A large part of Edward Locke's life was spent in Sutton. When he was a boy, he witnessed meetings at his father's house, Southfields, to discuss the building of *All Saints Church*, Benhilton. The chosen architect was Samuel S. Teulon (q.v.), but he died before the building was finally completed and Edward Locke, by that time a fully fledged architect, finished it, being responsible for the whole of the north side. On a more mundane level, Locke and his father designed and built the majority of the Victorian houses on Sutton Common.

Edward Locke was over thirty when he married. Jessie, his bride, was barely seventeen, but by the time she was nineteen she was the mother of two sons, Edward and Frank. The family lived at Ellerslie in Brunswick Road, which Edward Locke turned into a veritable treasure house, containing, as it did, his vast collection of pictures, antiquities and objets d'art. Paintings by Richard Wilson (q.v.), John Absolon and William Huggins hung on the walls, together with Locke's own architectural studies of English cathedrals. He had a large collection of ancient pottery, found during restoration work, and also some valuable items of Wedgwood ware, oriental porcelain, snuffboxes and swords. He once bought the whole carved brick front of a house (dated 1671) and kept it in his office.

Locke's style was Free Classical, with a predilection for Dutch gables. His designs, however, sometimes proved too elaborate for the building regulations and had to be modified.

Bibliog: Surrey Artists and their Homes. XVII. – Edward Locke. *Sutton and Epsom Advertiser*, 18 February 1888

LOTZ, Henry John 1883–1936

The Chestnuts, Mulgrave Road, Sutton 1912–1915

Hinrich Carl J. Lotz, who was later known as Henry J. Lotz, was a painter of landscapes, portraits and seascapes. Born in Lewisham in 1883, he was the son of William Frederick Lotz, a merchant; the Lotz family lived in Sutton from 1912 until William Lotz died there in 1915.

In 1913 Henry Lotz's painting *The High Road* was exhibited at the New English Art Club, submitted from Sutton. During the First World War he enlisted in the Artists' Rifles and after the war lived in London. He exhibited four paintings at the Royal Academy, including: *Cornish Landscape* (1929) and *Southampton Water* (1934). He died at Camberwell House, Camberwell, on 29 May 1936, leaving a widow, Wanda Hélène Lotz.

Exhib: G; GOU; LEI; NEA; RA; ROI
Bibliog: DBA

LUCAS, Edward George Handel 1861–1936

Montacute House, Blackwater, Sutton c.1880–1881

Handel Lucas, as he was known to the art world, was the son of a musician. He inherited his father's musical ability and sang in three choirs, one of which, appropriately enough, was the Handel Festival Choir. His father, Edwin Newton Lucas, a tailor as well as a musician, had a business at Croydon, Surrey.

Handel Lucas was born in Croydon on 4 May 1861 and was educated at Whitgift Middle School. His memorial portrait of *Head Master W. Ingrams*, painted in 1928, hangs in the Trinity School of John Whitgift, at Shirley Park, Croydon. Lucas studied art at Heatherley's and at St John's Wood Art School, and spent a year at the British Academy in Rome (1888–9).

He was only thirteen when his painting *Spring Beauties* was shown at the Society of British Artists' exhibition of 1875; he was only seventeen when he had his first acceptance at the Royal Academy. A painter of portraits, flowers, figures and landscapes, nearly all carried out in oil, he enjoyed a successful career, his style influenced by the artists Van Eyck and Gerard Dou. His other major interest was photography; he was a member of the Croydon Camera Club and was granted patents in colour photography.

Throughout his life he lived in or near Croydon and was a prominent member of the Surrey Art Circle (q.v.) which he joined in 1897. His stay at Sutton was brief. For a year or so he lived in Montacute House, where the householder then was E. Durrant Cecil (Pile); and he gave this address when he exhibited the paintings *The Poet's Corner* and *Homes of the Poor* with the SBA in 1881. Shortly after he left Sutton, he became a member of the Dudley Art Society (1883) but he refused nomination to both the RBA (1889) and the ROI (1905).

Today, there is a ready market for his paintings. Those sold in recent years include *Chapel of the Old Archbishop's Palace*, painted in 1880, which made £500 at auction in 1979; whilst another, *The Spirit of Purity*, painted in 1926, sold for £800 in 1978, the subject matter possibly accounting for the higher price of the latter. Today his paintings have reached the £2,000 – £3,000 bracket. One of his most important works: *Sairey Gamp's Treasures*, was presented to the Borough of Croydon in 1896 by Sir Frederick Eldridge.

Handel Lucas, who married Clara Mary Stunell, by whom he had two daughters, died on 4 April 1936.

Exhib: D; G; L; M; RA; ROI; SAC
Coll: London Borough of Croydon; Trinity School, Croydon
Bibliog: BEN; DBA; GW; TB; WOOD; *Who's Who in Art*, 1929; Surrey Artists and their Homes. II. – Mr. E. G. Handel Lucas. *Sutton and Epsom Advertiser*, 5 November 1887

*MADDER, E. Winifred 1883–1972

Sethella Lodge (later 64) North Street, Carshalton 1901–1909
Coombe Martin, 7 Prince of Wales Road, Carshalton 1914–c.1916
Westcroft Farmhouse, Westcroft Road, Carshalton 1920–1925
Farm Cottage, Westcroft Road, Carshalton 1926–1937–
Bramble Haw End, Westcroft Road, Carshalton –1962

'Miss Madder', as she was generally and respectfully known to local residents, was a noted Carshalton artist and archaeologist in the first half of the present century. Born at Westfield House, Trevelyan Road, Tooting, on 12 March 1883, she was christened Emily Winifred but only used her second name, presumably to avoid confusion with her mother Emily Jane Madder (née Baxter). Her father, Allen George Madder, was a Post Office official. When she was eighteen the family moved to Carshalton and between 1901 and 1909 lived in a large house called Sethella Lodge on the east side of North Street near the junction with Nightingale Road. They then appear to have left the district, but returned in 1914, and during the First World War lived at Coombe Martin, 7 Prince of Wales Road.

Winifred Madder's career as an artist was relatively short and only about forty of her paintings and drawings are known to have survived, all dating from between 1912 and 1921 when she was in her thirties. She had been a pupil of William Tatton Winter (q.v.) and was determined to continue his work in recording the historic buildings of Carshalton. When Tatton Winter died in 1928 she was able to arrange for some of his Carshalton pictures to be purchased by the Urban District Council. But unlike her mentor, she herself was clearly far more interested in buildings and street scenes than in the landscapes which Tatton Winter used so extensively to express feeling and emotion. Nevertheless there is ample evidence of his techniques in her own watercolours. She used the same muted colours (greens, browns and greys), and the same impressionistic treatment of trees, background buildings and white water. Her employment of central stretches of roadway, flanked by hedges to achieve a balanced effect, stemmed from her instructor. So, too, did her use of cloud effects to suggest movement, as seen in her picture of washing strung up to dry at Mill Green – a very Wintery attempt to show the sweep of wind across the land. In her best efforts she achieves the same blend of emotional recall combined with accurate visual record which we associate with Tatton Winter. But there were a number of occasions when the conflict between them went unresolved. It depended largely upon her own involvement and experience. Buildings which did not speak to her emerged as dull and lifeless. On the other hand, there is an intensity of emotion which transforms what would otherwise be a rather drab exercise into one vibrant with feeling when her own concerns were engaged.

Since half her paintings are undated (and her dating could itself be misleading) it is impossible to trace a clear progression in her work. But it may be suggested that the influence of Tatton Winter as an artist became stronger as the years went by, and the intention to record for historical purposes less apparent. From the latter viewpoint the most valuable pictures for us are the early but very accomplished attempts in 1912/13 to record cottages in the northern part of Carshalton, long ago demolished – Beevers Cottages and Hill Farm Cottages in Green Wrythe Lane or Strawberry Cottage in North Street. By contrast her late efforts around 1920 to sketch the rapidly vanishing Wandle watermills are so short on detail as to be almost worthless, although there is a rarity value in her reproductions of mill drawings made half a century earlier by H. Romer and now no longer extant in the original. But in 1914 she had begun to turn her attention to Carshalton High Street, where some of her best work was to be done, either producing very detailed and accurate descriptions of buildings or else using her skill to give an impression of architectural and ornamental detail with a few strokes of the brush. It seems likely that her concern for the historical record had already led her to develop the habit of using photographs to work from, perhaps those being produced by her friend Dr A. V. Peatling (himself an artist), and to do this to portray, as it had been, a building which was even then in the process of being altered or demolished. Thus the very attractive view of the range of old houses and shops from The Square to the old Post Office shows 18–20 High Street as Simmons' tearooms and general stores, which had been rebuilt in 1913. Studies of the churchyard, dated 1917, include the thatched barn behind the butcher's shop (Woodman Wine Bar), although this had collapsed and been removed in September 1916. An obvious error in the front gable of the *Greyhound* (1918) – in other respects a fine picture, and notable for including human figures – can only be ascribed to the effect of using a photograph which had distorted the angles of the roofline.

The Great War served to concentrate her attention on the parish church, and a quarter of her surviving paintings relate to the church and its surroundings. Here again there is an instructive contrast between early and late attempts to employ the same technique, in this case to use the Union Jack as a focal splash of colour to offset the plainness of pillars and stone walls. This is most impressive in her interior view of the church in 1917, a picture with a brooding emotional intensity which may show women mourning, possibly for their war dead. They may even be members of her own family, since in the church there is a brass plate to Second Lieutenant Robert Madder of the Gloucester Regiment and the Machine Gun Corps, killed at the Battle of the Somme on 20 July 1916. He was Winifred's younger brother, then aged 30, who had been a member of the church choir and in whose memory his relatives presented a processional cross. It was some time before her sombre mood lifted, and by the time the war was over she may have been suffering from trouble with her eyesight. Although the family's restless habit of moving house every few years continued, they now settled in the Westcroft Road area with which Miss Madder was to be particularly associated. This produced her last pictures, and these too are of markedly uneven quality. *Westcroft Farm Cottage*, painted in 1920, with its light colours and deftness of touch, shows her at her impressionistic best: the *Farm House* of the following year, her last dated painting, exaggerates the size of the building and the sweep of the road to such an extent that it is almost unrecognisable (and has in fact been wrongly identified). But she showed equal concern for the preservation of both pictures. She commanded that one should be given to the Urban District Council; the other to Dr. Peatling, and then returned to her if Peatling should part with it. He died the following year, and there appear to be no more pictures.

By now she was approaching forty: she would never marry, and she devoted herself to looking after her family and to taking an increasing part in local affairs. With her parents and sister she moved in 1920 into Westcroft farmhouse, the western half of a lovely seventeenth-century building known up to that point as The Croft, and their affection for the house can be gauged from the fact that when the time came to make another move in 1926 they simply transferred to the other half of the building, the Farm Cottage, and she remained there until after the Second World War.

When the first secretary of the recently-formed Beddington, Carshalton & Wallington Archaeological Society, Mr. H. V. Molesworth Roberts, resigned

unexpectedly in 1927, she (who had been a founder member in 1920) offered to help the Society over a difficult period by replacing him, and in fact remained as secretary for the next ten years. She wrote a booklet on the history of Roman London; she was very much involved in the bid to establish a Carshalton Museum, first in the 'cottage in the churchyard' and then in 1930 in Carshalton Library; and it was her custody of the Peatling Papers during the 1930s and 1940s which ensured the preservation of a major collection of local history records. It was a particularly active period in her life. She was elected as a local councillor in 1931 and served on numerous committees, especially those concerned with welfare matters and the maintenance of open spaces. Her musical evenings became a notable feature of social life in the village (although she had no time for the radio).

In 1936, however, there came a change. Miss Madder was now in her mid-fifties, and she began to resign from her commitments. There was talk of leaving Carshalton; her mother was seriously ill; her eyesight had become worse. Another war was to bring more sadness. Her much-loved sister, a talented pianist, died whilst giving a music lesson. Her father, now retired, was a picturesque figure in the locality clad in a Norfolk suit, cape and gaiters. She herself, also addicted to wearing a cape, was becoming the little dark, rather wizened figure recalled with great affection and much respect by old residents today: a little eccentric perhaps, but very kind and polite, even if precise and a firm upholder of old-fashioned virtues and values. She was positively obsessive about the need to keep the roads clear of litter (and always carried a small fork with which to spear offending pieces of paper). When the Bramble Haw estate, opposite Westcroft Farm, was sold for redevelopment in 1927, she had purchased the stables, a cottage and part of the back garden. These were converted into two separate residences (now no. 38 Bramble Haw End and no. 40 Bramblehaw Cottage): and after the War she moved across the road. Bramblehaw Cottage was sold in 1958; and Westcroft Farm Cottage also went to the sitting tenant; but she retained Bramble Haw End until she eventually moved to London in 1962 and bought a service flat at 54 Artillery Mansions in Victoria Street. She was now very frail, and lived quietly in retirement. Ten years later, having reached her ninetieth year, she died peacefully on 22 February 1972 at her London home.

Michael Wilks

Coll: Sutton LC
Sources: Sutton's Local Studies Collection

*MAISEY, Thomas, P.N.W.S. 1787–1840
Art Master at Cheam School pre-1830–1840
Thomas Maisey, a distinguished watercolourist, was the art master at Cheam School in Surrey during the first half of the nineteenth century. He also taught at a school run by the Misses Shepheard at Kensington. He was born at Beckford, Gloucestershire in 1787 and used to return there for sketching holidays. One of his

sketchbooks at the Victoria and Albert Museum, dated July 1839, is of 'Drawings from Nature in Gloucestershire and Worcestershire'. On 26 April 1823 he married Marianne Berthand, the daughter of a Swiss Calvinist Pastor. They had one son, Frederick Charles, born in 1825. Maisey died in 1840, after which his wife returned to Switzerland, where she died in 1864.

Maisey lived in London, and he was first represented in a major exhibition there in 1818. His watercolours were shown in various exhibitions up to his death, including five at the Royal Academy, two at the Old Water Colour Society and twenty-eight at the New Water Colour Society. An indication of his position in the art establishment of the time is his election as President of the New Water Colour Society in 1833.

It is not known exactly when Maisey started working at Cheam. He may have been there as early as 1826, when he exhibited the watercolour entitled *Nonsuch Park, Surrey* at the Society of British Artists' exhibition, an indication that he was by then familiar with the area around Cheam. In the Victoria and Albert Museum there is a set of photographs, taken from his drawings in a sketchbook entitled 'Cheam 1830–1840'. He was not resident at the school, but used to come down from London to take art classes. At Cheam he did several sketches and drawings of the village. The Cheam sketchbook contains drawings of the better known buildings of Cheam, including the *Old Cottage*, several of the school, and one of *Sutton Cross-roads*. The photographic compilation was made in 1923 by Dorothy Saward, Maisey's granddaughter, when Mary Mayo, to whom the originals belonged, gave them to an 'old resident of Cheam' (as yet unknown). Maisey also did two drawings of Cheam School of which engravings were made, and which are often reproduced. These show the early eighteenth century building surrounded by picturesque trees, with the charming detail of children playing in the foreground. They both date from around 1835.

Maisey's work shows a preoccupation with nature, the influence of Constable apparent in his treatment of trees. Some of his 'Drawings from Nature', which are attractive and confident, demonstrate his technical skill with a pencil. Maisey's other main subject was buildings. A third sketchbook in the Victoria and Albert Museum, dating from about 1836, contains rough sketches of rural scenes, and of famous London sights such as Buckingham Palace, then only recently remodelled. The Gloucestershire sketchbook has several detailed drawings of old buildings, particularly timber-framed ones. He seldom carried out portraits or figure studies.

Cheam School in the 1830s was, as it is now, a leading boys' private school. It was established by about 1645 by George Aldrich, traditionally in Whitehall in the centre of Cheam. In 1719 it moved to the site that is now occupied by Tabor Court, to the building drawn by Maisey. In 1826, probably just before Maisey started teaching at the school, Charles Mayo became the headmaster. He was a dedicated follower of Pestalozzi, with whom he had worked in Switzerland – there is no known connection between this visit and Maisey marrying a Swiss girl. He established a Pestalozzian system at Cheam, aiming to develop the whole personality and rejecting the narrow competitiveness and academic discipline of more formal schools. Curiosity about, and observation of nature was encouraged, and the atmosphere must have been more congenial to the teaching of art than in many schools. Cheam School eventually moved to Headley, near Newbury, Berkshire, in 1934.

Maisey died in 1840, at the early age of fifty-three, still exhibiting and teaching. His wife survived him by twenty-four years. He played a part in one of the exciting eras of Cheam School's history and has left us several important pictures of early nineteenth century Cheam.

Cynthia Bradley

Exhib: NWS; OWS; RA; SBA
Coll: Ashmolean Museum, Oxford; BM; V&A
Bibliog: BEN, LAMBOURNE; MALLALIEU; TB; WOOD; PEEL, E. *Cheam School from 1645.* Thornhill Press, 1974

MARKS, Henry Stacy, R.A., R.W.S., R.E. 1829–1898

Henry Stacy Marks, a brilliant pen-and-ink draughtsman, a realistic animal painter and one of the best bird painters this country has ever seen, had at least two links with Beddington in Surrey. His brother, John George Marks, had a cottage there in the 1860s, and in 1881 he himself was comissioned by Canon Bridges to design Shakespearian panels for the billiard room in Beddington House.

Henry's father was a coach builder who employed his son to paint heraldic bearings on his carriages. But it was his mother, against her husband's wishes, who encouraged Henry to enroll at Leigh's Academy in London and to study art in the limited spare time his father allowed him. At Leigh's he struck up a friendship with Frederick Walker (q.v.), whose twin sister Sarah married Henry's youngest brother John George, the young couple living in a cottage at Beddington for some years.

At the age of twenty-three Henry Marks entered the Royal Academy Schools and afterwards worked for the firm of Clayton and Bell, designing and painting stained glass windows. This was the firm which supplied the Bridges' memorial windows in St Mary's, Beddington, commissioned by Canon Bridges, but it is not known if Henry Marks designed any of them.

Henry Stacy Marks eventually left Clayton and Bell to devote the rest of his life to painting, etching, designing tiles and illustrating books, his inspiration often coming from the Middle Ages, or Shakespeare. After he had sold his painting *Toothache in the middle ages* he found he had enough money to get married, so in 1856 Helen Drysdale became his first wife. After she died he married the artist Mary Harriet Kempe.

In 1881, throughout the months of July and August, *The Architect* magazine published, one per issue, the coloured illustrations of Marks's eight circular plaques for the ceiling of the billiard room at Beddington House. Marks expressed the view that in such a place the most 'eligible' subjects would be those suggestive of mirth. He chose scenes from Shakespeare's *Comedies* and mentions the commission in his autobiography *Pen and Pencil Sketches* (1894).

Alexander Henry Bridges, who commissioned the plaques, was the Rector of Beddington Church from 1864 until his death in 1891. He inherited Beddington House – not to be confused with Beddington Park (the ancient home of the Carews) – from his father Sir Henry Bridges, enlarging and refurbishing it so that he could entertain in style his fellow clergy, his friends and local dignitaries. Since he was reputed to be one of the richest clergymen in England he could well afford it. But he is remembered in Beddington as a benefactor, kindly and approachable to all who asked for help. Canon Bridges's granddaughter Alys Mary married Henry Stacy Marks's nephew Geoffrey Marks, C.B.E. (1864–1938).

Beddington House was pulled down in the late 1920s after being used by the forces in the First World War. The Shakespearian plaques possibly perished then. If, by some miracle, they survived, their present location is unknown. A photograph of the house and garden can be found in *All Our Yesterdays* (1977), published by Sutton Libraries and Arts Services.

Henry Stacy Marks ('Marco') a member of the Arts Club from its early days, was a founder member of the group of artists known as the 'St John's Wood Clique' and was renowned for his practical jokes. Ruskin (q.v.) reproved him for that faculty which, he said, impeded Marks's progress as an artist, but even Ruskin was won over by the artist's open and cheerful personality. Throughout his life Marks treasured a tie-pin of a heron, carved from opal, which Ruskin had given him, and he even named his favourite dog 'Russ' after Ruskin.

In 1878 Marks was elected a full member of the Royal Academy, exhibiting regularly there until his death in 1898. Some of his work, which must have been seen by millions of Londoners and visitors to London, forms part of the terracotta mosaic frieze which encircles the outer dome of the Royal Albert Hall.

Exhib: B; BI; FIN; L; M; RA; RBA; ROI; RWS
Bibliog: BEN; DBA; DNB; ENGEN(1&2); HOUFE; LAMBOURNE; LISTER; TB; WOOD; MARKS, H. S. *Pen and Pencil Sketches*. 1894. 2 vols.; Henry Stacy Marks, R.A. Illustrated Interviews. No. II. *Strand Magazine*, vol. 2, 1891 pp. 110–120

MARLOWE, Florence Exhib: 1873–1888

Hartland House, Benhill Wood Road, Sutton 1873–1884
Florence Marlowe was a flower, still-life, and genre painter who lived at Hartland House, Sutton, the home of Charles and Juliet Robert, for about ten years. Her host and hostess, who were French, possibly inspired her Royal Academy painting. Entitled *In a foreign land* (1873), it bears a very long caption: "Our time passed sadly enough, sometimes a gazette came into our hands, and bringing our far-off home before us made our sojourn seem more weary than before." – *Journal d'un Emigré*, Coblentz, 1793.

Exhib: B; RA; RBA; ROI
Bibliog: DBA; WOOD

MARSHALL, Charles John, F.R.I.B.A. 1859–1943

Balvaird, Eaton Road, Sutton 1895–1901
Balvaird, 20 Burdon Lane, Cheam 1901–1943
Charles John Marshall, architect and local historian, was the son of Sir William Calder Marshall, R.A., the eminent sculptor whose *The Prodigal Son* was bought in 1881 under the terms of the Chantrey Bequest (q.v.). Sir William married twice. He had no children by his first wife, but by Margaret (née Calder), his second wife, he had four sons and two daughters. Charles, born in 1859, was the youngest. The Marshalls and the Calders had intermarried over the centuries and Charles was no exception, marrying a cousin, Charlotte Maria Calder.

After studying architecture at the Royal Academy Schools, he was articled to E. M. Barry, the son of Sir Charles Barry, architect of the *New Palace of Westminster and the Houses of Parliament*. Sir Charles died before the Houses of Parliament were completed but his son finished the job in 1862–8. Charles Marshall, through working for E. M. Barry, was able to acquire a large number of Sir Charles's original drawings for the Houses of Parliament. When the buildings were bombed in 1941 he unearthed the drawings and presented them to the Government in the hope that they would be useful in the rebuilding operations.

In 1895 Charles Marshall came to live in Sutton, which he had first seen when he was cycling home to London one summer evening in 1890. Freewheeling down the hill from Banstead, he had come across the old High Street and was struck by its 'picturesque qualities; quaint houses, trees overhanging the footpaths, two pleasant inns The Cock and The Greyhound; and beyond these an extensive view all over London'. However, he chose the wrong time to move to Sutton. Within a few years, despite pleas and petitions, a heavy building programme had completely changed the character of the High Street. It could then no longer, by any stretch of the imagination, be described as 'picturesque'.

He lived in Sutton for only six years and then moved to Cheam, where his house Balvaird, built to his own design, was, like his previous house, named after his ancestors. He lived there until his death in 1943. He designed other local houses, and also the *Cheam War Memorial* which, simple and dignified in form, stands in part of the old garden of West Cheam Manor House. The house is no longer there, but the Manor House boundary walls, lowered from their original height of twelve feet, surround the memorial. The central design is a cross on a column, the overall theme one of sacrifice.

Charles Marshall, a resident of this borough for almost fifty years, became more and more concerned, as the years went on, in preserving and recording its past. He wrote a history of Sutton and Cheam, a largely admirable work except that the author has caused a certain amount of confusion by stating that the artist Sir Edwin Landseer, R.A. once lived in Sutton where Landseer Road is now. Since there is no firm evidence to support this, we are reluctantly forced to the conclusion that in this instance, as inevitably, in some others, Marshall was wrong.

He was the President of the Beddington, Carshalton and Wallington Archaeological Society and an officer of St Dunstan's Church, Cheam. He helped to save the Old Cottage in Malden Road, Cheam, by arranging and supervising its removal to another site when it stood in the path of the 1922 road widening scheme. In 1929, Cheam Court Farm, which, according to Marshall, was originally attached to Nonsuch Palace and dated back to Tudor times, was due to be demolished; but in the same year the Rector and churchwardens of Cheam were considering building a church in Gander Green Lane. They decided to purchase the Court Farm buildings, including barns and cowsheds and to use the materials for the new church. Dedicated to St Alban, it is known as 'The Barn Church'. The joint architects were Charles Marshall and Edward Swann (of Oxted), who deserve praise for the sympathetic way in which they incorporated the old materials into the new building.

Local history absorbed much of Marshall's time. He took part in the 1923 excavation of the medieval pottery kiln at Parkside, Cheam, and also in the 1936 excavation at no. 19 High Street. He died on 4 December 1943, aged eighty-four, and is buried in St Dunstan's churchyard, close to the Lumley Chapel which he helped to preserve.

Published: MARSHALL, C. J. and ROBERTS-WEST, M. *History of the Village of Cheam with local guide . . .* [c.1924]; *The Family of Marshall.* Cheam: D. G. Rix, 1925; *A History of the Old Villages of Cheam and Sutton . . .* Cheam: Cryer's Library, 1936. Reprinted 1971; *A Medieval Pottery Kiln discovered at Cheam.* N.D. Reprinted from *Surrey Archaeological Collections,* vol. xxxv, 1924; *The Rate Book of the Parish of Cheam from 1730–1753.* 1941. Reprinted from *Surrey Archaeological Collections,* vol. xlvii, 1941; *The Story of the Churches of Cheam.* Rev. ed. Gloucester: British Pub. Co., 1964
Obit: *Sutton and Epsom Advertiser,* 9 December 1943
The Builder, 24 December 1943

*MARSHALL, John Fitz, R.B.A. 1859–1932
John Fitz Marshall, born in Croydon, was well-acquainted with this area. He was named after his father, the artist John Marshall, whilst his grandfather, who came from Merton, was a fabric designer. Fitz Marshall was educated at Whitgift School, Croydon, and studied art at South Kensington, at Heatherley's and at the British Museum.

He was a prolific artist, painting landscape, still-life, animal and genre studies in oil and watercolour. In 1896, the year his father died, he was elected a member of the Royal Society of British Artists, exhibiting a total of two hundred works with them. He was also a regular exhibitor at the Royal Academy. Various prizes came his way, including the Diploma of Honour, Edinburgh (1886) and a Gold Medal, London (1895). He won an Art Union prize for his painting *Total Abstainers,* exhibited at the RBA in 1912.

Fitz Marshall, known to his friends as 'Fitz', was an active member of the Surrey Art Circle (q.v.) and served on the committee. However, he was somewhat alarmed to discover that certain members of the Circle were planning a Bond Street exhibition at a cost of £100. This was during the 1890s when even the major London societies were experiencing poor attendances at their exhibitions. He wrote to a fellow committee member Tatton Winter (q.v.): 'Where, Oh where is that hundred quid to come from? We have nothing beyond a shilling or two . . .' and went on to say that the Circle lacked enough big names to draw a crowd. Then – ironically in view of what happened to him later – he blamed poor attendances at art shows on the latest craze – cycling. 'No one will talk art, or look at pictures lately, it's all Bike, Bike, Bike', he wrote.

One evening in 1898, he was cycling home from a meeting when he met with a serious accident. Two youths on a tandem, travelling at full speed, ran into him, the head of one of them striking him on the cheekbone 'knocking him off the machine senseless'. Fitz Marshall's wife Amelia, on her way to meet him, came across the sorry sight of the artist lying in the middle of the road surrounded by a crowd of onlookers. He was 'shaken to pieces', had a 'frightful face' and had broken his nose and collar bone. All this was related to Tatton Winter in a letter from another Art Circle member, John Burman (q.v.) (Tatton Winter family archive).

John Fitz Marshall eventually recovered and went on to paint many more works. A successful artist in his own lifetime, he is popular again today, his sentimental Victorian studies with titles such as *Old Age Pensioners* and *The Touch of a Vanished Hand* being much in demand. His painting of the mills at Butter Hill is now in Sutton's Local Collection. He lived in Croydon for most of his life, except for about ten years in Epsom (1894–1904) but he eventually retired to Oxfordshire, spending his last days at Shipton-under-Wychwood, where he died on 8 September 1932.

Exhib: B; D; M; NG; RA; RBA; RHA; ROI; SAC
Coll: Sunderland AG; Sutton LC; Melbourne, Australia
Bibliog: BEN; DBA; GW; MITCHELL; TB; WOOD; *Who Was Who 1929–1940*; Surrey Artists and their Homes. XI. – Mr. J. Fitz Marshall. *Sutton and Epsom Advertiser,* 31 December 1887

MARTIN,   Charles 1846–1910
Edwin 1860–1915
Robert Wallace 1843–1923
Walter 1859–1912
Studio Potters 1873–c.1923
The Martin brothers, recognised as the pioneers of British studio pottery, knew Sutton well. Nearly every year, from about 1898 onwards, their Christmases were spent at the home of their sister Frances, who was married to a stockbroker, J. F. Kelley. The Kelleys, with their five children, lived at Homestead in Grove Road until 1917.

Despite occasional mishaps, which included a disastrous fire in their studio, the brothers' pottery continued to flourish until the death of Edwin in 1915, the third of the brothers to die. After that the pottery limped along under Robert Wallace until the 1920s, but the later products have neither the originality nor the quality of the earlier pieces.

Their wares are usually signed 'R. W. Martin & Bros' or 'Martin Bros. London and Southall', together with the date of potting. Nowadays, some spectacular prices are paid for their most famous products, which are the 'Wally Birds', modelled by Robert Wallace Martin, the larger ones selling for over a thousand pounds at auction.

Bibliog: HASLAM, M. *The Martin Brothers, Potters*. Richard Dennis, 1978

MARTIN, Cicely Bridget, S.W.A. Exhib: 1899–1921
Delee, Park Road, Wallington 1902–1909

Cicely Bridget Martin, a painter in oil and watercolour of landscapes, figures and flowers, exhibited at several London galleries and at Birmingham and Liverpool. Most of her paintings, however, were shown at the Society of Women Artists' exhibitions, where she was elected an associate in 1904 while she was living in Wallington.

She exhibited at the SWA as 'C. Bridget Martin' until 1911 and thereafter as 'C. Hargrave Martin', showing four titles whilst she was living in Wallington, of which three were watercolours: *Summer Days* (1907), *Helen of Kirkonnel* (1907) and *Dickie* (1905). An oil, *Hardy Annuals*, was shown in 1906. In 1919, after she had left this area, she became a full member of the SWA.

Exhib: B; L; LS; RBA; SWA
Bibliog: DBA

MATHEWES, Blanche b. 1860
Camilla Lodge, Robinhood Lane, Sutton 1860–c.1912

Blanche Mathewes, a painter of portraits, landscapes and genre studies, was born in Sutton on 31 May 1860 and appears to have spent most of her life there. She was one of the seven children of John Mathewes and his wife Louisa.

John Mathewes, born in Ireland, came to England and married a London girl. His occupation has been variously described as 'Money dealer', 'Discount agent' and 'Accountant'; but whatever it was, it was successful; he made wise investments and lived well. He arrived at Sutton some time before 1860, buying a house in Robinhood Lane of sufficient size to accommodate himself, his wife, his son, his six daughters and three servants. Called Camilla Lodge, it had a garden large enough for him to employ a full-time gardener.

By the 1880s, when all the daughters had reached or passed the age of twenty, they started a school at Camilla Lodge called 'The Misses Mathewes Ladies' School for Nobility and Gentry' with Blanche, no doubt, teaching the young ladies to draw and paint. She was by then a successful artist who later, between 1888 and 1906, exhibited six titles at the Royal Academy. Apparently she visited France, as two of her RA pictures were entitled: *A rural spot in Picardy* (1888) and *Breton child* (1893).

Three of the Mathewes girls married, Mabel becoming the wife of the Rev. Edward Gates and Florence the wife of Major Robert Brocklehurst. Emma

Louise became Emma Louise Mortimer. But Constance Catherine, Alice Jane and Blanche were still spinsters in 1906 when their mother died. Louisa Mathewes died at 40 Norland Square, London, her husband having died some years earlier. In her will she expressed the wish that Camilla Lodge should not be sold but should continue to provide a home for her three unmarried daughters; but one rather gets the impression that Blanche was not her favourite. Louisa directed that if Blanche earned by her painting skills an income of more than £50 per annum, or kept a personal maid or 'lady help', she was to contribute £50 towards the expenses of the home.

Blanche's last RA painting, exhibited in 1906, the year her mother died, was entitled *My sister*, and was sent in from 40 Norland Square. The 'Misses Mathewes' continued to live at Camilla Lodge until 1912.

Exhib: RA
Bibliog: DBA

MATTHEWS, Lucy Roch d. 1945
Homecot, Burdon Lane, Cheam 1907–1915

Little is known about the landscape and genre painter Lucy Roch Matthews, whose name is not in any of the art dictionaries. She became a member of the Surrey Art Circle (q.v.) in 1913, when she exhibited three rural views and a case of miniature paintings at their annual exhibition. In 1917, again with the SAC, she exhibited a pastel entitled *Air Raid over London, October 1917*, and in 1918 another pastel, *Jeune Femme*, together with a watercolour entitled *Storrington, near Worthing*.

Her husband, Thomas George Matthews, died in 1910. After his death she continued to live at Homecot, a house in Burdon Lane, until 1915. Some years later, another artist, Amy Dimelow (q.v.), lived there. When Lucy Matthews died, on 29 May 1945, she was buried beside her husband in St. Dunstan's churchyard, Cheam.

Exhib: SAC

MAYERS, Miss A. R. Exhib: 1913
Abbotsthorpe, Park Road, Sutton c.1895–1919

Miss A. R. Mayers, the daughter of a Reverend Mr Mayers, appears to have exhibited only one work. This was shown at the Society of Women Artists' exhibition of 1913, sent in from the above address.

In April 1987, a large watercolour of a country scene with calves, by A. R. Mayers, was entered for sale at Burstow and Hewett's Auction Rooms at Battle in Sussex, where it failed to reach its reserve price and was 'bought in' at £950

Exhib: SWA
Bibliog: DBA

MEDLAND, James

The architect James Medland carried out alterations to *Beddington House*, Bridges Lane, Beddington, in 1813/14 for Sir Henry Bridges, its then owner.

Beddington House was pulled down in the late 1920s. (see also Marks, Henry Stacy (q.v.)).

Medland was the pupil of Charles Beazley and of Samuel Robinson.

Exhib: RA
Bibliog: COLVIN; TB

MIDDLETON, James Charles, M.M., A.M.C. 1894–1969
39 Montagu Gardens, Wallington 1934–
Carn Brae, 26 Osmond Gardens, Wallington –1969
James C. Middleton, an artist in oil and watercolour, an art teacher, a jeweller, a silversmith, and a craftsman in wood, was born in Redruth, Cornwall, on 7 May 1894. He was the son of James Middleton, a commercial traveller. Educated at Redruth County School, he then studied at Redruth School of Art under James Hancox, later attending the Royal College of Art at South Kensington.

During the First World War he served in France with the Royal Flying Corps, winning the Military Medal for bravery in action. After the war he became an instructor at the Southampton Education Command and then went on to teach at Coventry, both at the Art School and at the King Henry VIII Grammar School. Whilst he was living in the Midlands, he had the opportunity to study metalwork and jewellery under Robert Catterson-Smith, the renowned Principal of the Birmingham Art School, who had once assisted William Morris (q.v.) at the Kelmscott Press. In his turn, Middleton passed on Catterson-Smith's teachings to his own pupils at St Olave's School, Southwark, where he was art master from 1931 until he retired in 1960.

He spent the second half of his life in Wallington, Surrey, where in 1938 he received the news that his painting *Pudding Bag Lane, St Ives* had been accepted at the Royal Academy. From 1950 onwards he concentrated mainly on marine subjects, exhibiting with the Royal Society of Marine Artists almost every year from 1950 until 1963. Some of his RSMA titles were: *The Lady Brassey in dry dock* (1950), *A quiet Cornish cove* (1951) and *The slipway, Grimsby* (1963). He also belonged to the Wapping Group of Artists, the Langham Sketching Club and the Croydon Art Society.

His last years were marred by his own ill health and by the death of his only daughter. He died at St Helier Hospital, Carshalton, on 18 April 1969, leaving a widow Gladys (née Goldsworthy), a son and eight grandchildren.

Exhib: CAS; PS; RA; RI; ROI; RSMA; Arts and Crafts Exhibition Society; Wapping Group; Coventry and Warwick Society of Artists
Bibliog: DBA; GW; *Who's Who in Art* – several editions

MONTFORD, Marian Alice (née Dibdin) 1882–1969
Mayfield, Grange Road, Sutton 1890–1906
38 Cavendish Road, Sutton c.1939–1969
Marian Alice Montford spent two periods of her life at Sutton, the first starting in 1890 when she was eight years old. Her father, W. J. Dibdin, an eminent chemist, gave Sutton its sewage system, the family living at Mayfield in Grange Road.

Her artistic talent could have come from her two grandfathers, Thomas Colman Dibdin (q.v.) and Augustine Aglio junior (1816–1885); from her great-grandfather, John Absolon, R.I. (1815–1895); and from her great-great-grandfather, Charles Dibdin (1745–1814), amateur artist and composer of sea shanties.

She was educated at Sutton Girls' Public Day School and then entered Chelsea Polytechnic as an art student, falling in love with the modelling master, Paul Montford, fourteen years her senior and the son of the sculptor Horace Montford. They married in 1912 and had a son and two daughters, their son Adrian carrying on the family tradition by becoming a sculptor; he exhibited at the Royal Academy during the 1950s and taught at Sutton Art School from 1956 until 1962.

After Chelsea, Marian studied at the RA Schools under E. Borough Johnson and Sir Arthur Cope. An artist in oil, watercolour and pencil, she specialised in portraits, which included miniatures. Encouraged by her husband, she was also an occasional sculptress. Her first acceptance at the RA was in 1904 with *Portrait study of a lady*, and in 1912 she exhibited a portrait bust of her husband: *Paul Montford, Esq.*

Marian's husband was an eminent sculptor, his most important commissions in this country including the *Sir Henry Campbell-Bannerman Memorial* in Westminster Abbey and the *Kelvinway Bridge* sculptures at Glasgow. Of lesser importance, but of local interest, is his statue *Wounded* on the Croydon War Memorial. In 1911 he exhibited a portrait bust of his wife at the Royal Society of British Artists' exhibition, and in 1914, at the same venue, a bust of his father-in-law W. J. Dibdin.

The Montfords emigrated to Australia in 1923, living at Toorak, near Melbourne, where Paul spent most of his time working on the *Melbourne War Memorial*. He is regarded as an important figure in Australian art. When he died at Melbourne in January 1938, his obituary in *Art in Australia*, 1 March 1938, stated that 'No other sculptor has left his mark so definitely on the civic landscape in Melbourne as Paul Montford.'

Marian Montford was not idle whilst her husband was engaged on his important commission. She exhibited with the Victorian Artists' Society at Melbourne and also had her work shown at Sydney. After her husband died, she returned to England and once again lived in Sutton, this time in Cavendish Road, where she remained until shortly before her death in 1969. She continued to exhibit at the RA until 1956, nearly all her later works being portraits of her family and friends. They included *Letitia* (1945), *Paulina* (1946) and *The Artist's daughter* (1946). In 1968 she presented some interesting items, including a photograph of her father, W. J. Dibdin, to Sutton's Local Collection. Her death was registered at Brighton in 1969.

Exhib: M; RA; RBA; RMS; Australia
Bibliog: DBA; GW; *Who's Who in Art* – several editions

MOORE, Alfred J. Howell Exhib: 1899–1918
Clydesdale, 12 Clyde Road, Wallington c.1902–1912
Alfred J. Howell Moore, who painted genre, still-life and landscape studies, mostly in watercolour, lived in Wallington for about ten years. He exhibited a total of ten paintings at the Royal Academy, of which six were sent in from Wallington including *Isola Bella* (1903), *Amalfi* (1904) and *The Rialto* (1910).

His enchanting genre studies, which often portray children, can charm collectors into parting – quite happily – with fairly considerable sums of money. One such is a watercolour of a small boy playing with a litter of pigs (illus. *Antique Dealer and Collectors' Guide*, October 1986, Abbey Antiques advert.).

Exhib: RA; RI
Bibliog: DBA; WOOD

*MOORE, Dorothy Winifred 1897–1973
Dorothy Winifred Moore, a landscape and portrait painter in oil and watercolour, was born in Cork, Ireland, on 18 January 1897, the daughter of Lieut.– Col. W. F. Moore who married twice, giving Dorothy a sister, Mildred, and a half-brother, William. She was educated in England, at the Godolphin School, Salisbury, and subsequently studied at the College of Art, Edinburgh, living in Edinburgh for many years. She exhibited at galleries in London, Ireland and Scotland, and was the art mistress at the Wheelwright Grammar School, Dewsbury, leaving most of her paintings to the town of Dewsbury when she died.

Her final years were spent in Purley, Surrey, where she died on 17 January 1973, a day before her seventy-sixth birthday. Although most of her paintings went to Dewsbury, she left instructions that the rest should be offered to the boroughs adjoining Purley. Sutton selected six, one of which is Dorothy Moore's self-portrait, an oil carried out during the 1920s or 1930s. It shows a blue-eyed, rosy-complexioned young woman, whose blonde, plaited hair is coiled about her head.

Dorothy Moore's paintings reflect the styles of the periods in which they were painted, and she often used strong, vibrant colours for her landscapes. She had a predilection for blues and greens, colours which predominate in her watercolour *Forest Glen* (coll. Borough of Reigate and Banstead). This was on view in an exhibition at Reigate Town Hall on the 11 and 12 May 1984.

Exhib: ALP; L; RA; RHA; RSA; RWS; Reigate Town Hall
Coll: Dewsbury; Reigate Town Hall; Sutton LC
Bibliog: DBA; GW; V; *Who's Who in Art*, 1929

MOORE, Miss Jennie b.1851/2 Exhib: 1877–1918
1 Bath Villas, Carshalton Road, Sutton –1885
3 Western Villas, Carshalton 1885–1890
Born in London, Jennie Moore, a painter of genre, religious and classical subjects, was an artist by profession. Forever on the move, never settling in one place for long, she travelled restlessly from one part of the country to another, living briefly at addresses in London, Godalming, Eastbourne, Leeds, Birmingham, Sutton and Carshalton.

The 1881 Census shows her in lodgings at Godalming in Surrey. But shortly afterwards she moved to Bath Villas in Sutton, and by 1885 had moved yet again and was living at Western Villas, Carshalton.

Her first Royal Academy painting, *Delilah*, was hung in 1877. During the same year, she exhibited her first two paintings with the Society of British Artists. Titles exhibited whilst she was resident in this borough were: *Solitude* (RA: 1885), *Newark Mill* (RBA: 1887), *Chrysanthemums* (RI: 1885), *The Wreath* (RI: 1886) and *Aphrodite* (RI: 1887).

Exhib: B; D; L; RA; RBA; RI; SWA
Bibliog: BEN; DBA; WOOD

MOORE, Sidney Charles 1852–1912
5 Alcester Road, Wallington pre-1886–1890
Sidney Moore, born at Greenwich in 1852, lived in Wallington for about four years and thereafter at various addresses in South London. A landscape, genre and miniature painter, he knew many artists in this area, having joined the Surrey Art Circle (q.v.) in March 1888 when he was living in Alcester Road, Wallington. He remained a member for the rest of his life and served as Secretary when Sir Alfred Gilbert, R.A. was President, always carrying out his duties most conscientiously.

He often corresponded with his fellow member Tatton Winter (q.v.) on Art Circle matters, and also sought his advice on painting techniques. In 1898 he wrote to him in some agitation: 'Have been trying to get the arm and hand right in my Cigarette girl. I find it an awful twister to do out of my head'. Moore exhibited a painting entitled *Cigarette* at the SAC's exhibition in 1900, so he must have 'got it right' in the end.

An exhibitor at the Royal Academy and other galleries, his career was followed with interest by the local press, who reviewed his painting *At Beddington*, exhibited at Sutton Public Hall in 1889:

> *At Beddington* gives a faithful representation of the familiar water course in that neighbourhood, with a boy searching for minnows and a child watching the interesting occupation from the bank. The colours are harmoniously blended and the surrounding objects are reproduced with much fidelity. (*Sutton and Epsom Advertiser*, 2 March 1889)

Moore exhibited over seventy titles with the SAC. When he died at South Norwood in 1912, the Circle honoured his memory by including nineteen of his paintings – 'Works of the late Mr. Sidney Moore' – in that year's exhibition. Two were local scenes: *Beddington* and *The Snuff Mill*.

Exhib: M; NG; RA; RBA; ROI; SAC
Bibliog: DBA; WOOD

MOORE, Theo, A.A.S., B.W.S., P.C.A.S. b. 1879
Ravensbourne, Maldon Road, Wallington 1885–1897
Claremont, Stanley Park Road, Wallington 1897–1929
Born in Birmingham in 1879, Theo Moore came to live
in Wallington when she was six years old. The Moore
family remained in the area for over forty years, living
first in Maldon Road and then in Stanley Park Road.

Theo studied art in Paris, and attended various art
schools in this country, including one at St Ives,
Cornwall, and the Spenlove School of Art; she also
studied privately under Sir Alfred East, R.A. and
Terrick Williams, R.A. She enjoyed a successful career
as a landscape painter in oil and watercolour and
eventually became the Principal of the Cathcart School
of Modern Painting, and the President of the Cathcart
Art and Flower Society.

Her work was shown at the Royal Academy and
other galleries, a number of her paintings being hung
at the Society of Women Artists' exhibitions, where
two of her titles were: *A Moonlit River*, a watercolour,
and *Pont du Cheval*, an oil, both shown in 1911.

Exhib: AB; P; RA; ROI; SWA
Bibliog: DBA; GW; *Who's Who in Art* – several editions

MORGAN, Mary Elizabeth Taylor b. 1869
Cartref, 84 Mulgrave Road, Sutton – intermittently from
1880–1928
Mary E. T. Morgan, who studied art at L'Academie
Julian in Paris, was a niece of the Perrotts: Edmund
Perrott, a Sutton architect, and his wife Louisa. She
was born, like her aunt, at Caernarvon in North
Wales. The Perrotts, with no children of their own,
virtually adopted Mary, who was living with them at
the time of the 1881 census and again in 1896, when
her painting *Reverie* was hung at the Royal Academy.
Mary Morgan also exhibited in her native Wales (at the
Royal Cambrian Academy) and at the Royal Hibernian
Academy.

Her aunt and uncle were leading citizens of Sutton.
Louisa Perrott was Secretary of the Sutton branch of
the Primrose League and earned the admiration of
William Lewis Hind (q.v.), who dedicated one of his
poems to her. Edmund died at Sutton in November
1914, his wife at Littlehampton, Sussex, in December
1928. Their favourite niece, Mary Taylor Morgan,
inherited their house in Mulgrave Road, but does not
appear to have lived there after her aunt's death.

Exhib: RA; RCamA; RHA
Bibliog: DBA; V: WOOD

MORRIS, William 1834–1896
William Morris, who was one of the most remarkable
men of the nineteenth century, had many talents, but
we are concerned here with his skills as an artist,
craftsman and designer. He was influenced by John
Ruskin (q.v.), and after visiting churches in 1854/5 he
decided to become an architect. He entered the office
of George E. Street where he met and formed a lasting
friendship with Philip Webb (q.v.).

In 1861 he founded the firm of Morris, Marshall,
Faulkner and Co. (later Morris & Co.) which described
itself as 'Fine Art Workmen in Painting, Carving,
Furniture and the Metals'. The firm also produced
stained glass, tapestries and, later, fabrics and
wallpaper.

The organ-loft at St Mary's Church, Beddington,
was decorated by Morris & Co. in 1869 and is painted
with flowers and figures in the style of a minstrels'
gallery. Morris was also responsible for the interior
decoration and furnishings at no. 19 Park Hill, Carshalton (see Philip Webb (q.v.)) but they have not,
unfortunately, survived.

The firm of Morris & Co. continued to make stained
glass long after the death of William Morris. There is a
late example in St Barnabas Church, Sutton, dated
1938, which illustrates the *Sermon on the Mount*. Other
Morris & Co. windows, at All Saints' Church,
Benhilton, were destroyed during the war in 1944.

Jean M. Moore

Bibliog: SEWTER, A. *The Stained Glass of William Morris and*
his Circle. Yale, 1974

MOSTYN, Marjorie Florence, R.Cam.A., S.W.A. 1893–1979
Trelawney, 33 St James Road, Sutton 1917–1935
142 Mulgrave Road, Cheam 1935–1938
The Liverpool-born artist Tom Mostyn, R.B.A.,
R.O.I., who moved south to live in St John's Wood,
had three attractive, talented daughters: Ida, Marjorie
and Dorothy, who are featured in two of his oil
paintings, *The Hill Top* and *The Critic* (illus. in *The*
Studio, May 1912, pp. 268 and 269). They all, like their
father, became artists.

Marjorie Florence Mostyn was born on 31 August
1893. Educated privately, she then attended St John's
Wood Art School and proved to be one of its most
promising pupils. In 1912 she entered the Royal
Academy Schools where she met her future husband,
Leonard Fuller (q.v.). By coincidence, they both won
travelling scholarships and silver and bronze medals.
Their romantic, wartime wedding took place in 1917
when Leonard was serving in the forces; and for many
years they lived with Leonard's parents in St James
Road, Sutton. Marjorie exhibited a portrait of
Leonard's mother at the RA in 1916: *The Artist's Mother*
(Mrs I. Fuller).

More fortunate than many women artists of that
time, Marjorie was able to continue her career after her
marriage, painting portraits, flower studies and
interior scenes in oil and watercolour, her special
talent for interior design coming through in her
paintings. Her tutors at the RA Schools were John
Singer Sargent, R.A., George Clausen, R.A. and
William Orpen, R.A., all eminent portrait painters.
Gradually, Marjorie herself became recognised for her
sensitively painted studies of women and children,
and during the 1920s she designed a series of
'glamour' postcards for Raphael Tuck: *Girls of Today,*
Jewel Girls, Fair daughters of Eve and *Dream of Fair*
Women.

Known as 'Nancy' to her family and friends, she
lived in this area until 1938, when she and her

husband moved to Cornwall. Pretty, vivacious and good-humoured, she was a leading light of the Sutton Amateur Dramatic Society, tackling her roles with energy and enthusiasm. A very talented actress, almost of professional standard, she portrayed a wide variety of characters and continued her interest in amateur dramatics when she later lived in Cornwall. Stored away at St Ives are some photographs of the Fullers, showing them in their various dramatic roles, some even dating back to their Sutton days.

Jointly, Marjorie and Leonard Fuller ran the St Ives School of Painting until Leonard's death in 1973, after which Marjorie, assisted by Roy Ray (the present Principal) carried on alone until 1977. When she retired in February of that year, her students, past and present, gathered at St Ives to pay their respects and to toast her in champagne. For almost forty years she had played an important role in the promotion of artistic ideals in Cornwall, having been a founder member of the Penwith Society of Arts and also a member of the St Ives Society of Artists and the Newlyn Society of Artists.

Signing her work 'Marjorie Mostyn', she exhibited at galleries in this country and overseas. Many of her paintings were hung at the Royal Cambrian Academy, where she was a member. She died at St Ives in 1979, after a short illness.

Exhib: P; RA; RCamA; RP; SWA; Newlyn; St Ives; Penwith
Bibliog: DBA; GW; COYSH; *Who's Who in Art* – several editions; BAKER, D. V. *Britain's Art Colony by the Sea.* George Ronald, 1959

MUMMERY, Horace A. 1867–1951
Walden, 1 Lumley Road, Cheam 1940s–1951
Horace Mummery was a landscape painter in watercolour, influenced by Turner, by Brabazon and by the French Impressionists. The last few years of his life were spent in Cheam, where he lived with his sister Una Constance Tilney and her husband, the artist Frederick Colin Tilney (q.v.). Tilney and Mummery were sketching companions who often found inspiration in the countryside around Midhurst in Sussex.

Mummery, born in London in 1867, lived in Wood Green for many years. He attended Hornsey Art School where he formed a close friendship with the artist Robert G. D. Alexander, a mutual acquaintance being the highly acclaimed watercolourist Hercules B. Brabazon. Tall, thin and with an amiable disposition, Horace Mummery came from an artistic family. His brother was the architect John Charles S. Mummery, who was also the President of the Royal Photographic Society.

After Horace Mummery died at Cheam in 1951, some of his watercolours found their way to Derek James's antiquarian bookshop in Sutton, where they could be bought for a pound or two each. However, few of his paintings have appeared in the London salerooms since his death, with the result that today he is a somewhat neglected artist. This is a pity. Mummery was a watercolourist of considerable talent, who exhibited at the Royal Academy and other

galleries and who would return from trips abroad to France and Belgium with numerous brightly-coloured sketches painted rather in the manner of Brabazon, but showing more detail.

The late Sir John Witt, a renowned collector of watercolours, owned one of Mummery's paintings. It turned up in Lot no. 8 when the Witt Collection was sold at Sotheby's on 19 February 1987. Horace Mummery is represented in the National Watercolour Collection at the Victoria and Albert Museum by an impressionistic painting entitled *Landscape with Houses and a Rainbow*, donated by his old friend R. G. D. Alexander.

Exhib: RA; RBA; RI
Coll: V&A
Bibliog: DBA; LAMBOURNE; MALLALIEU; WOOD

NASH, Edwin 1814–1884
Edwin Nash, the father of the architect Walter Hilton Nash (q.v.), was the architect of *St Nicholas Church*, Sutton, when it was rebuilt in 1862–4. Erected on the site of a much smaller church, Sutton's parish church is designed in the Gothic style, apart from its spire. Its walls are of flint, with stone cornerings, and its windows are set in stone. A full description of the 'new' church can be found in Church's *Illustrated Sutton*, 1880 (re-published by Derek W. James, Sutton, 1978).

Edwin Nash was responsible for several ecclesiastical designs in the South of England and was often engaged in restoration work. He died in 1884, when an obituary in *The Builder* described him as 'a most excellent man and an architect of no mean power'.

Exhib: RA
Obit: *The Builder*, xlvii, 619, 8 November 1884

*NASH, Joseph, O.W.S. 1808–1878
Joseph Nash, a watercolourist and an architectural draughtsman, was born in Great Marlow, Buckinghamshire, on 17 December 1808, the son of a clergyman. He received his education from his father, who once kept a school at Croydon. Chiefly remembered today for his splendidly detailed views of the Great Exhibition of 1851, and for his numerous lithographed plates of old English mansions, he also illustrated novels and volumes of poetry.

He was a pupil of Augustus Charles Pugin, accompanying him to Paris to make drawings for Pugin's *Paris and its Environs* (1830). He also lithographed the plates for Pugin's *Views Illustrative of Examples of Gothic Architecture* (1830). Elected a member of the Old Water Colour Society in 1842, Nash exhibited with them, at the Royal Academy and at other galleries.

His most famous work was *The Mansions of England in the Olden Time*, published in four volumes. The first part appeared in 1839, to great acclaim. However, because of Nash's other commitments – mainly *Windsor Castle Sketches*, drawn by Royal Command – the last part was not published until 1849. It had a hundred lithographed plates and four decorative title pages, the interior scenes showing the mansions as they would have looked when furnished. Nash chose to set most of them in the Tudor period. His plate entitled *Beddington, Surrey: The Hall*, however, shows the Great Hall furnished with the tables, chairs, Chinese porcelain and family portraits of the early eighteenth century, with a gentleman dressed in the fashion of that time seen writing at one of the tables.

For hundreds of years, Beddington Manor was the home of the Carew family. When Nash visited it the occupant was Admiral Sir Benjamin Hallowell-Carew, who had served with Nelson at the Nile. Later on in the nineteenth century it became the Female Orphan Asylum; today it is Carew Manor School.

When Joseph Nash died on 19 December 1878, his daughter Mary Dorothy, who had cared for him during his last years at Bayswater, inherited all his possessions. His son, Joseph Nash junior, was a landscape painter and illustrator.

Exhib: BI; NWS; OWS; P; RA
Coll: Fitzwilliam Museum, Cambridge; Glasgow AG; Greenwich AG; Levens Hall, Cumbria; Maidstone AG; Sutton LC; V&A
Published: See HOUFE
Illus: See HOUFE
Bibliog: BEN; ENGEN(1&2); HOUFE; LAMBOURNE; LISTER; MACKENZIE; MALLALIEU; WOOD

NASH, Walter Hilton 1850–1927

Southfields, Sutton Common, Sutton pre-1880–1906
Walter Hilton Nash, an etcher and architect, was born in Lewisham in 1850. He was the son of Edwin Nash (q.v.), the architect who designed *St Nicholas Church*, Sutton, when it was rebuilt in 1864. His father took him into his practice as his partner, one of the buildings they designed together being the *Old Vicarage* extension in Lewisham High Street (1879–81). After his father died in 1884, W. H. Nash continued to practice at Adelaide Place, London Bridge.

Shortly before 1880 he settled in Sutton, living in a house called Southfields on Sutton Common, built by and formerly occupied by Anthony Locke, the father of Edward Locke (q.v.). Nash exhibited three architectural designs at the Royal Academy whilst he was living in Sutton: *Residence, Sutton, Surrey* (1889), *Convalescent Home for Ladies, Bognor* (1889) and *Entrance to public building* (1903).

One of his pupils, later his partner, was Lionel G. Detmar (q.v.), who was tragically killed in a riding accident in 1910. Nash retired from practice in 1905 and left Sutton shortly afterwards to live in London. He died at Kensington on 18 December 1927, leaving a widow, Elizabeth Nash.

Exhib: RA
Bibliog: DBA; LISTER; TB

NASMYTH, Patrick Milner, S.B.A. 1787–1831

Patrick Nasmyth, the son of the artist Alexander Nasmyth, was born in Edinburgh on 7 January 1787. A landscape painter like his father, he came to London when he was twenty, and proceeded to paint many views of the London area and the Home Counties. Dorking, Copthorne, Worth, Dulwich, East Grinstead and Carshalton are some of the place-names mentioned in his titles.

Left-handed because of an early accident to his right hand, he was also deaf, and he suffered from ill-health of one form or another throughout his life. His various handicaps tended to make him feel isolated, so to compensate he drank rather heavily. In 1831 he caught a chill whilst painting by the Thames and he died shortly afterwards at Lambeth, his death taking place during a thunderstorm. His friends raised him in bed so that he could watch it. He is buried in St Mary's churchyard, Lambeth.

Influenced by Hobbema and the Dutch School, Nasmyth painted luminous landscapes with fine skies. He was a founder member of the Society of British Artists, exhibiting with them, and also at the Royal Academy and the British Institution. After his death, his paintings rose rapidly in price, by 1848 selling for sums of £200 upwards. When his view entitled *Carshalton Mill* (showing Culver's Mill), painted in 1811, appeared at Tooth's Sale in 1871, it was sold for £288–15–0, a considerable sum in those days. Under its full title, *The Water Mill, Carshalton*, this oil painting is now in the Guildhall, London. A copy of it, painted prior to 1911 by A. F. Compton, is in Sutton's Local Collection. Nasmyth painted another view of Carshalton: in 1833 his oil painting, *View near Carshalton*, lent by G. B. Potts, was exhibited at the SBA's exhibition.

Exhib: BI; RA; SBA; Edinburgh
Coll: Birkenhead AG; Birmingham AG; BM; Fitzwilliam Museum, Cambridge; Nat.AG, Scotland; Newport AG; Sutton LC (copy); V&A
Bibliog: BEN; DNB; SEGUIR, F. P. *Dictionary of the Works of Painters*. 1870; JAMES, R. N. *Painters and their Works*. 1897, 3 vols.

NEEDHAM, Jonathan 1822–1887

3 Sunningdale Villas, Robinhood Lane, Sutton c.1870–1876
Hazeldene, St James Road, Sutton 1876–1887
Reputed to be 'a gentle and retiring man, precise in all his habits', Jonathan Needham was an engraver, a lithographer, a landscape painter in oil and watercolour and a drawing master. Born at Westminster on 10 April 1822, he was educated in Newbury and in Brighton. At the age of fourteen he was apprenticed to Robert Brandard of Islington, one of the finest line-engravers of the nineteenth century. He later took up lithography, when his drawing master was James Duffield Harding, whose most famous pupil was John Ruskin (q.v.). Needham lithographed two plates after Harding: *Dunmoor Castle* and *Goat Fell*; these were registered with the Printsellers' Association and published by Gambart in 1850.

Harding opened Needham's eyes to the beauties of the Surrey countryside, accompanying him on sketching trips to the area around Dorking. One of Needham's earliest attempts at a coloured drawing was a view of Sutton, carried out near the house in St James Road where he later lived. His watercolours were nearly always executed in pencil and coloured washes.

On completing his training, Needham worked for Day & Son, Lithographers to Queen Victoria, staying with the firm for two years (1850–52). He then branched out on his own, doing work for such firms as Marcus Ward & Co., and editing and illustrating *Vere Foster's Drawing Books*. When J. D. Harding died in 1863, some of his pupils transferred to Needham. Amongst them were members of the nobility, who included Lady Sybil Lumley, Lady Georgiana Churchill, the Marquis of Lorne, the Countess of Roslyn and Lady Onslow. Needham was also a drawing master at the military academies of Woolwich and Sandhurst. He abandoned lithography in 1875 to devote more time to teaching and painting.

He often visited Wales, usually staying at Portmadoc. On one such visit he met David Cox at the Royal Oak, Bettws-y-coed; the famous landscape painter gave him some friendly advice and encouragement. But a visit to the West Country nearly ended in tragedy, when the coach in which Needham and his son were travelling overturned at Boscastle, throwing them both out. As if this was not enough, a fall of rock at Lynmouth landed just ahead of where Needham was painting.

Jonathan Needham lived in Sutton for about twenty years, first in Robinhood Lane, next door to the etcher Robert Kent Thomas, and then in St James Road, where his studio window overlooked fields towards Wimbledon. He was a familiar figure to passengers on the train journey from Sutton to London; London was where he gave drawing lessons and carried out his business. He exhibited with the Dudley Art Society, with the Society of British Artists and at the British Institution. A member of the Langham Sketching Club from its early days, he formed friendships there with the artists John Mogford, E. M. Wimperis, William Simpson (the artist/war correspondent) and the marine artist Walter William May, an executor of his will.

Needham, who married twice, was survived by his second wife, Mary Ann, and by his son Henry William Needham. He died at Hazeldene, in St James Road, on 17 January 1887, his final illness brought on by a severe attack of the rheumatism from which he had suffered for many years. Over the years, with a characteristic thoughtfulness, he had put aside some of his best works so that when he died, these could be sold for the benefit of his family. More than a thousand finished works were found in his studio after his death. Today his lithographs, according to their subject matter, sell for between £15 and £300 each.

Exhib: BI; D; SBA
Published: NEEDHAM, J. *Studies of Trees*. Blackie & Sons, N.D.

Bibliog: BEN; ENGEN(1); LISTER; MACKENZIE; WOOD; Surrey Artists and their Homes. VIII.–Mr. J. Needham. *Sutton and Epsom Advertiser*, 10 December 1887

NELSON, Harold Edward Hughes, S.G.A. 1871–1948
Brockenhurst, Prince of Wales Road, Carshalton 1902–1906

Harold Nelson was a painter, an etcher, a designer, an advertising agent and a lecturer. He lived in Carshalton for the brief period of four years, yet during that time he carried out some of his most important work: he published two books, illustrated others and designed many book-plates. Born on 22 May 1871 in Dorchester, a town where Nelsons had lived since the eighteenth century, he trained at Lambeth School of Art and at the L.C.C. Central School of Arts and Crafts, studying etching under Luke Taylor, R.E. at the latter.

He worked as a black-and-white artist for *The Graphic, The Sphere, The Queen* and many other magazines, but is chiefly remembered for his book-plates, his first important one appearing in 1897, inspired by Dürer; many of these plates were illustrated in *The Studio*. Designing both for individuals and institutions, he took pleasure in matching each plate to the name or character of the owner. Thus, on Joan Phillips's book-plate we see St Joan of Arc, on Gerald Knight's a knight in armour. Nelson's book-plate for St Andrew's, his local church at Carshalton, has a simple Celtic design incorporating a drawing of the Scottish saint (illus. in *Harold Nelson; his Book of Book-plates*, 1904). St Andrew's, the daughter church of All Saints', Carshalton, was pulled down after 1958, the priest-in-charge having resigned following a doctrinal disagreement with his superiors. A block of flats was put up on the site. Other local book-plates by Nelson include one for Doris Shorter of Sutton, who must have loved her garden, since she is portrayed standing by a sundial in the midst of flowers; and one for Carshalton's local historian, Dr A. V. Peatling, who appears on his as a medieval bibliophile.

Although Nelson trained in the traditions of William Morris (q.v.), he was able to adapt his style to each new art movement as it came along, entering easily into the spirit of Art Nouveau; then, instead of a chaste medieval damsel, he would draw a seductive enchantress with long, flowing hair, like the one on Charles Alfieri's book-plate (illus. in *The Studio*, March 1918, p. 67). During the 1920s and 1930s he worked in the Art Deco style, his most notable design from this period being his chunky Wembley Lion, backed with a 'setting sun motif', on the British Empire commemorative postage stamps of 1924 and 1925. However, his impressive drawing of St George and the Dragon on the £1 stamp for the Postal Union Congress, 1929, harks back to his earlier style.

Of the several books illustrated by Nelson, one is particularly interesting because of its author, Queen Elizabeth of Roumania. In 1890 she paid a memorable visit to Britain, where in Wales she was made a bard; some streets in Llandudno are named after her. Under the pseudonym 'Carmen Sylva' she wrote a number of books, including a volume of verse, and she chose Harold Nelson and Garth Jones to illustrate the English edition of *A Real Queen's Fairy Book*, published by George Newnes in 1901. The illustrations were described in *The Studio* as 'clever, powerful and beautiful'.

On the commercial side, Nelson did advertising work for Selfridge's, Dewar's and Cadbury's, his style becoming simpler as the years went by. Several examples of his work can be found at the headquarters of the Art Workers' Guild in London, where he served as Secretary for many years; after his death his wife Margaret took over this duty. Nelson lived in London for most of his life and died suddenly, in Regent Street, on 25 February 1948, leaving a widow and a daughter, Winifrede.

Exhib: AWG; L; RA; RI; RMS; SGA
Coll: AWG
Published: NELSON, H. *His Book of Book-plates*. Otto Schulze, 1904; *25 Designs by H. N.* Otto Schulze, 1904
Illus: See HOUFE; and PEPPIN
Bibliog: BEN; DBA; GW; HOUFE; PEPPIN; V; WOOD; *Who's Who in Art*, 1929; HORNUNG, C. P. *Book-plates by Harold Nelson*. Batsford, 1929
Obit: *The Times*, 28 February 1948

NICHOLSON, Alexander 1815–1887
Robinhood Lodge, Robinhood Lane, Sutton pre-1864–1871
Winterbourne, Reigate Road, Sutton 1878–1885

Alexander Nicholson, born in Scotland in the year of Waterloo, would today be described as a 'Sunday Painter'. He was a wealthy shipowner, stone merchant and ship insurance broker who traded with his partner, George Allen, at 66 Mark Lane, London; and who painted watercolours as a change from making money. Nicholson exhibited with the Society of British Artists and at the Royal Institute of Painters in Water-Colours.

He married Annabella Bessie Harriett Colclough, who had been born in Canada, and they came to live in Sutton in about 1864, when they already had four children: three boys and a girl. Their youngest, Ellen, was born at Robinhood Lodge, Robinhood Lane, shortly after the family arrived in Sutton. In 1871 they moved to Caterham and after that lived in Kent for a brief period. They returned to Sutton in 1878, when they moved into Winterbourne, a large house in the Reigate Road. Reigate Road has since been renamed Brighton Road and there is now a block of flats called Winterbourne, close to the site of Nicholson's old home.

One of Nicholson's friends, and his senior by a year, was John Henry Mole, the Vice-President of the RI. They used to paint together in the Dorking area of Surrey. Mole, an artist by profession, exhibited well over a hundred works at the major galleries, whereas Nicholson exhibited a mere handful – some views of Surrey, Devon and the Lake District – his shipping and other interests taking up most of his time.

Two years before he died, Alexander Nicholson left Sutton to live in Barnes, Surrey, again naming his house Winterbourne. He died at Barnes on 10 September 1887, aged seventy-two.

Exhib: RBA; RI
Bibliog: DBA; WOOD

NORTON, Charles William, R.I., R.Cam.A., A.R.W.A. 1870–1946
68 Malden Road, Cheam c.1940–1946

Charles William Norton, a landscape and genre painter in oil and watercolour, was born in Beverley, Yorkshire, in 1870, and studied art at the Regent Street Polytechnic and at L'Academie Julian in Paris. He was a member of the Royal Institute of Painters in Water-Colours, the Royal Cambrian Academy and the London Sketch Club; and was an Associate of the Royal West of England Academy.

He exhibited eleven paintings at the Royal Academy between 1912 and 1934, two of these being: *"Lapt in oblivion sweet, forgetful of the day"* (1919) and *A joy for ever* (1928). Although his work rarely appears on the market, in 1979 *"Oh, merry goes the time when the heart is young"* (RA: 1919) was sold at Sotheby's Belgravia for £220.

Charles Norton's final days were spent in Cheam, where he is said to have found inspiration in Cheam Park. Throughout these last years he continued to paint and to enjoy his other main interests, which were gardening and fishing. He died in Sutton District Hospital on 21 November 1946, leaving a widow, Gertrude, and two daughters, his only son having died before him.

Exhib: AR; GI; M; P; RA; RCamA; RI; RWA
Bibliog: DBA; GW; TB; WOOD; *Who Was Who 1941–1950*
Obit: *Sutton and Cheam Advertiser*, 5 December 1946

NOWLAN, Carlotta, R.M.S. 1863–1929
The Elms, London Road, North Cheam c.1881–1929

Carlotta Nowlan, christened at St Pancras Old Church, London, on 26 March 1863, was the daughter of Susannah and Frank Nowlan (q.v.) and the sister of Pauline Nowlan (q.v.) and Rose Kathleen Nowlan. A member of the Royal Miniature Society, she exhibited over a hundred titles at their exhibitions; her diploma painting, *Youth*, a sensitive study of a young woman, is illustrated in *The Art of the Miniature Painter* by G. C. Williamson and P. Buckman (1926). This painting, carried out in the 'mixed method', may be a self-portrait, or perhaps a study of one of her sisters. Queen Mary saw, admired and bought her painting *Monthly Roses*, exhibited at the Royal Academy in 1925; Carlotta's painting *A Bit of Colour* is in the Canadian National Gallery.

For most of her life, Carlotta lived with her family at The Elms, North Cheam; and although she never married, she had numerous interests which, as well as painting, included gardening and music. Some of her miniatures were of her friends and acquaintances in Cheam. In 1899 she exhibited one of *Mrs. Frederick Cavendish Bentinck* at the RA – the Cavendish Bentincks had strong links with Cheam – and in 1900 she exhibited one entitled *Our Rector*. A miniature of *The Rev. A. E. Shewring* was shown at the 1919 exhibition of the RMS.

Two years before she died, she gave Frederick Walker's (q.v.) 'watercolour box for the pocket', left to her by her father, to the Victoria and Albert Museum. She died in New Malden, Surrey, on 23 December 1929, survived only by her sister, Rose Kathleen, the last of the Nowlans to live at The Elms.

Exhib: L; NG; RA; RI; RMS
Bibliog: BEN; DBA; GW; TB; WOOD; *Who's Who in Art*, 1927 and 1929

NOWLAN, Frank 1835–1919
The Elms, London Road, North Cheam c.1881–1919

Frank Nowlan, who lived at The Elms, North Cheam (near to where St Anthony's Hospital is today) for about forty years, was born in County Dublin, Ireland. He came to London in 1857 and studied art at Leigh's Academy, where he formed a friendship with Frederick Walker (q.v.), whose portrait of him, entitled *Frank Nowlan*, carried out in 1858 when they were both students, is in the British Museum. After Walker's untimely death, Nowlan treasured the former's travelling paintbox until he himself died, willing it to his daughter Carlotta (q.v.).

Frank Nowlan's bachelor days came to an end on 10 September 1861, when he married Susannah Maxley at St Pancras Old Church, London. They had three daughters, who all remained spinsters and lived with their parents at Cheam. Nowlan was a genre and portrait painter in oil and watercolour, exhibiting with the Royal Miniature Society and at the Royal Academy and other venues. Apparently, he put much time and effort into the invention of unforgeable cheques. A skilful restorer of miniatures, he was patronised by Queen Victoria and King Edward VII, who bought his paintings and employed him to restore the royal miniatures.

He died at The Elms, Cheam, on May Day 1919. Shortly before he died, his portrait was painted by his daughter Pauline (q.v.), who named it *Eighty-Four* and exhibited it with the RMS in 1920. Two watercolours by Frank Nowlan, both dated 1886, are in the Bethnal Green Museum (Dixon Bequest): *Lady wearing a Lace Veil and holding a Fan* and *Head of a Girl wearing a Yellow Head-dress*. Only a few paintings by Frank Nowlan have appeared on the market since his death; many may still be in private hands. In 1976 his pencil and wash drawing, *His First Story*, was sold at Phillips for £100; and in July 1985 his watercolour *The Village Shop* realised £990 at Sotheby's, Pulborough.

Exhib: RA; RBA; RMS
Coll: V&A (Bethnal Green)
Bibliog: BEN; DBA; FOSKETT; GW; LAMBOURNE; MALLALIEU; WOOD

NOWLAN, Pauline Louise 1867–1922
The Elms, London Road, North Cheam c.1881–1922

Following in the footsteps of her father, Frank Nowlan (q.v.), and her older sister, Carlotta (q.v.), Pauline Nowlan was a talented miniaturist, her sensitive portraits showing an almost photographic quality.

She lived in Cheam with her parents for most of her life, exhibiting at the Royal Academy and with the Royal Miniature Society, her RMS titles including: *Mrs Arthur Brock* (1903), *My Mother* (1903) and *James* (1906). She painted two portraits of her father: *The Artist's Father* (RA: 1913) and *Eighty-Four*, the latter being exhibited at the RMS exhibition of 1920, a year after he had died. Pauline only survived him by three years, dying of cancer on 8 March 1922, aged fifty-five.

Exhib: RA; RMS; RP
Bibliog: DBA

NYE, Elsie Louisa 1876–1956
Camperdown, 56 Woodcote Road, Wallington c.1895–

For over thirty years, Thomas Nye and his family lived in Wallington, in a large house called Camperdown, which has only recently been pulled down to make way for re-development. Nye, a member of the Stock Exchange, had a son and three daughters. His daughter Elsie Louisa, named 'Louisa' after her mother, was an artist who specialised in painting miniatures, although she also painted some full-size landscapes and seascapes in watercolour.

She exhibited six portrait miniatures at the Royal Academy. They were all shown whilst she was living in Wallington, and included one entitled *Hilda* (1906), a miniature of her married sister, Mrs Sydney Holyman, who lived in Stanley Park Road. Two of the others: *Geoffrey* (1909) and *Ralph* (1910) were possibly portraits of Geoffrey and Ralph Dadd, the sons of the artist Frank Dadd (q.v.), whose home at Wallington was quite close to where the Nyes lived. Elsie Nye's seascapes are colourful and lively, somewhat in the style of Charles Dixon. Her watercolour *Mediterranean Coast Scene* was sold at auction in 1980 for £30.

When Thomas Nye died in 1927, his son Gerald inherited Camperdown, continuing to live there with his sisters Elsie and Leila. The sisters later lived in a cottage at Chiddingfold in Surrey. Elsie Nye died on 26 June 1956.

Exhib: AB; RA; RMS
Bibliog: DBA; FOSKETT

OAKEY, Miss H. Exhib: 1923–1924
Mayfield, Christchurch Park, Sutton 1907–1936

Miss Oakey, a resident of Sutton during the first half of this century, exhibited three paintings at the Society of Women Artists' exhibitions: *The Snake Charmer* (1923), *Pirates* (1924) and *Wings of Night* (1924).

Exhib: SWA
Bibliog: DBA

OSMOND, William Henry, S.A.M. 1865–1943
Principal, Sutton and Cheam Art School, 1901–1930
William Henry Osmond enjoyed the distinction of being the first Principal of both the Epsom and the Sutton Art Schools, Epsom being founded first in 1896. A few years later, in 1901, an art school was established at the Sutton County School for Boys, later transferring to the Institute in Throwley Way. Since at that time neither school provided full-time tuition, Osmond was also able to teach art at Epsom County School for Boys. When he retired in July 1930, David Birch was appointed Principal at Epsom and Miss Howard-Mercer (q.v.) took over at Sutton.

Osmond, a member of the Society of Art Masters, was an examiner to the Science and Art Department at South Kensington. He gained medals and other prizes for 'architectural drawing', 'modelling' and 'figure painting'; and taught a wide variety of subjects, which included clay modelling, geometrical drawing and general art work. Amongst his many pupils were the late David Birch (his successor at Epsom), and the politician, the late Rt. Hon. James Chuter Ede, who was one of Epsom and Ewell's most famous citizens – born there in 1882, Charter Mayor in 1937 and later an Honorary Freeman of the Borough.

During the 1890s, Osmond lived in Fulham; but he later moved to Epsom, living at Inglefield Cottage, St Martin's Avenue, until his death on 22 April 1943. He left a widow, Bertha Emily Osmond.

Source: Epsom School of Art and Design archive

PACE, Percy Currall 1871–1945
Malvern Villa, Worcester Road, Sutton 1871–c.1880
16 Maldon Road, Wallington 1942–1945
Percy Currall Pace, an artist in oil and watercolour, was born in Sutton in 1871, the son of Alfred Octavius Pace, a Brighton-born banker's clerk who had settled in Sutton shortly before 1869. Percy lived at Malvern Villa in Worcester Road for the first nine years of his life, until his family moved to Redhill in Surrey.

He was educated at Reigate Grammar School for Boys, excelling at both science and art, years later being granted two patents for 'hydraulic-petrol-air-gas machines'. He studied art at the Royal Academy Schools, and also attended Croydon Art School, under Walter Wallis, the headmaster there for over forty years. Pace carried off the most coveted prize of all from Croydon when he married the head's daughter, Elsie Dora Wallis, one of the first women to exhibit with the Surrey Art Circle (q.v.); Pace himself was a member of the Art Circle from 1900 until the late 1920s. They were married at St Peter's Church, South Croydon.

Walter Wallis appears to have made a habit of encouraging his most promising pupils to attend the Antwerp Academy. His son-in-law was no exception and benefited from tuition at this famous establishment which had a reputation for producing fine landscape painters. Pace carried out many landscapes, but was a skilful portrait painter as well, and also produced some fine still-life studies, some of which were exhibited at the RA, including: *Mushrooms* (1926), *The copper pot* (1927) and *Bread and Honey* (1935). He once shared an exhibition at the Ryder Gallery, London, with his friend of Croydon Art School days, Joseph F. Percy Rendell, showing views of Surrey and Sussex.

The Pace family spent many years in Sussex, where Percy was a member of the Brighton Arts Club. Living first in Steyning (where Pace conducted outdoor painting classes during the summer months) and then in Eastbourne, their various homes were always tastefully furnished and contained an abundance of books, statuary and antiques. A few years before his death, Pace returned to the area of his birth and lived in Wallington, where he died on 26 August 1945, survived by his widow and his two daughters. He is buried in Bandon Hill Cemetery.

Exhib: B; GOU; L; LS; M; P; RA; ROI; SAC; Brighton; Eastbourne; Ryder Gallery, London
Bibliog: DBA; GW; V; WOOD; *Who's Who in Art*, 1929
Obit: *Sutton and Cheam Advertiser*, 30 August 1945

PEAKE, Mervyn Lawrence 1911–1968
Woodcroft, 55 Woodcote Road, Wallington 1922–c.1932 and 1952–1960
Mervyn Peake is perhaps best known as a novelist; the author of *Titus Groan*, *Gormenghast* and *Titus Alone*. However he was a man of intense creativity and his artistic achievements encompassed not only novel-writing but also short-story writing, the writing of plays and, above all, the arts of drawing and painting. It is these latter on which this entry concentrates.

The artist was the younger son of Congregational medical missionaries, Dr Ernest Cromwell Peake and Amanda Elizabeth Peake (née Powell), and was born on 9 July 1911 at Kuling in the province of Kiang-Hsi, China. His artistic ability, which does not seem to have been inherited, showed itself early in a compulsive talent for drawing and a keen interest in colours and shapes of objects. It is very likely that his unusual and individual artistic vision had its roots in the circumstances of his early life.

In 1922 the family returned to England on leave but, since Mrs Peake was in poor health, they decided to remain. Dr Peake bought a practice at Wallington and the family moved to a large Victorian house named Woodcroft which was at 55 Woodcote Road – now the site of a block of flats, Surrey Court.

The following year Mervyn Peake went as a boarder to Eltham College where his brother Leslie was already a pupil. The artist showed himself a good athlete, cricketer and rugby player, but his academic abilities did not match his sporting skills, although the art master believed him to be a genius.

School-days ended in 1929 and the young artist enrolled, with family approval, at Croydon School of Art. However in December 1929 he was accepted for a five year course at the Royal Academy Schools, where the art course of the time was extremely conventional, rigid and formal. Peake used to commute daily from Wallington to Piccadilly, and occupied the journey by sketching his travelling companions. He was now eagerly engaged in painting and other artistic activities: in 1930 he illustrated a book by a former school friend, Gordon Smith; in the same year he won the Arthur Hacker prize (a silver medal and thirty pounds) for a painting of a lady in an evening gown; and in 1931 he had a painting *Cactus* accepted for the Royal Academy – the only time he ever submitted work.

From December 1931 to January 1932, together with other young painters comprising the Soho Group, he exhibited twelve paintings at the Regal Restaurant, Greek Street. This was followed immediately by an exhibition at the Wertheim Gallery by the Twenties Group in which Peake showed three paintings. A perceptive reviewer in the *Birmingham Post* advised his

readers to buy the artist's work and, in fact, Peake was able to sell his work at moderate prices. In this year a new field of artistic endeavour for Peake was the designing of costumes for Capek's *Insect Play* which was performed by a repertory company at the Tavistock Little Theatre in November. In June the Wertheim Galleries put on a second exhibition by the Twenties Group, including a portrait *The wild duck* by Peake, who now decided to leave the Royal Academy Schools.

Mervyn Peake now moved to Sark in the Channel Islands where there was an artistic community and exhibition gallery. The first exhibition in the gallery commenced on 30 August 1933 and included twenty-three pictures by Peake which were enthusiastically reviewed by the local papers. This led to an exhibition of 'Paintings by the Sark Group' at the Cooling Galleries, New Bond Street in May 1934, followed immediately by a 'First exhibition, second season' at the Sark Gallery in May and June 1934.

In April 1935 Peake exhibited a painting at the Royal Society of British Artists' Exhibition. Later that year he took up the post of teacher of life drawing at Westminster School of Art which necessitated his return to London. While teaching at the school he met his future wife Maeve Gilmore, who was a pupil; they became engaged in 1936 and were married in December 1937.

In 1936 Peake underwent an appendectomy performed by his father at the Cottage Hospital, Carshalton. Artistic activities continued with a revival of the *Insect Play* at the Little Theatre by Nancy Price, whom Peake persuaded to use his designs from the earlier production, which were praised by James Agate. Following this he was invited to design

MERVYN PEAKE Indian ink 182×115mm.
Illustration from *The Hunting of the Snark*.
Reproduced by permission of the Mervyn Peake Estate

costumes for a play at the Arts Theatre Club.

March 1938 saw Peake's first one-man exhibition which was held at the Calman Gallery, St James's Place and included oils, watercolours, sketches and some drawings of monsters. Then from 22 February to 10 March 1939 there was an exhibition of drawings and portraits at the Leicester Galleries, which sold well and brought some publicity. In June 1939 the Delius Giesse Gallery, Bennet Street, St James's had an exhibition 'Satirical drawings of our time' which included some work by Peake. A summer exhibition at the Leicester Galleries included a *Nude figure* by Peake. The same gallery held an exhibition in December 1939 entitled 'Six by eight' which also contained work by the artist. At about this time *Captain Slaughterboard drops anchor*, a children's book with text and illustrations by Mervyn Peake was published, to mixed reviews.

With the outbreak of the Second World War, the Westminster School of Art moved to the country, which meant the loss of the teaching post. In October 1939 Peake's mother died, and just after Christmas he and his wife moved to Sussex where their first son was born on 7 January 1940. Peake now tried for an appointment as a war artist but without success; soon he was called up for the Royal Artillery and on 29 July 1940 was posted to an anti-aircraft establishment on the Isle of Sheppey, the first of several inappropriate and unsuitable postings which culminated in a nervous breakdown and discharge on medical grounds on 30 April 1943.

During his army service Peake managed to continue his artistic work with book illustrations and had an exhibition of drawings at the Leicester Galleries. Various employments followed the end of his army career. For a time he worked for the Ministry of Information for whom he did paintings, drawings and propaganda leaflets. During June 1944 some of his paintings were exhibited at Peter Jones department store in Sloane Square and he continued with book illustrations.

At last, after the war had ended in 1945, Peake was appointed as an accredited war artist commissioned to tour Western Europe. He brought back many drawings, but one legacy of his visit seems to have been the shattering effect on his mind of conditions in Germany and, more particularly, the Belsen Concentration Camp.

From 1946 to 1949 the Peake family lived in a large house on Sark but this proved to be too expensive and too remote from London, and in the autumn of 1949 they returned to England where the artist took up a teaching post at the Central School of Art, Holborn. The following year the Peakes bought a large house in Kent but had to sell it within two years when they found the mortgage to be a serious financial burden. When Dr Peake died he left his house in Wallington to the artist, who moved there in 1952. However the Peakes did not enjoy living at Wallington, finding it arid, claustrophobic and culturally isolated, and in 1960 they sold the house for development and moved to Fulham.

Artistically the years 1945 to 1954 were busy and productive with many commissions for illustrations for books and the *Radio Times*, the publication of the artist's own illustrated books, and exhibitions. Recognition came in the form of a feature in *Picture Post*, a BBC talk on his work as an illustrator and a published collection *The Drawings of Mervyn Peake*.

After 1954 there was a lessening of interest in Peake's work, although he had a financially successful exhibition in 1956. It was about this time the first symptoms of illness appeared, in the form of slight tremors in the hands; the disease was at first thought to be nervous in origin, but after the failure of the artist's play *The wit to woo* in 1957, he suffered a complete nervous collapse and Parkinson's Disease was diagnosed. It has been suggested that the illness resulted from an epidemic of sleeping sickness in 1917 during Peake's boyhood in China, although he did not become ill then; or that it was the delayed result of a mild attack of encephalitis when he was twenty-two. Despite the illness, which confused his mind and eventually made it physically impossible for him to draw, Peake managed to produce two further works before lapsing into illness and obscurity. He spent the remaining years of his life in nursing homes until his death in November 1968.

Mervyn Peake was a many-talented artist of enormous creativity; John Watney in his introduction to *Peake's Progress* compares him to William Blake, but Blake with a sense of humour, while his compulsive childhood enthusiasm for drawing reminds one of the young Bewick obsessively drawing on any available surface, or Turner continually sketching as he travelled around. Peake's boyhood in the strange surroundings of China clearly influenced his work both on the surface and at deeper psychological levels: the many strange creatures that he drew, and which a critic described as 'at the same time terrifying and captivating' could perhaps be seen as descendants of Chinese dragons; the atmosphere of grotesque fantasy that pervades much of his work probably results from the juxtaposition of Western and Eastern cultures, from living in a small European community surrounded by the strange, alien and half-understood Chinese world. However grotesqueness and fantasy are not the only elements in Peake's work; it is also informed with tenderness and sympathy as can be seen particularly in his drawings of children; with humour as in his children's books and the illustrations to *Droll Stories*; with a sinister atmosphere, as in his illustrations to *Treasure Island* and *Dr Jekyll and Mr Hyde*, which complements perfectly the feeling of the books. It is this genius for complementing a book which makes Peake such a great illustrator; as he said in a radio interview, the artist had to be a good designer and draughtsman with passion and compassion 'but above all things there must be the power to slide into another man's soul', and in pursuit of this power he studied the work of the great illustrators – Rowlandson (q.v.), Cruikshank, Hogarth, Blake, Doré, Dürer and Goya whose influences can be detected in all his work. However Peake was no mere imitator, he was a unique artist with a moving, intensely personal vision which captivates and fascinates and is certain to be valued more by posterity than in his life-time.

Patrick Ford

Exhib: LEI; RA; RBA; Soho Group; Sark Group; Twenties Group
Published: PEAKE, M. *Rhymes without Reason.* Eyre & Spottiswood, 1944; *Letters from a Lost Uncle.* Eyre & Spottiswood, 1948; *Captain Slaughterboard Drops Anchor.* Academy Editions, 1967; *A Book of Nonsense.* Peter Owen, 1972. Collected works: *The Drawings of Mervyn Peake.* Davis-Poynter, 1974; *Peake's Progress: selected writings and drawings.* Academy Press, 1974
Illus: See PEPPIN
Bibliog: BEN; DBA; GW; PEPPIN; TB; *Who's Who in Art,* 1934; GILMORE, M. *A World Away.* Gollancz, 1970; WATNEY, J. *Mervyn Peake.* M. Joseph, 1976

PERCY, Amy Dora b. 1860

Woodseat (later 34) Mulgrave Road, Sutton 1879–1886

Amy Dora Percy, the youngest daughter of the artist Sidney Richard Percy (q.v.), was herself an artist of sufficient merit to have one painting hung at the Royal Academy and three at the Society of British Artists' exhibitions, all shown whilst she was living in Sutton. Two were West Country scenes: *Fish Street, Clovelly* (SBA: 1883) and *At Stragnel, Cornwall,* which was 'hung on the line' at the RA in 1884.

She was born in Wimbledon in 1860, and her birth was registered as 'Amy Dora Percy Williams', since her father was a member of the famous 'Williams' family of painters. However, like most of that family, she dropped the 'Williams' from her name. After her marriage to Frederick Reynolds, a prominent Quaker, she concentrated on writing novels and became more famous as a novelist (writing under her married name 'Mrs Fred Reynolds') than as an artist.

Her first book was published in 1890, her last, when she was in her seventies, in 1936. At least two of the many works by Mrs Fred Reynolds which are listed in the British Museum *Catalogue* have Quaker themes: *Quaker Wooing* and *The Lady in Grey.* During the early years of the present century she lived in Yorkshire, where her address was 'Hill Carr, Ilkley' (*Literary Yearbook,* 1907). Her elder son, who had studied at Newlyn under Stanhope Forbes, R.A. was, like so many other promising young artists, killed during the First World War.

Amy's granddaughter, Jan Reynolds, has given us a fascinating account of this remarkable family in her book *The Williams Family of Painters,* Antique Collectors' Club, 1975.

Exhib: RA; SBA
Bibliog: DBA; WOOD

PERCY, Herbert Sidney b. 1863

Woodseat (later 34) Mulgrave Road, Sutton 1879–1886

Herbert Sidney Percy, the younger son of Sidney Richard Percy (q.v.), was born in Great Missenden, Buckinghamshire in 1863. He lived with his parents until 1886, the year his father died.

When the Percys came to live in Sutton, Herbert was still in his teens and about to embark on a career in which he was following in the footsteps of his father, his grandfather and numerous other relatives. In 1880 his watercolour *The brook that brawls along the wood,* sent in from Sutton, was hung at the Society of British Artists' exhibition, the first of eight he exhibited with them up to 1885.

He painted far fewer works than his father, and never quite reached the same standard in landscape painting, tending instead to specialise in genre studies. Some charming, if rather sentimental pictures with titles like *Sunshine and Shadow* (RBA: 1884) and *Days that are no more* (RBA: 1885) came from his brush. *Tea Time,* an oil on canvas (illustrated in the *Antique Dealer and Collectors' Guide,* December 1983) is a typical example of his style; it shows a little girl totally absorbed in the task of giving tea to her dolls. Later on in his career he was a successful picture restorer and worked on some of the country's important collections.

After his father died, the Sutton house was sold and the family went their separate ways, Herbert, a lifelong bachelor, living in London. He submitted his only Royal Academy picture, *The top of the village* (1900), from an address in Shepherd's Bush. He had a large circle of friends, who included the writer G. K. Chesterton, and he enjoyed a reputation as a raconteur. He died at Hammersmith during the 1940s.

Exhib: L; M; NG; RA; RBA; ROI
Bibliog: DBA; WOOD; REYNOLDS, J. *The Williams Family of Painters.* Antique Collectors' Club, 1975

PERCY, Sidney Richard 1821–1886

Woodseat (later 34) Mulgrave Road, Sutton 1879–1886

Sidney Richard Percy Williams, born in Lambeth in 1821, was a member of the Williams family of painters. However, to avoid confusion with all the other artists of that surname exhibiting in Britain during the nineteenth century, he dropped the 'Williams' to become Sidney Richard Percy.

The artists James Ward, R.A. and George Morland were his great-uncles. His father was the landscape painter Edward Williams (1782–1855) who, known as 'Old Williams', and held in high regard by his children and grandchildren, lived at no. 32 Castlenau Villas, Barnes, Surrey. It was at Barnes Parish Church, on 30 June 1857, that Sidney Richard Percy married Emily Charlotte Fairlam, the beautiful daughter of Richard Fairlam, a wealthy jeweller. Jan Reynolds relates in *The Williams Family of Painters* how Emily, accustomed to a life-style of fine clothes, large houses and servants, told her father that she would not consider a suitor with less than £2,000 a year. Sidney, thirty-six when he married her, must have fulfilled this requirement since by then he was an established oil painter, who subsequently did all he could to keep her in the style she expected, even if it meant painting the odd 'pot boiler' to pay the bills.

Their first married home, shared with Sidney's brother, Alfred Walter Williams, was Florence Villa in Wimbledon Park. Within six years of marriage five

98

SIDNEY R. PERCY Oil 457×635mm
Cattle in a Highland Valley. 1853. Photo courtesy Sotheby's

children had been born, and they moved to a larger house, called Hill House, in Buckinghamshire, which had splendid views of the surrounding countryside. During this period Emily's extravagances were indulged to the full. The Percys had a carriage and pair, numerous servants and holidayed in Italy with the William Callows who lived close by. Sadly, two of their children died at Hill House and they left Buckinghamshire to live in Redhill in Surrey.

From 1873 until 1879 their home was Bickley Lodge in Meadvale, Redhill. Sidney's brother Alfred was already established in nearby Reigate, and a number of important artists lived in the neighbourhood at that time, including John Linnell and his son-in-law Samuel Palmer. In fact the Percys' home in Meadvale was quite close to Samuel Palmer's.

Sidney Richard Percy's final residence was at Sutton in Surrey. In 1879, with his wife Emily and his surviving children Edith Maud, Amy Dora (q.v.), and Herbert Sidney (q.v.), aged nineteen, eighteen and sixteen respectively, he moved into Woodseat in Mulgrave Road. Although the house was fairly large, the family's life-style was more modest than the one they had enjoyed at Hill House; they employed only two servants, a cook and a housemaid.

Seven years after moving to Sutton, Sidney Percy met with a serious accident. In 1886 he fell from his horse, injuring his knee. The wound failed to heal and infection set in. After an uncomfortable illness, a desperate remedy was suggested. A surgeon was summoned from London to amputate the artist's leg, but the shock of the operation, which took place in a room at Woodseat, proved too great and he died of a heart attack on 13 April 1886. Brief notices of his death 'suddenly at his residence, Woodseat, Sutton, Sidney Percy, aged 64' appeared in the local newspapers, but no mention was made of his artistic reputation. Owing to earlier extravagances, he left less than £1,000. The house was sold and a studio sale of his paintings was held at Christie's on 27 November 1886.

He enjoyed popularity and success in his own lifetime; and today his paintings are experiencing a return to favour, selling for between £2,000 and £6,000, sometimes more. Sidney Percy's finely-detailed lake and mountain views of Devon, the Lake District and Wales are well-designed, atmospheric, nearly always serene. Although his skies often threaten a storm, he seldom, if ever, painted one. His paintings have a photographic quality; this is hardly surprising since he took up photography during the 1850s and had his own darkroom at Hill House.

He was a prolific artist, exhibiting hundreds of paintings, the majority of which were shown at the Society of British Artists' exhibitions. Purchasers were as diverse as the Maharaja of Baroda and the City Art Gallery, Salford. Although he lived in the South of England all his life, there are remarkably few paintings by him of this area. One or two of Dorking were exhibited, some of Wimbledon, some of Kent, and one with the title *Near Reigate, Surrey* (SBA: 1859).

His very last painting, *Llyn Idwal, North Wales*, was hung at the Royal Academy in 1886, shortly after he died. Woodseat, his home at Sutton, was demolished in August 1969.

Exhib: L; M; RA; SBA; TOO
Coll: Bath AG; Hull AG; Leeds AG; Leicester AG; Nottingham AG; Sheffield AG; Sunderland AG; York AG; Montreal AG, Canada; Baroda, India
Bibliog: BEN; DBA; TB; WOOD; REYNOLDS, J. *The Williams Family of Painters*. Antique Collectors' Club, 1975

*POLLARD, James 1792–1867

One of the most famous of all English coaching artists, James Pollard, was born in London in 1792, the son of Robert Pollard. Robert was born and brought up in Newcastle but came to London to study engraving under Isaac Taylor, got married and settled in Islington where he started up his own engraving business.

Islington was well placed for the young James Pollard to watch the comings and goings of the stage coaches, and by 1820 he was specialising in coaching scenes, exhibiting his first at the Royal Academy in 1821. The famous Newcastle engraver Thomas Bewick, Robert Pollard's friend, sent James advice on how to paint the legs of galloping horses, a tricky problem before the age of photography.

At first James Pollard worked for his father, but he later branched out on his own, taking commissions from dealers and private collectors alike. Until 1840 he was very successful. But in 1840 his wife Elizabeth (née Ridley), whom he had married in 1825, died; so too did his youngest daughter. This double tragedy plunged him into a grief from which he never fully recovered. His work suffered in consequence and never quite reached the standard of earlier years. He died at Chelsea in 1867.

He knew this part of Surrey well. James Pollard's best known works of this area – apart from his many paintings of the Epsom Races – are *The Lord Nelson Inn, Cheam* and *The Cock at Sutton* (from the series 'Scenes on the Road, or a Trip to Epsom and back'), painted in 1838 and later engraved by J. Harris; both the original oils are now in America, privately owned. Fishing was his favourite form of relaxation and he painted a series of fishing scenes by the River Wandle. One particularly interesting title is his oil *Fishing for Trout at the Pinch of Snuff Inn, Beddington*, dated 1839. This is the only mention we have that there was once an inn of that name, and Pollard may well have used artistic licence for his title. If it ever existed, the Pinch of Snuff Inn might have taken its name from the snuff mill on the bank of the Wandle at Beddington, owned at the time by the Lambert family. The painting itself, originally in the A.N. Gilbey collection, was sold at Christie's on 25 April 1940. Other titles in this series include *Fly Fishing for Trout at Beddington Corner*, and *Trout Fishing at Beddington Corner*, both oils, and both undated.

Because they show such fine detail, James Pollard's paintings are of great interest and importance to historians. More than three hundred of his works were engraved: a hundred and forty-six by Pollard himself, the rest by R. Reeve, Charles Hunt and John Harris.

99

Exhib: RA
Coll: BM; Museum of London; National AG, Scotland;
Sutton LC; Tate AG
Bibliog: BEN; ENGEN(1); MACKENZIE; MITCHELL; TB;
WOOD; SELWAY, N. C. *The Regency Road; the Coaching Prints
of James Pollard.* Faber, 1957; *James Pollard 1792–1867 . . .* F.
Lewis, 1965

POLLENTINE, Richard John b. 1830

Richard John Pollentine, a member of the Pollentine
family of artists – Alfred was the most famous – was a
painter of animals, game and landscapes. Born in
London in 1830, he was the son of William and
Caroline Pollentine, and the brother of the shipping
and coastal painter William Henry Pollentine.

Living in London with his wife Mary and son
Richard, he made frequent sketching trips to the
Surrey countryside and was one of the many artists
who found that a popular – and lucrative – subject to
paint was 'fishing for trout in the River Wandle'. James
Pollard (q.v.) painted several versions. Richard
Pollentine was responsible for at least two: *Trout from
the River Wandle*, shown at the British Institution in
1857 and *A Trout Stream, Surrey*, exhibited at the Royal
Academy in 1858.

The River Wandle was famous for its trout, but by
the end of the nineteenth century their number was
dwindling rapidly. In 1914, before he drowned on the
Lusitania, Charles Dingwall of Shepley House,
Carshalton, told the local historian Dr Peatling that he
used to take five hundred trout each year from the
Wandle on his estate, but since the tarring of the roads
the fish had gradually died off (Jones).

A stuffed trout in a glass case in Sutton's Local
Collection has a label which informs us that it was one
of the last trout caught on the Wandle before they were
all killed off by pollution.

Exhib: BI; RA; SBA
Bibliog: BEN; WOOD

*PORDEN

A watercolour entitled *Cheam School*, signed 'Porden',
was painted either by William Porden, a distinguished
architect and a pupil of James Wyatt (1746–1813); or by
his nephew Charles Ferdinand Porden (1790–1863); or
by some other, as yet unrecorded, 'Porden'. The
favoured candidate is William Porden, an
acquaintance of Jeffry Wyatville (1766–1840), the
architect of Samuel Farmer's Gothic-style mansion
Nonsuch Park, Cheam; he may have visited Cheam
with him.

William Porden, born in Hull in about 1755, died in
London in 1822. His designs are mostly in the Gothic
style, but for his most important commission, *Eaton
Hall* in Cheshire, he used the Greek Revivalist style.
From 1778 until 1813 he was a frequent exhibitor at the
Royal Academy, but was an unsuccessful candidate
for the associateship. A vast quantity of his original
designs are housed in the RIBA Library.

Exhib: RA
Coll: Croydon PL; RIBA; Sutton LC
Bibliog: COLVIN; DNB; TB

POTTER, Frank Hayden, N.S. 1896–1979

3 Lewis Road, Sutton 1896–1908
Cobo, Benhill Avenue, Sutton 1908–c.1918

Frank Potter, artist and art teacher, was born in Sutton
in 1896. His family were then living in Lewis Road but
they later moved to Benhill Avenue. His father was a
builder with a yard in Throwley Way; his grandfather,
who married twice, had a harness shop. Frank could
trace his family back to 1374, when one of his ancestors
was a master craftsman at Cheam. One of his earliest
memories was of seeing his mother receive a telegram
which informed her that her brother had been killed in
the Boer War. Another early memory was of spending
every August by the sea at Littlehampton.

After a happy childhood, some of which was spent
riding his own pony through the lanes of a more rural
Sutton, he entered Sutton County School for Boys,
where one of the masters described him as 'a most
intelligent boy but a perfect nuisance', and where he
first developed his interest in art. He later studied at
Heatherley's, at Westminster, at the Slade and at the
Central School of Arts and Crafts, two of his tutors
being Henry Tonks and Walter Bayes. Frank had a
fund of stories, often risqué, about his contemporaries
at the Slade and the famous models who posed for
them there.

At the start of the First World War, Frank was just
eighteen. He joined the army as a trooper in the
cavalry and spent most of the war in France where he
experienced the horror of the trenches. After the war
he taught at Pocklington School in Yorkshire and then
at St Peter's School, York, thereafter maintaining a
strong affection for Yorkshire and its forthright
inhabitants, returning to the county from time to time
on sketching holidays. Between the wars he served in
the army reserves and in 1925 was commissioned in
the 8th Hussars.

In 1929 he was appointed art master at Whitgift
School, Croydon, where he remained until he retired,
introducing new subjects to the curriculum and
achieving an excellent record of scholarships, mostly
in architecture. During the Second World War, when
he did some work for the Baynard Press, he founded a
Department of Typography at the school. He also
inaugurated an art society for Old Whitgiftians called
'The Majorca' after a restaurant, long since gone, in
Brewer Street, London. Speakers at their annual
dinners included Sir John Betjeman, Dame Ninette de
Valois and Denys Sutton.

Frank Potter used to take parties of schoolboys on
cultural trips to France, the country he regarded as his
spiritual home. His affection for France embraced her
art, her literature, her food and wine – Banyuls was his
favourite aperitif – in fact the whole unique ambience
of the place.

In England he wore a beret in the French style,
painted in the manner of Bonnard, Segonzac, Derain
and Sisley, the artists he most admired, and could
extoll at length, to anyone who cared to listen, on the
virtues of the French artists of the nineteenth and
twentieth centuries, whom he admired long before it
was fashionable to do so. He always stayed at the same
hotel in Paris, The Athenée in the Rue de Roch,

which he had first discovered in 1925 and was still recommending to friends in the 1970s.

Mainly a portrait and landscape painter, he exhibited at the London galleries and also with his local art societies, his portrait subjects including politicians, actors and ballet dancers. A portrait which he particularly enjoyed painting was one of Martin Jarvis, an Old Whitgiftian, whose performance as Jon Forsyte in the television drama series *The Forsyte Saga* is still remembered. Not surprisingly, Frank's wife, Ethel Lily Potter, was his model on numerous occasions. His landscapes and interiors were sometimes carried out in pen-and-wash, and show the influence of André Dunoyer de Segonzac, whom he once met in the South of France.

For many years, up to his death, Frank lived in Reigate, contributing to the cultural quality of life there by founding the Reigate Society, and the Reigate Society of Artists, and serving as Chairman of the Civic Society. With one or two others, he was instrumental in persuading the Borough of Reigate to buy Reigate Priory for the town. In 1963 he designed the poster for an exhibition, which he also helped to organise, at Reigate Town Hall, on the lives and works of John Linnell, and Linnell's son-in-law, Samuel Palmer, Reigate's most famous Victorian artists.

During his long retirement he continued to mark examination papers for various boards, and was always full of energy, even after he had passed his eightieth birthday; travelling by train from Reigate to London to paint in his studio and/or visit his club, the Savage. In 1976 he had a one-man exhibition in the Europa Gallery of Sutton Library, and in the same year delivered two lectures at the library – recollections of his childhood and youth in the borough.

He died at Reigate on 9 February 1979 and is buried at Balcombe in Sussex. Reigate paid homage to him in 1984 by inviting Sir Hugh Casson, President of the Royal Academy, to deliver the inaugural lecture of the 'Frank Potter Memorial Fund' at Reigate Priory. Frank's son carried on the artistic tradition by having a position at Agnew's in Bond Street, whilst his daughter, a nurse, had her portrait painted by her father which, entitled *The Artist's Daughter*, was hung at the Royal Academy in 1965.

Exhib: Army Art Society; LG; NEA; P; RA; RP; Sutton PL
Bibliog: GW

*POWELL, Joseph, P.N.W.S. c.1780–c.1834
Joseph Powell was the first President of the New Society of Painters in Water-Colours, his failure to win election to the Old Water Colour Society possibly accounting for the active part he played in the founding of the new one. A drawing master, a topographical artist and an etcher, his dates of birth and death are uncertain: c.1780 for the former and c.1834 for the latter. His charming – though slight – brown-wash drawings of Southern England, Wales and the Lake District were exhibited at various galleries, including the Royal Academy.

Samuel Redgrave, Powell's pupil, who really

JOSEPH POWELL   Pencil drawing 108×152mm
A farm at Carshalton.   Sutton's Local Collection

should have known better, listed him as 'John Powell' in his *Dictionary of Artists of the English School*, 1874. Redgrave's misnomer was continued in later art dictionaries, with the result that until the mistake was spotted by Jonathan Mayne in the 1940s, Joseph Powell's works, including some of those at the Victoria and Albert Museum and at the British Museum, were attributed to a 'John Powell'.

Six of Powell's sketches are in Sutton's Local Collection, one showing the Old Priest's House at Carshalton. Known locally as 'Dame Duffin's Cottage', it stood near All Saints' Church. It was demolished in 1836 to make way for a new building to house the fire engine. Powell's sketch is thought to date from 1792, but if this is correct, then Powell must have been born before 1780, or been a twelve-year-old prodigy when the drawing was carried out. His other sketches at Sutton include two drawings of an unidentified farm at Carshalton, and two drawings of a Carshalton mill, the latter being identified as the snuff mill which was later the Grove Iron works. Shortly before his death, he visited this part of Surrey again, painting *Study of Ashtead Church, Surrey*, and *Study at Leatherhead, Surrey*, both exhibited at Suffolk Street in 1833.

Exhib: AA; NWS; OWS; RA; SBA
Coll: BM; Chester AG; Manchester City AG; National Library of Wales; Newcastle AG; Sutton LC; V&A
Bibliog: BEN; HARDIE; HOUFE; LAMBOURNE; MALLALIEU; WATERHOUSE; WILLIAMS; MAYNE, J. *Joseph Powell. Burlington Magazine*, xc, 1948, pp. 267–8

PROSSER. Henry c.1802–
Henry Prosser, in collaboration with his colleague John Staff (q.v.), enlarged *St Nicholas Church*, Sutton, in 1825. With hindsight, this was largely a wasted effort, since the church was demolished and rebuilt some forty years later.

Prosser lived near Sutton, at Crown Hill, Croydon. In 1822, at the age of twenty, he entered the Royal Academy Schools, and in 1828 his design for a military college was exhibited at the RA. Some architectural drawings by him are in Guildford Library.

Exhib: RA
Bibliog: COLVIN

PUCKLE, Ethel Mary b. 1865
The Grennell, Grennell Road, Sutton c.1876–
Ethel Puckle was born in London in 1865, the daughter of Edmund Puckle, a Sutton insurance clerk. She was the eldest of six children, three boys and three girls, who were brought up mainly by their aunt, their mother having died when they were young. The family lived in The Grennell until about 1923.

In 1885 a painting by Ethel Puckle, entitled *Christmas roses*, was accepted for exhibition at the Royal Academy.

Exhib: RA
Bibliog: DBA; WOOD

REID, Nina Margaret Winder, F.R.S.A., R.S.M.A. 1891–1975
Hawthorndene, 25 Burdon Lane, Cheam 1914–1932
Born in Hove, Sussex, on 26 May 1891, Nina Winder Reid, who studied at St John's Wood Art School, was a well-known painter of landscapes and seascapes, mostly in oil. An exhibitor at most of the major galleries, in 1938 she was a founder member of the Society of Marine Artists (later 'Royal'), showing three paintings at their inaugural exhibition: *The Crested Wave, Atlantic Rollers* and *Atlantic*. In April 1939 an exhibition of her work was held at Walker's Galleries in London, where coastal scenes, mainly of Sussex and priced at between six, and forty guineas each, were shown.

Her strong, vigorous style can be seen in paintings like *Homeward Voyage*, the subject suggested to Nina by a cargo boat she had seen in the South Atlantic. It forms the frontispiece to *The Studio* magazine, March 1934, and conveys so realistically the movement of the sea that one feels sea-sick merely through looking at it. One of her favourite sketching grounds was Cornwall, its wild, rugged coast providing the inspiration for many of her paintings.

For nearly twenty years she lived at Hawthorndene in Burdon Lane, Cheam, a house owned by her father Frederick John Reid, who also owned a property in Norfolk. Reid's only son having died before him, on Reid's death in 1929 Nina inherited Hawthorndene and continued to live there for three more years. She died at Eastbourne, Sussex, in 1975.

Exhib: AR; B; L; P; RBA; RCamA; RHA; ROI; RSA; RSMA; WG
Coll: Kidderminster
Bibliog: DBA; GW; HART (2); TB; V; *Who's Who in Art –* several editions

RICH, Alfred William, N.E.A., I.S. 1856–1921
Alfred Rich was an important, prolific and well-respected watercolourist who lived in Croydon, Surrey, for many years. He appears here because of

two local views, both exhibited at the New English Art Club: *In Beddington Park* (1899) and *On the Wandle* (1901), present ownership unknown.

Influenced by the great landscapist Peter De Wint, but tending to paint in a looser, more impressionistic style, he exhibited at most of the major galleries and wrote a standard work on painting technique: *Watercolour Painting*, Seely, Service & Co., 1918. He died on a painting trip to Tewkesbury in 1921.

Exhib: AG; ALP; BA; CAR; DOW; FIN; GI; GOU; I; L; LEI; M; NEA; RBA; RSA; RWS; WG
Bibliog: BEN; DBA; GW; LAMBOURNE; MALLALIEU; TB; WOOD; LOCK, H. R. Alfred William Rich: water-colour painter. *Walker's Quarterly*, vol. 3, no. 9, 1922–3

ROBERT, Caroline Exhib: 1884–1893
Hartland House, Benhill Wood Road, Sutton 1884–1893
Caroline Robert was the half-sister of a French merchant, Charles Alphonse Robert, who settled in England during the nineteenth century and lived at Hartland House in Sutton from the 1870s until his death there in 1922. Caroline Robert seems to have regarded Hartland House as her own home from about 1884 until 1893, when she moved to Sidcup in Kent. Florence Marlowe (q.v.) was another artist who lived with the Roberts during this period.

A painter of landscape, flower and still-life studies in oil and watercolour, Caroline Robert exhibited nine works with the Society of Women Artists but only one painting at the Royal Academy, *A shady corner in the garden* (1886), possibly inspired by the garden at Hartland House. She eventually married, changing her name to Caroline Moffatt, and had three sons who no doubt occupied so much of her time that she was left with little in which to paint. Her last work was exhibited in 1893, when she was still Caroline Robert. Following the deaths of her half-brother Charles Robert and his wife Juliet, she inherited most of their property at Sutton.

Exhib: RA; SWA
Bibliog: DBA; WOOD

ROBERTSON, Charles Kay Exhib: 1888–1931
The Nest, Park Hill, Carshalton 1898–1900
The Scottish artist Charles Kay Robertson, husband of Jane Kay Robertson (q.v.), lived in Carshalton for about two years, having moved south from Edinburgh, where he exhibited fifty-seven paintings at the Royal Scottish Academy.

Robertson, a painter of portraits and flowers, joined the Surrey Art Circle (q.v.) when he was living in Carshalton, in 1898 exhibiting a portrait entitled *Daughter of G. H. McCausland, Esq.* He moved to Wanstead in 1900, during that year exhibiting a painting entitled *Professor Tobias Mathay, R.A.M.* at the SAC's annual exhibition.

Exhib: GI; L; RA; RSA; SAC
Bibliog: BEN; DBA; WOOD

ROBERTSON, Henry Robert, R.E., R.M.S. 1839–1921

Henry Robertson was commissioned by Alfred Smee, one of the borough's most famous gardeners, to illustrate the latter's book, *My Garden*. Smee, in his preface to the book wrote: 'The artistic drawings of the various views in 'my garden' were made by Mr. H. Robertson and the faithful manner in which Mr. Palmer has rendered them needs no commendation'. One of the most attractive illustrations in the book is Robertson's drawing of a game of croquet.

A watercolourist and an etcher, specialising in Thames scenes, Robertson – like Smee's other illustrator Charles Holloway (q.v.) – lived in the Bloomsbury area of London. He wrote several books on painting technique and died at Brighton on 6 June 1921.

Exhib: B; GI; L; M; NG; RA; RBA; RE; RI; RMS; ROI
Bibliog: BEN; ENGEN(1&2); GW; HOUFE; MACKENZIE; MALLALIEU; WOOD

ROBERTSON, Jane Kay Exhib: 1885–1923

The Nest, Park Hill, Carshalton 1898–1900

Jane Robertson, the wife of Charles Kay Robertson (q.v.), painted portraits and flower studies. She lived in Carshalton for about two years, during this period, in 1898, exhibiting three portrait miniatures at the Royal Academy: *Mrs. Watson, Mrs. John C. Turnbull* and *Elsie, daughter of Professor Bedson*. All her other RA paintings were submitted from addresses in Chelsea and Wanstead.

Exhib: RA; RSA; SWA
Bibliog: DBA

ROBINS, William Palmer, R.E., R.W.S. 1882–1959

Nutford, 69 Benhill Avenue, Sutton 1925–1929

'Not a dilettante but a working craftsman' was how Martin Hardie described William Palmer Robins – a fair appraisal of this etcher, watercolourist, oil painter and teacher who exhibited at the Royal Academy every year except one from 1912 until 1960.

Born in Southwark on 21 July 1882, the son of a schoolmaster, he was educated at Roan's School, Greenwich, where, whilst wandering through the park and strolling by the river, he experienced his first desire to paint. He studied architecture under Banister Fletcher at King's College, London, where he won a silver medal for the history of architecture; and he later attended, at various periods, St Martin's School of Art, the Royal College of Art (under Sir Frank Short, R.A., P.R.E.) and Goldsmiths' College.

Robins, who lived in Sutton during the 1920s, married three times. His first wife, a promising student of sculpture and etching at Goldsmiths', died during the First World War whilst Robins was serving in the forces. Miriam Gladys Matthews was his second wife. His third was the artist Marjory Forbes, a painter of miniatures and pastel studies.

Learning his craft under Sir Frank Short, Robins became an accomplished exponent of the aquatint, the lithograph and the etching, playing his part in the great etching revival which swept through this country during the last quarter of the nineteenth century and reached its peak in the first half of this. He taught at his old school, St Martin's, and also at the L.C.C. Central School of Arts and Crafts, where he was the head of the etching department from 1921 until 1947.

Attracted to architectural subjects such as old mills, bridges, cottages and theatres, he also painted and etched harbour views of Kent, Suffolk and Sussex. His aquatint of a local scene: *Headley Downs*, is illustrated in *The Studio*, April 1913, p. 222. Many honours and awards came his way, including the National silver medal in 1911 and the Logan Medal for Etching (Chicago Arts Institute) in 1925. He was a prolific artist, exhibiting over a hundred works both at the RE and the Fine Art Society; and fifty at the RA. One-man shows were held at London, Edinburgh and New York, and he became well known internationally by exhibiting at Venice, Leipzig, Florence, Paris, Zurich, Los Angeles and Australia.

An accomplished watercolourist, who admired the early masters such as Thomas Hearne, Robins painted in a loose, free style, using a limited palette of about ten colours. Elected a member of the Royal Society of Painters in Water-Colours in 1955, he served as Hon. Treasurer from 1955 until 1958 and devoted the last years of his life to the interests of this society.

His book *Etching Craft* is still a standard work on the subject, and in 1924 he edited *The Artists' London*, in which one of his illustrators was H. M. Livens (q.v.). He died at 16 Fitzroy Square, London on 14 July 1959.

Exhib: CG; FIN; G; GI; I; L; LEI; NEA; RA; RCamA; RE; RHA; RSA; RWS and abroad
Coll: BM; V&A; Uffizi AG, Florence; Congress AG, Washington, U.S.A.
Published: ROBINS, W. P. *Etching Craft*. Bookman's Journal, 1922; *The Artists' London*. John Castle, 1924; *How to Draw Bridges*. The Studio, 1957; *Notes on water-colour*. *Studio*, vol. cvii, no. 492, March 1934, pp. 131–136
Bibliog: BEN; DBA; ENGEN(2); GW; LAMBOURNE; MACKENZIE; TB; V; *Who's Who in Art* – several editions; *Who Was Who 1951–1960*; *Studio*, vol. lviii, no. 241, April 1913, pp. 221–223
Obit: *The Times*, 15 July 1959; BURY, A. Ed. *The Old Water-Colour Society's Club Thirty-Fifth Annual Volume*, London, 1960

ROBINSON, Robert d. 1706

The Painted Parlour at Carshalton House, Carshalton, and the overmantle paintings in the Library and in the Oak Room there, are attributed to Robinson.

Robert Robinson, a mezzotint artist and a decorative painter, was also a master of theatrical illusion, his scenery gracing the stage of Drury Lane Theatre and his 'fantastic' painted rooms enlivening the homes of seventeenth century gentlemen. Robinson would surely have been delighted, had he been alive today, to witness the startling effect two of his rooms, both in schools, have on today's audiences. One is in this borough at Carshalton House (now St Philomena's School). The other is in

London at the Sir John Cass School in Duke's Place, Aldgate.

The greater surprise is at the latter, since this is a fairly typical school of the Edwardian period, and still serves the local population. Visitors arriving to see the painted room often have to pick their way through the hordes of children dashing about the playground, before they can enter the building. Then, walking past classrooms decorated with the usual examples of children's art work, they arrive at a locked room on the ground floor. A man with a key opens it and steps aside to allow the visitors to enter. They are transported, as in a time-machine, to the seventeenth century. Some stand silent in amazement; others gasp involuntarily. For this really is an astonishing room. All four walls are decorated with painted wooden panels, thirty-three in total. One is signed and dated; 'R. Robinson 1696'. The immediate impression is one of colour – a harmonious blending of light greens, yellows and browns.

Gradually the subject matter becomes clear. Against backgrounds of classical architecture, Wren city churches and Chinese pagodas, all kinds of races and improbable beasts disport themselves; with Indians, elephants and rhinos living happily alongside grand European ladies of fashion. The room was originally part of a London mansion in Botolph Lane, built in 1669 and demolished in 1906. The painted room, with its fine fireplace and plaster ceiling, was rescued and placed in the Sir John Cass School, the house in Botolph Lane having belonged to the Sir John Cass Foundation. Robinson's panels and door had become uniformly brown over the years and little could be discerned of their content until 1913, when they were restored by E. W. Tristram. The room now serves as the school's committee room.

The Painted Parlour at Carshalton House is another delightful surprise, and again the way to the room is through classrooms. Carshalton House was built at the beginning of the eighteenth century by Edward Carleton, who possibly bought the paintings from Robinson before the latter died in 1706. The Painted Parlour, a small, intimate room on the ground floor, is approached via the Library and the Oak Room, both these rooms having overmantle paintings attributed to Robinson: the Library has one showing Neptune and Amphitrite, the Oak Room one of a romantic landscape.

Most of the hundred or so panels in the Parlour, which have recently been restored after damage from a burst radiator in 1978, are painted with landscape scenes. The decorative stiles separating them are good examples of chinoiserie and have strong affinities with Robinson's work at the Sir John Cass School. The panels vary in size from a few inches to several feet, three standing out from the rest. One is a bird painting in the style of Bogdany, another a seascape of fighting ships in the Dutch style (recently attributed to Isaac Sailmaker, not Robinson). However, the most striking painting of all is a capriccio of an imaginary house and garden, where figures looking more like cardboard cut-outs than real people are placed at random in the carriageway and gardens. It is stiff and formal

compared with the panels in the Sir John Cass School; yet it does resemble a backcloth for a stage set, and Robinson was, of course, a scene painter.

Other examples of Robinson's style can be seen in a set of panels in Room 56 of the Victoria and Albert Museum, purchased from Christie's auction rooms in 1955. Robinson is also known to have painted a still-life of a fish for the Hall of the Painter-Stainers' Company, of which he was a member.

Robinson was one of the earliest mezzotint artists in this country. Examples of his work, including still-life studies, landscapes, classical subjects and seascapes, can be seen in the British Museum. Some of his mezzotints were engraved after his own paintings, but one entitled *The Bombarding of Diep by their Majities Bomb-ships, 1694*, is after a painting by Col. J. Richards.

His career as a scene painter is known through a contract he entered into with Elkanah Settle in 1699 to paint scenery for Settle's new opera at Drury Lane, Robinson receiving £130 for his efforts.

Little is known about his personal life except that in 1695 the Robinson family – Robert, his wife Elizabeth, his son Samuel and his daughter Sarah – were living in the Parish of St Bride's, Fleet Street, London. Robert was buried at St Bride's Church on 6 December 1706. His name appeared in the minutes of the Painter-Stainers' Company in 1674 when he was made free 'by redemption'. He had eleven apprentices, bound between 1677 and 1699, a Joshua Ross and his own son Samuel amongst them.

Most art dictionaries have dismissed Robinson with a couple of lines or so; but he has become better-known since an article about his work appeared in *Country Life* in 1955, and through his name being mentioned in recent books on decorative painting. Now that his work is more widely known, other examples may come to light. This borough is extremely fortunate in having, still in its original setting, such an important example of Robinson's work within its boundaries.

Bibliog: BEN; TB; TRISTRAM, E. W. A Painted Room of the 17th Century. *Walpole Society Annual Volume*, no. 111, 1914; MURRAY, E. C.–. An English Painter of Chinoiseries. *Country Life Annual*, 1955

ROOKE, Herbert Kerr, R.B.A. 1872–1944
Trenowith, Egmont Road, Sutton 1900–1914

Herbert Kerr Rooke, who trained at the Royal College of Art and at the Slade, was a marine artist, a poster designer and a woodcut artist, his colourful posters of Putney and Greenwich decorating the L.C.C. tram-cars of the inter-war years. Born in Greenwich on 24 December 1872, the son of P. A. Rooke, he was a nephew of the watercolourist Thomas Matthews Rooke (1842–1942) and a cousin of the artist Noel Rooke (1881–1953).

He settled in Sutton in 1900 and lived in a house named Trenowith in Egmont Road until the outbreak of the First World War. Artistically, this was his most creative, most prolific and most successful period. He was already a member of the Royal Society of British Artists when he came to Sutton, and whilst he was living in Egmont Road he exhibited over a hundred works at their exhibitions – sketches, watercolours and oils. Coastal views of Dorset, Hampshire, Sussex and the West Country were amongst them, and also some French and Norwegian scenes. In 1904 his watercolour of a local scene, *Old Cottages, Beddington*, was shown at that year's RBA exhibition.

Rooke had his first Royal Academy acceptance in 1898; in 1901 one of his major works was hung there: *Her late Majesty Queen Victoria's last voyage*, showing the Queen's body being brought back to England from the Isle of Wight.

Soon after the start of the First World War, Rooke left Sutton to live in Wimbledon, where during the war he worked as a turner in a munitions factory. He returned to 'civilian life' in 1918, but from then onwards exhibited far fewer works, having resigned from the RBA in 1912. A woodcut by Rooke, *Steamer at Sea*, is illustrated in the book *Modern Woodcuts and Lithographs by British and French Artists*, The Studio, 1919.

Although Rooke never married – or perhaps because he never married – he had many interests and hobbies. He played the cello, he was a keen cyclist, and he built and sailed model boats. His death occurred at Brixham, Devon, on 22 March 1944. Having no family of his own, he left everything to his cousin, Noel Rooke.

Exhib: GOU; L; M; RA; RBA; RI; London Sketch Club
Bibliog: BEN; DBA; GW; TB; WOOD; *Who's Who in Art* – several editions from 1927 onwards; *Who Was Who 1941–1950*

*ROWLANDSON, Thomas 1756–1827

The best-loved caricaturist and depictor of the comic scene in England is undoubtedly the watercolourist and printmaker Thomas Rowlandson. Born in London in 1756, he spent two years in Paris (1771–2) studying art at the expense of his rich French aunt, and then entered the Royal Academy Schools, where he won a silver medal in 1777. He carried out a vast number of works, ranging in subject matter from large, busy scenes of London life to small pen-and-ink sketches of individual characters. Although he is mostly remembered for his humorous, even bawdy, drawings, he was also capable of producing some fine, serious studies.

His favourite drawing instrument was the reed pen, dipped in black or brown ink and watered down so that it flowed freely. His drawings were then covered over with thin, simple washes of primary colours. Although he was an innovator, whose methods were copied by other artists, his style never changed throughout his life.

Travelling extensively at home and abroad, often with friends, he exhibited at the RA from 1775 until 1787 and was in work almost until the end of his life. He gambled and drank away most of a considerable fortune inherited from his aunt, but still managed to leave £3,000 when he died.

Some of his best known illustrative work was done for Rudolf Ackermann, who published the *Dr Syntax* books. Dr Syntax is thought to be based on the Reverend William Gilpin (q.v.), famous headmaster of Cheam School and exponent of the 'picturesque'. Dr Syntax's first appearance was in *Tour of Dr. Syntax in Search of the Picturesque*, published in book form in 1812. Its success was such that two more adventures were published (in 1820 and 1821). The text was written by William Combe, and Rowlandson etched the plates, which were then hand-coloured according to his instructions.

Rowlandson visited Sutton in 1789, when he and his friend Henry Wigstead were journeying from London to Brighton. Travelling along the old Brighton Road, they wined and dined at all the post houses, and admired the scenery and the barmaids as they went along, eventually arriving at Brighton. The following year they published a book about their travels: *An Excursion to Brighthelmstone in the Year 1789*; Henry Wigstead wrote the text and Rowlandson provided the 'eight engravings in Aqua Tinta from views taken on the road'. Here is Wigstead's description of Sutton:

> The Cock, kept by Fuller, is an excellent Inn, where the Traveller may be supplied with good Chaises, and able Horses. – This village is very pleasantly Situated; and the Air is so pure and Healthy, that with the additional inducement of eating the celebrated Banstead-Down Mutton, many of the Citizens of London resort here on Sunday.

Rowlandson's aquatint of Sutton shows the first Cock Hotel, with a coach and horses by the door, another just arriving. As a contrast to the affluent coach passengers, Rowlandson has placed a poor family travelling on foot in the foreground of his picture. The father, leaning heavily on a stick, carries the baby on his back and is leading a donkey, which bears the weight of the rest of the family. A small dog trails behind the pathetic little group.

The Cock of Rowlandson's day was pulled down in 1898, after another of that name had been built beside it. Eventually, however, even this 'new' one was demolished to make way for re-development. Now, only 'The Cock' sign in the High Street acts as a somewhat wistful reminder of the great coaching days at Sutton.

Exhib: RA
Coll: BM; V&A; and most of the other important art galleries in this country
Illus: See HOUFE
Bibliog: BEN; HARDIE; HOUFE; LAMBOURNE; LISTER; MACKENZIE; MALLALIEU; MITCHELL; TB; ROE, F. G. *Rowlandson*. F. Lewis, 1947; BURY, A. *Rowlandson's Drawings*. Avalon Press, 1949; FALK, B. *Thomas Rowlandson; Life and Art*. Hutchinson, 1949; HAYES, J. *Rowlandson Watercolours and Drawings*. Phaidon Press, 1972

RUSKIN, John, M.A., H.R.W.S. 1819–1900

Ruskin Road, Ruskin Drive, Ruskin Hall, the Ruskin Players – these are but a few of the many reminders of the enduring influence in this area of John Ruskin, one of the most important figures in the art and social scene of Victorian England. He himself was a watercolourist of exceptional talent. The late Sir Kenneth Clark, introducing the 1949 edition of Ruskin's *Praeterita* (1885–89), mentions 'some of the most beautiful architectural drawings ever executed'. Renowned as a social reformer, Ruskin spent much of his own fortune in improving the conditions of the working man. As an art critic he formed the taste of many Victorians.

He is honoured in Carshalton because of his campaign to clean up the 'pools and streams' of the River Wandle which, by 1870, had become, according to Ruskin, 'ghastly'. In his famous work *Crown of Wild Olive* (1866), Ruskin rages against the 'human wretches of the place' who 'cast their street and house foulness; heaps of dust and slime, and broken shreds of old metal, and rags of putrid clothes' into the waters of Beddington and Carshalton which, twenty years earlier, had been sweet and clear. Nothing changes. Even today, as this is being written, posters are on display calling for volunteers to join in a 'clean up the Wandle' operation.

John Ruskin, who knew and loved the Carshalton area, did more than merely write about the situation. He personally put in hand the purification of the natural spring and pool of water behind Carshalton police station (on the corner of Pound Street and West Street), the work being carried out in about 1872. Variously known as Margaret's Well (its true title), Lady Margaret's Well – even St Margaret's Well – the pool is named after John Ruskin's mother, who was born and brought up not far from Carshalton.

Ruskin's mother, Margaret Cock (Ruskin always referred to the surname as 'Cox'), was born in 1781, the daughter of William Cock, the landlord of the Old King's Head in Market Street, Croydon. William Cock, who had also been a sailor involved in the herring trade at Yarmouth, was only thirty-two when he died – crushed against a wall by his horse as he was riding into Croydon. His wife then took over the running of the inn and brought up their two daughters: John Ruskin's mother and her sister Bridget. The latter married a Mr Richardson who had a baker's shop in Market Street, Croydon. Some of Ruskin's happiest childhood memories were of days spent at the bakery, where he played with his Croydon cousins and was spoiled by his homely, witty and loving Aunt Bridget.

Ruskin's mother, Margaret Cock, married her cousin John James Ruskin; he was a partner in the firm Ruskin, Telford and Domecq, wine shippers, and made a considerable fortune which John Ruskin, an only child, inherited.

Millions of words have been written by and about John Ruskin; his writings are to be found in almost every library and bookshop in the country. Brantwood, his home in the Lake District, has become a shrine visited each year by pilgrims from all over the world. Art galleries, halls and institutions bear his name. Even a pottery – William Howson Taylor's famous Ruskin Pottery – was named in his honour. Here in this borough he is partly and indirectly responsible for the existence of Little Holland House, the former home of Frank Dickinson (q.v.), who lived out his whole life according to Ruskin's principles.

John Ruskin had two good friends in this area, one being William Hale White, the writer 'Mark Rutherford', who lived at Park Hill in Carshalton from

GEORGE RICHMOND   Engraving by Francis Holl
Portrait of John Ruskin.

the 1860s until the 1880s. When Ruskin fell out with George Brightling, the first custodian of Margaret's Well, he placed this precious shrine to his mother's memory in the care of Hale White. His other friend in the borough was the Pre-Raphaelite artist Arthur Hughes (q.v.), whose paintings Ruskin greatly admired and recommended to his friends.

As a final word on Ruskin's connection with Carshalton, mention must be made of a commission which was never carried out. In 1872 he asked Sir George Gilbert Scott, the celebrated architect of the *Albert Memorial*, to design a fountain for Carshalton, obviously intending it to be a 'Margaret Memorial' in honour of his mother; but for some reason nothing came of this, which is rather a pity.

Exhib: D; RHA; RWS
Coll: Abbot Hall AG, Kendal; BM; Fitzwilliam Museum, Cambridge; Ruskin Museum, Coniston; Tate AG; V&A; and others
Illus: See HOUFE
Bibliog: BEN; DBA; DNB; FISHER; HALL(2); HARDIE; LAMBOURNE; MALLALIEU; WOOD; ABSE, J. *John Ruskin the Passionate Moralist*. Quartet, 1980 (this contains an excellent bibliography)

SACHSE, Edward John.   Exhib: 1884–1898
Lived in Sutton c.1893
Edward Sachse, who lived in Sutton during the 1890s (address unknown), had earlier lived in South

Norwood, Surrey, and then at Heath Cottage, Brighton Road, Banstead, Surrey. Heath Cottage, built of flint between 1844 and 1866, was demolished in 1973 to make way for the dual carriageway on the A217.

Sachse was acquainted with William Tatton Winter (q.v.) who, when he died, left amongst his personal papers some cuttings from a Winchelsea newspaper – articles on art, nature and local history, written by Sachse. In one of these, Sachse tells of how he was first inspired to paint when he was a boy on holiday at Whitby, where he met an elderly painter who had brought up a large family on an income earned by painting ships' portraits for ships' captains. As he watched the old man paint and listened to his tales, Edward vowed that one day he, too, would be an artist. He grew up to fulfil this ambition by making art his profession, exhibiting oils and watercolours at the Royal Academy and other galleries.

In about 1896 the Sachse family – Edward, his wife Rosina and their several children, one of whom, Conrad Maris Sachse, grew up to be a cartoonist – left the London area to live at Garden Cottage, Winchelsea, Sussex, where Edward soon became part of the local scene. He wrote a series of somewhat whimsical articles for the local newspaper and painted views of Winchelsea, which were exhibited at the RA. Sachse also visited Suffolk, after which he exhibited *Summer afternoon, near Southwold* (1887) and *Marshes on the Suffolk coast, Walberswick* (1890) at the RA.

After his wife's death – Rosina Sachse died in the December of 1905 – Edward moved back to the London area and lived in Clapham. He died circa 1920.

Exhib: D; NEA; RA; RBA; RI
Bibliog: DBA; WOOD; Tatton Winter family archive

SANFORD, S. Ellen, A.S.W.A. Exhib: 1886–1921

Ayshford, North Street, Carshalton 1900–1904
Miss Ellen Sanford, a member of the Sanford family of Nynehead Court, Wellington, Somerset, came to live in Carshalton in 1900 and remained there for four years. She occupied a house in North Street called Ayshford, a family name of the Sanfords. Painting portraits, landscapes, still-life studies and genre subjects, she exhibited fifty-five paintings at the Society of Women Artists' exhibitions and was elected an associate of this society whilst she was living in Carshalton. She also exhibited at the Royal Academy and other galleries, two RA titles being: *"Grow old along with me"* (1894) and *"Love's young dream"* (1904).

In 1904 she left Carshalton to live at Ascot in Berkshire, but by 1917 she was back in Surrey, living at Rose Cottage on Redhill Common. Her last known address, in 1921, was at Ockley, near Dorking.

Exhib: L; M; RA; RI; RID; RWS; SWA
Bibliog: DBA; GW; WOOD

SEARLES-WOOD, Herbert Duncan, F.R.I.B.A., F.R.San.I. 1853–1936

The Arches, Angel Hill, Sutton early 1880s
Benfleet Hall, Benhill Wood Road, Sutton late 1880s–1890s
The Nook, Benhill Road, Sutton pre-1896–1900
Blakesley, Christchurch Park, Sutton 1900–1936
Herbert Duncan Appleton, an architect and watercolourist who changed his surname to Searles-Wood on 5 July 1890, designed many notable buildings, including the *Painter-Stainers' Hall and Chambers* in London (when it was rebuilt in 1915) and more modest ones in his home town of Sutton, where he lived for most of his life.

Born in Stockwell in 1853 and educated at Stockwell Grammar School, he matriculated at King's College in 1868 and entered the Royal Academy Schools in 1870. In 1871 he was articled to the celebrated church architects H. Jarvis & Son, and was only twenty years old when he designed the *Hill Road Baptist Chapel*, Sutton, built in the Ornamental Gothic style at a total cost of £2,250. Opened in 1873, it was pulled down in 1934 to make way for an extension to Shinners Store (now Allders). Another design from this period was his *London and Provincial Bank* in the High Street at the junction with Hill Road (now Town Square). The building still stands, but today houses a shop on the ground floor and offices above. In 1875 he started his own practice at 157 Wool Exchange, London.

Herbert was the third son of William Appleton, the owner of Benfleet Hall, Sutton, which stood amidst acres of landscaped gardens in Benhill Wood. Today Benfleet Close occupies the site of the grounds. The richly furnished Hall had paintings by David Roberts, R.A., Marcus Stone, R.A. and other eminent Victorian artists hanging on its walls. During the First World War, after the Appletons had left, the Hall was commandeered as a war hospital. A postcard showing it as such is in Sutton's Local Collection.

Herbert Appleton married Bessie, the adopted daughter of Searles V. Wood, F.G.S. They had three children: Valentine, Christine and Sadie. Under the terms of his father-in-law's will, Herbert was obliged to assume the name Searles-Wood, and thus caused confusion in art circles by exhibiting at the RA as 'Herbert Appleton' until 1890 and thereafter as 'Herbert Searles-Wood'.

Specialising in the 'problems of construction', he rose rapidly to the top of his profession, becoming President of the Architectural Association (1888-9) and a Vice-President of the RIBA. He had a great admiration for the architects T. G. Jackson (q.v.) and Ernest George, who were both associated with the Queen Anne style; he himself designed buildings in this style and also in the Elizabethan and in the Baronial styles. Searles-Wood was the architect of two local hospitals: *Epsom County Hospital* and the *Cuddington Isolation Hospital*, as well as designing the *Sutton Board School* (in West Street, since pulled down) and the *Banstead Board School*. Three of his designs were exhibited at the RA: one for a house at Sutton, *Dolce, Sutton* (1898); one for the *Sutton Public Offices* (1895), since pulled down and replaced by a store. The other was for the *Sutton Technical Schools* (1895) in Throwley Way, also since demolished. Another domestic building in Sutton by this architect was a house named *Haslemere* (next door to Wellesley Lodge in Brighton Road) designed for Mr W. K. Appleton.

He also enjoyed restoration work, a visit to Italy in his youth having awakened his interest in old buildings.

Later on in his career, he practised in Sutton at no. 14 High Street and was active in local affairs, serving on several committees and enjoying the distinction of being the first Chairman of the Sutton to Wimbledon Railway. His many interests included archaeology and photography, and he was a member of the National Liberal Club. For thirty-six years, up to his death, he lived in a house named Blakesley in the Christchurch Park area of Sutton. He died, aged eighty-three, on 22 December 1936, and his funeral service was held at Christ Church. As Bessie, his wife, had died five years earlier, Searles-Wood's fine collection of paintings went to his children, who inherited some of the famous pictures which had once hung in Benfleet Hall, and some studies of cathedrals, painted by Searles-Wood himself. He bequeathed an important painting by David Roberts, *Houses of Parliament*, to his only son, Valentine Searles-Wood, a retired naval commander.

Exhib: RA
Published: APPLETON, H. D. *Carpentry in Building Construction.* The Architect's Library. Vol. 1. Longmans Green & Co., 1910–13; SEARLES-WOOD, H. D. Ed. *Modern Building.* Gresham Publishing Co., 1921–3. 6 vols.
Bibliog: DBA, *Who Was Who 1929–1940*; *Surrey Artists and their Homes.* xii.– Mr. H. D. Appleton, F.R.I.B.A. *Sutton and Epsom Advertiser*, 14 January 1888.
Obit: *The Times*, 23 December 1936; *Sutton and Cheam Advertiser*, 24 December 1936

*SKELSEY, Maud   Exhib: 1918–1923

Greenhayes, 32 Hillside Gardens, Wallington 1913–1920
Maud Skelsey, a painter of landscape and genre studies, exhibited at the Dudley Gallery, London, and with the Society of Women Artists. In 1918, when she was living in Wallington, she exhibited a painting entitled *Going to Market* at the SWA's annual exhibition, whilst her painting of the former Rectory in Carshalton High Street is now in Sutton's Local Collection.

Although she herself left Wallington in 1920 to live in Milford, Surrey, other members of her family continued to live at Greenhayes for many more years.

Exhib: D; SWA
Coll: Sutton LC
Bibliog: DBA

SKELTON, Jonathan, or John d. 1759
Painted the following watercolours of this area:
The Church at Cheam. N.D.
Carshalton Church. N.D.
A Mill nr. Carshalton in Surrey. 1757 [Coll. BM]
A Sandpit nr. Croydon in Surrey. 1757 [Identified as the one at Beddington. Coll. BM]
Jonathan Skelton, whose death occurred on 19 January 1759, is buried in an unmarked grave at the foot of the Pyramid of Cestius, the accustomed burial place of English Protestants dying in Rome. On the afternoon of that day he had walked with friends in the Trinita del Monte; by midnight he was dead. He had been in Italy for just over a year. Although that year is well documented through the letters he sent to his friend and mentor William Herring of Croydon, hardly anything is known of his life prior to 1757. Even his paintings were virtually unknown before this century. Most of his surviving works, acquired by Thomas Blofeld in the eighteenth century, had been locked away at Hoveton House in Norfolk. They came to light in April 1909 when items from the Blofeld collection, including eighty-four watercolours and drawings by Skelton, were sold at Hodgson's sale rooms in London. The artist was described in the catalogue as 'apparently unknown'. Apart from a study of *The Archbishop's Palace, Croydon*, discovered in Dorking, these paintings and two which are still at Hoveton House, are the only known works by Skelton.

Everything we know about Skelton has been gleaned from his letters and from the dates and locations of his English landscapes. His earliest dated painting, *The Archbishop's Palace, Croydon* (1754), has a note on the back to the effect that it was done by a footman in 'His Grace's family', 'His Grace' being Archbishop Herring, the Archbishop of Canterbury. Since a number of Skelton's watercolours are of places the Archbishop would have visited in the course of his duties, it does appear likely that Skelton was in his employ. Also, in 1757, the year the Archbishop died, Skelton packed his bags and went to Italy, encouraged and financed by William Herring, a distant cousin of the Archbishop. Skelton appears to have enjoyed a close friendship with the Herring family. In one of his letters from Italy he enquires affectionately after 'the Young Misses', Herring's daughters.

Once Skelton had been rediscovered, it became obvious that here was an English watercolourist of importance, to be classed alongside his contemporaries, one of whom was William Taverner (1703–72), the 'Father' of English watercolourists. Taverner, as well as being an artist, was the Procurator of the Court of Arches at Canterbury, and Skelton may have met him there. Indeed, his style is not dissimilar to Taverner's, although George Lambert (1710–65) is thought to have been his drawing master – Skelton, in his letters from Italy, mentioning a 'Mr. Lambert'.

Skelton's purpose in going to Italy was to develop his own style and to study the paintings of Claude and Piranese. On both counts he was successful. Yet his year in Italy was beset with problems. He failed to sell enough paintings to stay out of debt and his superior talent aroused jealousy in others, three artists in Rome putting about a rumour that Skelton had Jacobite leanings. He tended to be shunned by his compatriots until a letter from William Herring, clearing him of the allegations, arrived in Rome. Incidents like this, and his tendency to starve himself to save money, may have contributed to his early death. Although rumours at the time said that he had been poisoned, this has been discounted by a doctor this century, who diagnosed, after reading an account of his death, that the artist had been suffering from a duodenal ulcer.

JONATHAN SKELTON Watercolour
A Mill at Carshalton. 1757. British Museum

109

His birth and background remain a mystery. His only known relative was an uncle, Jonathan Beck, mentioned in his will. The year of his birth has been put at circa 1735, on the assumption that he was in his twenties when he died. The main proof of his youth is in a letter sent from Italy to William Herring, shortly after Skelton died, where his death is described as a 'happy release to a very good young man'. However Skelton's closest friend in Italy, Andrew Lumisden, thirty-eight at the time, was once described by William Herring as a 'Young man of uncommon knowledge'. So in the eighteenth century the term 'young man' did not necessarily mean someone in his twenties.

It is tempting to wonder if Skelton was born within what is now the London Borough of Sutton, where Skeltons, or Skiltons have lived for centuries. He appears to have been well-acquainted with this area; he painted views of Cheam and Carshalton and wrote nostalgically of the 'pure air of Beddington'. The 'Mr. Lambert' mentioned in his letters may have been one of the local mill-owning Lamberts and not George Lambert the artist. Indeed, the mill in Skelton's *A Mill nr. Carshalton in Surrey* was possibly owned by one of the Lamberts.

There was a John Skelton, the son of Isaac and Joan Skelton, who was christened at Beddington Church on 29 August 1717. His mother Joan died in 1727, followed by Isaac, his father, two years later, leaving John Skelton an orphan at the age of twelve. A mortuary fee was paid for Isaac Skelton, indicating that he was a man of property. Although both Isaac and Joan Skelton were buried at Beddington, there is no record of their son being buried there. The main argument against the Beddington John Skelton being the artist is his age; he would have been forty-one in the year the artist died, and it has always been assumed, as mentioned above, that the latter was in his twenties when he died.

Whatever his background, Jonathan Skelton was an important figure in the history of the English watercolour – the first Englishman to paint a significant number of watercolours of Rome, one of the earliest to paint in oils – though none seem to have survived – out of doors, directly from nature. In Italy his style matured, became broader and less parochial. Particularly admired are his views of Tivoli.

Coll: Aberdeen AG; BM; Croydon PL; Fitzwilliam Museum, Cambridge; Leeds City AG; V&A; Whitworth AG, Manchester
Bibliog: FISHER; HARDIE; LAMBOURNE; MALLALIEU; WILLIAMS; PIERCE, S. R. Jonathan Skelton and his watercolours; FORD, B. Letters of Jonathan Skelton written from Rome and Tivoli 1758. Both these articles are in the *36th Volume of the Walpole Society 1956–1958*. 1960. **N.B.** The Skelton letters were published by permission of Mr Edward Holland-Martin

SPRULES, Arthur Crossingham 1885–1968
Cressingham Villa, Clifton Crescent, Sutton 1885–c.1890
Trelawne, 1 Camborne Road, Sutton c.1890–
The Sprules and Crossingham (or Cressingham) families have lived in this area for at least a hundred and fifty years, several generations of the Sprules family being associated with the local lavender industry.

The two families were joined in marriage in the nineteenth century, when Mercy Crossingham became the wife of Alfred Sprules, an accountant. They had a large family, eight of Alfred's children surviving him when he died in 1930, including his daughter Dorothy Winifred Sprules, a contributor to the Surrey volumes of the Victoria County History series; she was educated at Sutton High School for Girls and had a distinguished career as a headmistress.

One of Alfred's sons was the artist Arthur Crossingham Sprules, who, born at Cressingham Villa, Sutton, in 1885, painted genre studies in oil and watercolour, often using body colour in the latter. He exhibited two paintings at the Royal Academy: *Life's little things* (1915) and *Memories* (1916). Others were shown in Liverpool and at the Royal Institute of Oil Painters' exhibitions. After living to be eighty-three, he died at Hove, Sussex, on 5 December 1968.

Exhib: L; RA; RI
Bibliog: DBA

*STACEY, Doris Marion
St Peters, Beeches Avenue, Carshalton 1909–
Born in Clapham, early this century, Doris Stacey, one of the two daughters of William Charles Stacey and Marianne Harriett Stacey, was seven years old when she came to live in Carshalton. St Peters, a house in Beeches Avenue, has been her home ever since. An early neighbour was the architect Robert Atkinson (q.v.), whose little boy, John, took a great interest in the baby next door – Doris's younger sister Angela.

After attending a local kindergarten, Doris spent a brief period at Wallington County School and then became a pupil at the Old Palace School, Croydon, where the nuns recognised and encouraged her artistic talent, possibly inherited from her grandfather's cousin J. W. Ebsworth, M.A., F.S.A., an artist and writer, who painted some family miniatures which are still in Miss Stacey's possession. On leaving the Old Palace School, she enrolled at Goldsmiths' College in London, hoping to become a fashion illustrator, but on her arrival she was asked to join the etching class, under-subscribed that year.

This accidental propulsion into printmaking resulted in her being singled out for praise by Malcolm Salaman, the noted authority on etching, who wrote in his article on Goldsmiths' College (*The Studio*, September 1918, p. 124): 'One student Miss Stacey has etched a portrait of an old man which is of remarkable quality in true Rembrandt tradition'; and in 1920 her etching *Study of an Old Woman* (illus. in *The Studio*, September 1920, p. 74) won her a British Institute Scholarship. A contemporary at Goldsmiths' was Graham Sutherland (q.v.) who, like Doris, lived in this area. They sometimes travelled home on the train together.

In 1920 she left Goldsmiths' and was about to enrol at the Royal College of Art when she discovered that since her father had an income of over £400 per annum, he would have to pay her fees. Wishing to be independent, she applied to the Royal Academy Schools, where the tuition was free, and was admitted at a time when the schools were experiencing a period of change, and where discipline was becoming hard to maintain. Doris, as one of the two student curators, was expected to exercise some control over the other students, and on one memorable occasion she was called upon to intervene in a brawl between two male students. They were quarrelling over a remark one had made about the other's sister. Displaying a confidence which was mostly bluff, she succeeded in separating them with a few well-chosen words, icily delivered: 'We don't have fighting here!', she said.

At the Academy Schools she studied under Sir George Clausen, R.A. who taught her the technique of 'wax painting', a method which involves mixing paraffin with the paint vehicle. The resulting matt finish can then be polished to a shine if required. Her first Royal Academy painting, *A flower-seller*, was hung in 1919; four more were exhibited between 1923 and 1936. Two were in tempera: *Adoration* (1923) and *Fantasy* (1925). These were carried out in the decorative style of the day, the Stacey's housemaid at Carshalton posing for one of the figures in *Adoration*. Doris won the Landseer Scholarship at the RA Schools and was a runner-up for the Prix de Rome. She later attended the L.C.C. Central School of Arts and Crafts.

On completing her training she took up teaching and also carried out a number of private commissions. She was asked to make an etching of *Judge Sir Horace Edmund Avory, K.C.* (1851–1935), showing him presiding over a case at the Old Bailey. From her special seat near the Judge's box, she was able to observe the great man in action, and she completed a brilliant character study of 'England's most feared judge'. He was noted for the shabbiness of his gown, having worn the same one for so long that its original crimson had turned into a dingy purple.

Living near her at Carshalton was the artist Frank Dickinson (q.v.), whose old home is now open to the public. They collaborated on various commissions, one of which was to design murals for the cinema restaurant in Dorking. Doris Stacey recalls with amusement that Frank was 'put out' when he discovered that his murals had been placed high near the ceiling where they were difficult to see. She enjoyed a good working relationship with this amiable artist who, she says, used to quote Ruskin on every conceivable occasion.

At the outbreak of the Second World War she joined the W.V.S. but found herself stitching pyjamas as part of her war effort. Considering this to be a waste of her artistic talent, she decided to apply for a job in camouflage. When William Gaydon, the Principal of Sutton Art School heard of this, he invited her to work for him instead. She started at the school in January 1942 and for twenty-six years taught general drawing, life studies and portrait painting, retiring in July 1968. Her ex-pupils remember her with gratitude and affection.

Doris Stacey is no longer a practising artist; but visitors to her home can appreciate what a wide range her talents embraced. The house is filled with her watercolours, oils, etchings, decorated furniture, sculptures and embroideries. Portraits of her own family, painted by Doris, are prominently displayed; they include two of her sister, the late Mrs Angela Simms, who embroidered, to Doris's design, the wall hangings, seat covers and cushions in the house. A couple of watercolours of Rye are a reminder of the days when Doris Stacey once owned a cottage there.

Exhib: I; NEA; RA; RP
Bibliog: DBA; *Who's Who in Art*, 1929

STAFF, John

John Staff and his partner Henry Prosser (q.v.) had an architectural practice in Croydon, Surrey. Together, they produced designs for the enlargement of the old *St Nicholas Church* at Sutton, Surrey (1825). John Staff also repewed and repaired *Betchworth Church*, Surrey (1789–90) and is thought to have designed *Juniper Hill*, Mickleham, Surrey for a Mr Jenkinson (c.1780).

Bibliog: COLVIN

STAMFORD, Alfred 1826/7–1894

2 Fortescue Villas, Croydon Road, Beddington c.1876–1894
On 9 January 1886, the artist Alfred Stamford and his wife Augusta were the witnesses at the register office wedding of Edith Constance Fox Hudson and William Tatton Winter (q.v.). Alfred was more than twenty years older than Tatton Winter, and the latter, who had lost his own father when he was a boy, possibly looked upon Alfred Stamford as a father figure. The close friendship between the two families continued up to and well after Alfred's death.

Alfred Stamford, who was born in London, exhibited oils and watercolours of the River Thames, Hampstead Heath, Suffolk and the Lake District at the British Institution (1851–6) and with the Society of British Artists (1852–63). Shortly before 1876, accompanied by his wife and their three children – Bertha, Henry and the baby, Frank – he came to live in Beddington, where he made a living by giving drawing lessons and restoring and framing pictures. He placed this advertisement in the *Sutton Herald*, 3 January 1880: 'Alfred Stamford – Drawing master and landscape painter – gives lessons in Drawing, Water Colour and Oil Painting – Water Colour drawings repaired Mounted and Framed – Oil paintings Cleaned and restored'.

In 1884, when the Science and Art Classes, held at Shepley House, the home of Alfred Tylor, were discontinued after Tylor's death, Tatton Winter established some others at Carshalton-on-the-Hill. He invited his friend Alfred Stamford to take charge of them and assisted him by taking some of the classes.

When Stamford died in 1894, his widow was left with a number of pressing financial problems and found herself obliged to sell some paintings. Tatton Winter helped her enormously at this time (and also over the next few years) by making sure that she obtained the best possible prices for her pictures, one or two of which turned out to be real treasures. There were some enamels by George Stubbs, A.R.A. and a portrait of Stubbs by Ozias Humphry, R.A. The National Portrait Gallery bought the portrait of Stubbs for £105, Tatton Winter negotiating the deal (on behalf of Augusta Stamford) with Lionel Cust. In her 'thank you' letter to Tatton Winter, Augusta wrote that she hoped 'our next transaction may prove equally fortunate' (Tatton Winter family archive).

Exhib: BI; SBA
Bibliog: WOOD

STANTON, William 1639–1705

The tomb of Dorothy, Lady Brownlowe, in St Nicholas Church, Sutton was for many years attributed to the sculptor Cibber from an unsigned drawing in the Victoria and Albert Museum's collection. Recent research seems to point more positively to it being the work of William Stanton, a well known mason and statuary, who was working for the Brownlowe family at Belton in Lincolnshire during the last quarter of the seventeenth century. There is a memorial to Sir John and Lady Brownlowe in the church at Belton, also by William Stanton. Lady Brownlowe inherited the manor of Sutton from her father Sir Richard Mason and was buried in St. Nicholas Church on her death in 1700. She married Sir William Brownlowe, 4th Baronet of Belton.

The magnificent tomb in Sutton cannot now be seen since it is completely obscured by the organ which was installed in 1899. Unfortunately, it is a good organ so that the chances of removing it are remote.

The tomb was delightfully described by William Hone in 1831 as 'gorgeous', and representing, above Lady Dorothy's recumbent figure 'three sorrowing infants and four cherubs above, in a sort of hasty pudding, garnished with slices of gilded gingerbread'.

A recent publication by the Victoria and Albert Museum suggests that the Victorians did not look too kindly on the lady's generous curves and provocative posture; but it must be pointed out that when St. Nicholas Church was rebuilt in 1864 great care was taken to preserve, re-erect and refurbish the tomb and to place it in the best possible vantage point to be observed and enjoyed by the majority of the congregation attending Divine Service. It was not until a later generation, possibly more musical, but not necessarily more prudish, that the Brownlowe monument was entombed.

Note: The inscription on the tomb spells out the Brownlowe name with a final 'e': it is more often spelled without it.

Jean M. Moore

Bibliog: BEN; GUNNIS; TB

*STARLING, Albert 1858–1947

Widmerpoole, Grove Road, Sutton 1879–1911
Brierley, Tate Road, Sutton 1911–1947

For sixty-eight years Albert Starling, a portrait, marine, landscape and genre painter in oil and watercolour, lived in Sutton. He was born in Hastings, Sussex, on 17 November 1858, the son of the engraver Matthew J. Starling (q.v.), and he showed artistic talent from an early age, leaving school at the age of sixteen to enter the then newly-opened Hastings School of Art. However on leaving the art school he did not immediately embark on a career in art but went into business. It was only when some of his friends in the art world convinced him that he was wasting his talent that he abandoned the world of commerce to enter Heatherley's Art School in London.

After early misgivings, when his progress at Heatherley's was, in his own words, 'merely moderate', one of his drawings, *After Work*, was accepted by the Society of British Artists. It was exhibited in 1879, the year the Starling family left Hastings to live in Sutton. They moved into a house in Grove Road called Widmerpoole, where Albert's father died ten years later.

In 1880 Albert went to Switzerland to convalesce from an illness, and he occupied his time by sketching the mountain scenery. On his return to England, some of these sketches were published in the *Graphic*. After a short spell at the School of Art, South Kensington, he returned to Switzerland where he completed some more drawings. He next attended St John's Wood Art School where he met the landscape painter Charles Wilkinson, with whom he later shared a studio in Fitzroy Street. In 1883 they entered the Royal Academy Schools together and Starling spent the next three years mastering all aspects of drawing and painting; he passed all his exams without difficulty and won the first prize for the 'six best drawings from the life'. He was still a student when his painting *Miles Standish* was hung at the RA in 1884. This was sold immediately on Private View Day, Starling subsequently receiving four more offers for it.

In December 1887 there was an article about him in the *Sutton and Epsom Advertiser*, the writer stating that 'Mr. Starling . . . is well on the way to making a name and a place among – not only Surrey – but English artists of the nineteenth century'. A year later, at the inaugural meeting of the Surrey Art Circle (q.v.), Albert Starling was elected a member of the committee, his first duty being to assist the Secretary, George Flemwell (q.v.), who had also spent some time in Switzerland because of ill health. Starling's long association with the Circle lasted well into the 1920s. He exhibited over a hundred titles with them, mostly marine subjects.

His love of the sea took him back to it constantly. The coasts of Cornwall, Sussex, Suffolk and Yorkshire appear over and over again in his paintings. He visited Yorkshire many times, painting views which were later exhibited at the Surrey Art Circle's exhibitions: *Cliffs at Flambro'* (1898), *Herring Fleet, Whitby* (1900) and *In Whitby Harbour* (1903). He also visited Italy, in 1909 exhibiting *On Lake Como* and *In Rapallo Bay* at the SAC's annual exhibition. Starling's inland subjects were the moors, the marshes and the rivers – again nearly all in Suffolk or Yorkshire. His genre studies included the titles: *The Skipper had taken his little girl to bear him company; Hale and Hearty* and *News from her soldier son*, this last title appearing at the RA in 1887.

In 1889 his oil painting *Strangers in a Strange Land*

was bought by the Walker Art Gallery, Liverpool. Starling had been asking £250 for it but he agreed to let the gallery have it for £150. The painting shows two Italian travelling musicians, and their monkey, entertaining the customers of The Three Mariners, an inn by the sea. A long pier juts out to sea in the far distance. Starling has used artistic licence. The inn, which he knew well, was not by the sea but on the River Alde at Slaughden in Suffolk, kept by a retired sergeant-major in the artillery.

There are three paintings by the artist in Sutton's Local Collection. One shows the Barrow Hedges or Banstead Downs area; another the Hackbridge on the River Wandle; the third shows Westmead Farmland at the bottom of Highfield Road. In addition, there is a colour slide of *The Tithe Barn, Sutton* (private coll.). Until the 1940s this ancient building stood at the side of St Nicholas Church; it was pulled down to make way for a Civil Defence car park.

Recently, Starling's works have gained in popularity and value, particularly his marine views. Some of his finest works, however, are to be found amongst his portraits, conveying, as they do, the rapport he so obviously enjoyed with his sitters. He exhibited at various galleries until the end of the 1920s, after which little was heard of him in the art world. Few of his paintings have appeared on the market in recent years, even though he was a prolific artist. Some may still be in private hands at Sutton, where he spent most of his life. He lived at Widmerpoole in Grove Road until 1911, and then moved to a house called Brierley in Tate Road, where he remained until his death. Brierley had a lucky escape in the Second World War, when a bomb fell on Tate Road, demolishing the two houses next door.

Starling married late in life, his wife Cecilia being some years his junior. They had two daughters: Mary and Nancy; the latter was present at her father's death on 9 December 1947.

One or two Sutton residents can still recall how the elderly artist used to ride a rather ancient bicycle about the town. In recent years his old home has been without a name, but the present occupants have called it Brierley again, in memory of the artist who once lived there.

Exhib: B; L; M; RA; RBA; RI; ROI; SAC
Coll: Sutton LC; Walker AG, Liverpool
Illus: *Royal Academy Pictures 1892*, p. 92
Bibliog: BEN; DBA; GW; TB; WOOD; Surrey Artists and their Homes. X.– Mr. Albert Starling. *Sutton and Epsom Advertiser*, 24 December 1887

*STARLING, Matthew James 1805–1889

Widmerpoole, Grove Road, Sutton 1879–1889
Matthew J. Starling, born in Islington, London, in the year of Trafalgar, was one of a number of steel engravers of that surname working in England during the nineteenth century, and he may have been the son of Thomas Starling (fl. 1820–1840), an engraver living in Islington. Matthew specialised in landscape and interior views and was a prolific artist, successful both artistically and commercially; he bought stocks and shares and owned properties in England and Wales. He married Anna Brittain, and was the father of a daughter, Letitia, and four sons.

From the 1830s onwards, Matthew Starling carried out countless book illustrations, some appearing in Gastineau's *Wales Illustrated* (1830) and in Shepherd's *London and its Environs* (1829–31). On several occasions he collaborated with Thomas Allom, engraving his drawings for Brayley's *History of Surrey* (1850), which contains the plate: *The Hall, Beddington House* (interior of the Hall). Others by Starling, after Allom, can be found in Beattie's *Scotland Illustrated* (1838) and Britton and Brayley's *Devonshire and Cornwall Illustrated* (1832).

The Starling family lived in Hastings, Sussex, for many years, moving to Sutton in 1879, when they took up residence in a house named Widmerpoole in Grove Road. Matthew, seventy-four when he came to Sutton, was by then no longer a practising engraver; but he no doubt sat back and took pride in the success his son Albert (q.v.) was beginning to experience in the art world, especially when his son painted his portrait: *M. J. Starling*, which was exhibited at the Royal Academy in 1886.

Although Albert and his sister Letitia still lived with their parents in Sutton, Matthew's other three sons had, by then, gone their separate ways, one having qualified as a medical doctor. Ten years after moving to Sutton, Matthew died suddenly, at his home, on 25 March 1889.

Coll: Sutton LC; V&A
Illus: See HUNNISETT
Bibliog: BEN; HUNNISETT; LISTER; MACKENZIE; TB

THE SURREY ART CIRCLE
Founded at Sutton, Surrey in 1888
The Surrey Art Circle was founded at Sutton on the last day of January 1888. The inaugural meeting was held at Highfield in Cheam Road, home of George Jackson Flemwell (q.v.), an artist noted for his paintings of Alpine scenes. Highfield was demolished some years ago and the site is now the public car park adjacent to Sutton Baptist Church.

Four of the Circle's eight founder members came from Sutton. They were: Edward Henry Corbould (q.v.), George Flemwell, Albert Starling (q.v.) and Edward Frampton (q.v.). The others were William Tatton Winter (q.v.) from Carshalton; Walter Wallis and Maurice Page from Croydon; and an S. Drewett, who was possibly 'S.D.', the art critic of the *Sutton and Epsom Advertiser*. Edward Corbould, former tutor in historical painting to the Royal Family, was the most distinguished artist present. He was elected President, with George Flemwell, assisted by Albert Starling, the Secretary, and Maurice Page the Treasurer.

A set of rules was drawn up. To keep the standard above mediocrity it was decided that amateurs should be excluded and that prospective members should submit examples of their work before being elected. Architects, sculptors, painters on glass, engravers, wood carvers and metal workers – as well as painters – all were eligible. It was decided that the Circle should

ALBERT STARLING Oil 241×495mm
Westmead farmland, at the bottom of Highfield Road. c. 1900. Sutton's Local Collection

W. TATTON WINTER Watercolour 273×419mm
Butter Hill, Carshalton. Sutton's Local Collection

114

embrace the areas south of Sutton so that artists from Dorking and Guildford could be included. Corbould designed the Circle's badge – seen on their notepaper and exhibition catalogues – and the subscription was set at ten shillings per annum. Before the end of the first meeting George Earl, a sporting artist from Banstead, was elected a member.

At the second meeting, in March 1888, three more members were admitted: the painter Sydney Moore (q.v.) from Wallington, the sculptor Domenico Tonelli from Croydon, and William Cheshire (q.v.) from Sutton, a wood engraver.

The Circle's first anniversary was celebrated in great style. It took the form of a conversazione, and was held at Sutton Public Hall in February 1889. It must have been one of the most lavish affairs ever seen there. Mr W. C. Truncheon and Mr A. Reynolds, Upholsterers, High Street, Sutton, transformed the Hall into a large drawing room, where an air of warmth was imparted to the cold February evening by the walls being hung with a rich, red fabric. Comfortable chairs and sofas beckoned invitingly from the centre of the room. Carpets, rugs and matting covered the floor. The stage was a conservatory where guests strolled amidst banks of foliage, lilies and potted plants, plundered from George Flemwell's father's garden. Suspended from the gallery were crimson and white curtains festooned with garlands of blue silk which, when parted, revealed a sumptuous buffet supper. The Royal Standard was extended over the gallery.

The main focus of the evening was, of course, the Art Circle's exhibition, and over a hundred works of art were admired by three hundred and fifty guests. The cream of Sutton society mingled with important guests such as W. P. Frith, R.A., the painter of *Derby Day*, there with his second wife; she had been his mistress when his first wife was alive. One of the main attractions at the exhibition was a portrait of Frith, painted by his pupil George Flemwell. Tatton Winter exhibited some views of Carshalton and Edward Frampton some designs for stained glass. There were one or two fine wood engravings from William Cheshire, whilst the programme, a 'work of art in itself', was designed by Edward Corbould. The evening was brought to a close with an entertainment of songs and humorous recitations which included a rendering of 'Beauty's Eye' (violin obligato by Mr Hills) by the Reverend Courtenay Gale, a prominent supporter of the local art scene.

After such a promising start, the Surrey Art Circle went on from strength to strength, gaining new members, some of national importance. Annual exhibitions were held – first in Sutton or Croydon, later in London. Sketching tours abroad were arranged for the summer months.

The cartoonist John Proctor followed Edward Corbould as President. Then, from the 1890s until well into the 1920s, Sir Alfred Gilbert, M.V.O., R.A. was their President. His famous statue of *Eros* in Piccadilly Circus, London (the *Shaftesbury Memorial Fountain*) known throughout the world, was restored to its former glory as recently as 1986. That same year, the Royal Academy mounted a major exhibition of Gilbert's work, confirming his place as a sculptor of international importance.

Gilbert was born in 1854. His rapid rise to fame was as spectacular as his fall from grace, when he failed to complete a number of commissions contracted in the 1880s and 1890s for which he had accepted 'down payments'. He was attacked as being dishonest, went bankrupt and fled to Bruges, the night before he left England taking up a mallet and smashing some of the unfinished works in his studio.

His exile lasted from 1904 until 1926; but throughout this period his fellow members of the Surrey Art Circle remained loyal. They kept him on as their President throughout his long, unhappy years of exile. Then he surprised everyone by making a triumphal return to England at the age of seventy-two. He finished the *Clarence Memorial*, first started in the 1890s and rose again to the peak from which he had tumbled when he was fifty. He died in 1934.

Toward the end of the 1920s the Surrey Art Circle, which had then been in existence for some thirty-odd years, was incorporated with the Southern Society of Artists. The Surrey Art Circle's Exhibition Catalogues (from 1898–1921, with one or two gaps) are in the National Art Library at the Victoria and Albert Museum.

Bibliog: *Sutton and Epsom Advertiser*, 4 February 1888; 2 March 1889

SUTHERLAND, Graham Vivian, O.M., A.R.E. 1903–1980

Adenholme, Camborne Road, Sutton 1910–1914
Storrington, Camborne Road, Sutton 1914–1922
Four Winds, Upland Road, Carshalton 1922–1924

Graham Sutherland, one of the major figures of British painting in the twentieth century, lived in Sutton from 1910 until 1924. He was born on 24 August 1903 in Streatham. His father, George Humphreys Vivian Sutherland, was a Civil Servant working for the Land Registry Office, and later for the Board of Education. By 1907 the family – George, his wife Elsie and their young son Graham Vivian – were living in Merton Park, and in 1910 moved to Sutton. This move indicated an improvement in their standard of living as they moved from a semi to a large detached house called Adenholme, at the junction of Stanley Road and Camborne Road (the house is no longer standing). However, this advance was short-lived as they had to move four years later, in 1914, when the rent was increased. They moved to a smaller house almost opposite, called Storrington. The Sutherlands' uncertain ascent of the social scale was resumed when they commissioned an architect, who had already built them a holiday home at Rustington in Sussex, to build them a substantial house in Carshalton Beeches. This was Four Winds, now no. 39 Upland Road. Two more children were born: Humphrey in 1908 and Vivien in 1913.

The first school Graham Sutherland went to was a kindergarten at Clanricarde House in the Brighton Road. The school was where Sutherland House now stands, but it would be an over-simplification to say that the new building was named after Graham Sutherland as there was, three houses away, a doctor's house already called Sutherland House when he was at the kindergarten. The young Graham then had a governess at home who taught him a restricted range of subjects. From 1912 to 1917 Sutherland went to Homefield Preparatory School, where he was very happy. The school, which is now in Western Road, was then in Grove Road. It was run by two men who were already friends of the Sutherland family: Rupert Gray and Charles Walford, the latter being a major influence on the atmosphere of the school. Sutherland later remembered it as being like a smaller, friendlier version of a public school.

In 1917 Sutherland went to Epsom College. There he suffered a conspicuous lack of success and left after two years, as soon as he reached his sixteenth birthday, because he was considered 'not university material'. He felt the pupils were not encouraged to learn, and was not helped by the emphasis the school put on sciences rather than arts. Also, many of the best teachers were away at the war, so the school was at a rather low ebb.

So the outward trappings of the Sutherland family's life were typical of an upper-middle class suburban family. But it is the underlying currents and attitudes that leave their mark on growing children. Graham Sutherland was living at Sutton from the age of seven until he was twenty-one (with a break from 1919–21) – the most formative years of his life. One of the major influences in his early life was the constant feeling of tension in the family home – his brother Humphrey said that 'it was not a happy home', and Graham remembered the rancorous quarrels his parents would have. The tension and drama he grew up with found strong expression when Sutherland eventually found his true style in painting. However, the angst was initially masked by a feeling for whimsy. Arthur Rackham was a friend of the family, and an early influence on Sutherland, who was also influenced by the E. V. Lucas series, *Highways and Byways in . . .* which all had charming illustrations by people like F. L. Griggs, the Cotswolds artist who had close connections with the last, and more romantic, generation of the Arts and Crafts movement. Added to this was the tacit encouragement of a slightly arty environment at home – his aunt was interested in Beardsley; his father's family were keen amateur painters. Although Sutherland showed no particular artistic promise at school, his mother encouraged him to make sketches on his walks in the local countryside.

These walks in the country, as the Carshalton Beeches area then was, were another major influence in the development of Sutherland's visual sense. He went butterfly-catching with his father, or on his own, as his siblings were young enough for him to feel slightly isolated from them. He became used in this way to observing nature closely, and nature became and remained the main subject of his work, through various changes of style.

After leaving Epsom College Sutherland was sent as an apprentice to the family engineering works in Derby. In 1921, after two years that convinced him he could never be an engineer, he came back to the family home in Carshalton Beeches. In Derby he had spent some time painting and drawing, and on returning home persuaded his parents that he wanted to spend his life in Art. He went to Goldsmiths' College, commuting up to New Cross from Carshalton Beeches.

It was at Goldsmiths' that Sutherland felt he got his true education – he became more interested in music and literature, and did classes in book illustration, still-life, and life drawing but not portrait painting. His main interests were drawing and etching, and he became increasingly influenced by Samuel Palmer, as well as being introduced to the work of Cezanne and Matisse. 'One began to feel', he later said, 'that there was more to drawing than copying more or less what we thought we saw'. He was already conscious of the possibilities of introducing a strong emotional content in nature studies.

In 1923 Sutherland exhibited for the first time at the Royal Academy. His submission was selected to be 'hung on the line' at the Summer Show, and was a small (6″ × 8″) dry-point of a *Barn Interior*; the subject was an old barn in Carshalton Beeches. His brother recalled that Sutherland showed some embarrassment at being discovered sketching a subject which, he felt, might be considered an unworthy one. He had etchings in every RA show until 1930 – rural scenes in a slightly whimsical, Palmerish style. Unfortunately, little of this early work is known to remain.

In 1924, while still at Goldsmiths', Sutherland had his first exhibition, at the 21 Gallery in London. We can safely assume that the exhibition contained paintings and etchings of local views, including an etching of Barrow Hedges Farm, one of the few he did direct onto the plate with no preliminary sketches. The exhibition was well reviewed in, for example, the *Morning Post* and *The Times*, and was the start of Sutherland's early career as an etcher.

Also in 1924, Sutherland moved from Carshalton Beeches to Blackheath, to be nearer Goldsmiths' and to get independence. He shared a flat with Oliver Grey, later a successful designer. The Sutherland family's local connections were finally severed in 1928 when they moved away to their holiday home in Sussex. Graham stayed at Goldsmiths' until 1927, but was already getting teaching jobs – in 1925–6 he taught at Kingston School of Art, and in 1927 at Chelsea School of Art, where Henry Moore was a colleague. In 1927 he married a fellow-student Kathleen Frances Barry, under whose influence he had become a Catholic. They moved to Shoreham in Kent – Samuel Palmer country.

Sutherland's early work has none of the power of his established style – the first suggestion of his true voice is in the 1930 etching *Pastoral* – there is no human presence, and the trees evoke a threatening, dramatic tension. The paintings of his maturity, prompted by a visit to the dramatic landscape of Pembrokeshire in 1934, have all the angst and idiosyncratic observation of nature for which the foundations were laid in his childhood in Sutton.

GRAHAM SUTHERLAND   Oil 959×959mm
Lord Goodman. 1973.   Tate Gallery

He went on to become a leading figure in British painting – he was an official war artist during the Second World War (using his experience in Derby to draw heavy machinery), became a close friend of Kenneth Clark, and was awarded the Order of Merit. However, he never became predictable, and his two most famous commissions – the portrait of Winston Churchill in 1954 and the Coventry Cathedral tapestry (1955–62) were surrounded by controversy.

Sutherland settled in Kent, in an eighteenth century weather-boarded house, The White House, in Rottiscliffe. From 1955 he also had a house in the South of France, where the bright light encouraged his already daring sense of colour. His life was rich in intense and developing artistic activity, enhanced by a deeply supportive and happy marriage. He seems to have been a man of charm, whose anguish was expressed in his paintings rather than his everyday life. He died in London on 17 February 1980.

Cynthia Bradley

Exhib: ALP; BA; CHE; GI; LEI; NEA; RA; RE; Twenty-One Gallery
Coll: BM; Brussels; Paris; Tate AG; V&A; Vienna
Illus: See PEPPIN
Bibliog: BEN; DBA; GW; LAMBOURNE; MACKENZIE; PEPPIN; TB; V; *Who's Who in Art* – several editions; *Who Was Who 1971–1980*; TASSIE, R. *The Complete Graphic Works of Graham Sutherland*. Thames & Hudson, 1978; BERTHOUD, R. *Graham Sutherland*. Faber and Faber, 1982

THOMAS ROWLANDSON
Engraving 222×292mm
Sutton [The Cock Inn]. 1790.
Sutton's Local Collection

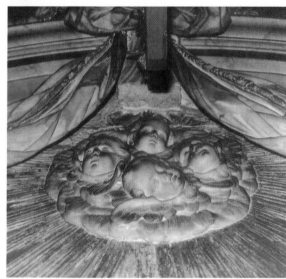

WILLIAM STANTON
Detail from the tomb of Dorothy, Lady
Brownlowe, in St Nicholas Church, Sutton.
Photo Nigel Moore

NORAH K. TRAVERS
Watercolour 171×248mm
Cottages in Malden Road, Cheam.
Sutton's Local Collection

*SWAN, Laura Exhib: 1890
Miss Laura Swan, who exhibited with the Society of Women Artists, lived at Indiana, Avondale Road, Croydon, during the 1880s and 1890s, and trained at Croydon Art School, where in 1889 she won a prize for 'painting from still-life' (*Croydon Advertiser*, 7 September 1889). She later moved to Sydenham.

Her painting entitled *Carshalton Mill*, painted circa 1890, is in Sutton's Local Collection, and shows a rear view of the mills at Butter Hill (Lower Mill site). They have been identified as Ansell's and Denyer's Mills.

Exhib: SWA
Bibliog: DBA

TAYLOR, Mrs B. V. Walden Exhib: 1910–14
Wynberg, Carshalton Road, Sutton 1914–1929
Mrs Taylor, a portrait painter, exhibited three works at the Royal Academy, of which two were shown in 1914 when she was living in Sutton: *Kathleen, daughter of Charles Irwin, Esq.* and *Alice, daughter of S. Hunnings, Esq.*

Pile's *Directories* list H. J. Taylor as the householder at Wynberg, Sutton, from 1914 until 1929.

Exhib: RA
Bibliog: DBA

TAYLOR, Maud Winifred Exhib: 1904–1913
Rusthall, Park Hill, Wallington 1905–1908
Adversane, Woodcote Avenue, Wallington 1908–1929
Maud Taylor's most important work, an oil painting entitled *"Seventy years ago, my darling, seventy years ago"*, was exhibited at the Royal Academy in 1909. It was later reproduced as a black-and-white print by Forman of Nottingham and must have graced many a front room parlour in the years between the two world wars.

The painting was exhibited at the RA a year after the Taylor family had moved from Rusthall in Park Lane, Wallington, to live at Adversane in Woodcote Avenue; so the sitting room of one or other of these houses may have formed the background of the picture. Its subject matter is the contrast between old age and youth. A very old lady, a shawl draped over her shoulders, is showing some family treasures to her granddaughter, a beautiful young woman aged about twenty. They are looking at a portrait of the old lady as a girl – hence the title. Despite its sentimentality, it is an appealing picture; and the various fabrics – the curtains, the carpet, the costumes of the old lady and the girl – are convincingly painted. A preliminary sketch for the oil, *Long Ago*, was exhibited at the Society of Women Artists' exhibition in 1908.

Maud Taylor was the daughter of Octavia and James

Benjamin Taylor. Her father was employed by the Bank of England. She had three brothers and two sisters. According to her father's will one of her brothers, Thomas Harold Cottingham Taylor, was also an artist, although his name does not appear in any of the art dictionaries. However in the Local Collection at Sutton there is a pen-and-ink drawing by a 'Cottingham Taylor', showing the *Fellowes Memorial, All Saints Church, Carshalton*. After their father's death in 1918, Maud and her sisters continued to live at Adversane until 1929.

Exhib: L; RA; SWA
Bibliog: DBA

TEULON, Samuel Sanders 1812–1873
Noted for his highly original Victorian Gothic style, S. S. Teulon was the architect of *All Saints' Church, Benhilton, Sutton* (1863–6). He also designed other churches south of London, including *Christ Church, Croydon* (1851–2) and *Christ Church, Wimbledon* (1857–60)

Of Huguenot descent, he was born in Greenwich in 1812. After attending the Royal Academy Schools, he was articled to George Legg and later became an assistant in the office of George Porter, establishing his own practice in 1838.

Teulon's clients included the Archbishop of Canterbury and three dukes: Bedford, Marlborough and St Albans. His most illustrious client was Prince Albert, the husband of Queen Victoria, who commissioned Teulon to design estate buildings in Windsor Great Park, including cottages for the farm workers (1854).

During the 1860s a committee was formed at Sutton to discuss the building of a new church at Benhilton, which was then a well-wooded area of scenic beauty between Sutton and Rose Hill. Meetings to discuss the church were held at Southfields on Sutton Common, the home of Anthony Locke. Locke's young son Edward (q.v.) was also present at the meetings. Years later, after Teulon's death, Edward Locke completed the church, being responsible for the whole of the north side.

All Saints' Church, with its high, broad tower dominating the area, heralds the approach to Sutton for travellers journeying south from London. A somewhat restrained example of Teulon's style, it has a wide nave, cruciform piers with chamfered corners, and attractive, circular, clerestory windows. Bomb damage in 1944 lost the church its Morris & Co. windows; but in 1965 some impressive, modern stained glass windows by J. & M. Kettlewell, and by John Hayward, were installed there.

Today the church presents a sorry sight, once again undergoing restoration work. In the early hours of Monday, 11 August 1986, a violent storm raged over Southern England and lightning struck the roof of All Saints' Lady Chapel. The ensuing fire spread to the chancel and caused extensive damage to the roof. Fortunately, the tower remained intact; and due to the prompt action of the vicar and other valiant helpers, many treasures from the Lady Chapel were saved.

Bibliog: The late Mr. S. S. Teulon, Architect. *The Builder*, vol. 31, no. 384, 1873

TILNEY, Frederick Colin 1864–1951

Walden, Red Lion Street, Cheam 1909–1912
Walden, 1 Lumley Road, Cheam 1912–1951

Frederick Colin Tilney, painter, etcher, photographer, author, designer and musician, was certainly an artist of Cheam, living there for forty-two years. Whether he was a Cheam artist, implying that he was part of the art culture of Cheam, is arguable.

He was born on 28 December 1864 – some reference works erroneously quote 1870 – at no. 34 Brooke Street, Holborn, just beyond the City of London boundary. His father, William Walden Tilney, was a grocer and cheesemonger; his mother, née Catherine Ellen, came from Bonnington, a village near Ashford in Kent. The Tilneys had three other children, all girls. As far as is known there were no traditions of art or music in the family.

Frederick may have attended a local Church of England school at Holborn, before going on to study at the London Mechanics' Institute (now Birkbeck College, part of London University). Such institutions, as well as helping working-class children to supplement their elementary education, had a tradition of offering excellent tuition in art and music. Frederick Tilney was both artistic and musical, and during the 1880s – by that time the family had moved to North London – he entered Westminster School of Art where he studied under Professor Fred Brown.

In 1894 his etched book-plate for a ship-owner's library was accepted at the Royal Academy, his first work to be shown there. In the same year, a new edition of Elizabeth Barrett Browning's *Sonnets from the Portuguese* was published, with an introduction and illustrations by Tilney. A portrait of his future wife, Una Mummery, to whom he dedicated the book, illustrates Sonnet 27.

Una and Frederick were married at Wood Green on 21 August 1897 and set up home at Winchmore Hill, in a house called Unaleigh. Una, a gentle, cultured person, was well versed in the classics and intensely musical; but after the birth in 1900 of the Tilneys' only child, John Walden Tilney, who was physically handicapped throughout his forty-two years, Una had to devote most of her time to looking after him. One of Una's brothers, John C. S. Mummery, was the President of the Royal Photographic Society; another brother was the artist Horace Mummery (q.v.) who lived with the Tilneys at Cheam from the 1940s until his death in 1951.

Needing to find gainful employment now that he was married, Tilney took up a teaching post at Hornsey School of Art in 1897 and remained there for twelve years. During this period he was also the Art Director at the London branch of Swan Sonnenschein & Co. and a designer for Löwenbräu of Munich. He pursued an operatic career, too, acting and singing with the Carla Rosa Opera Company and with Beecham's Tours. He had a good singing voice, but his short physique prevented him from playing any leading romantic parts, so he had to make do with the less attractive and secondary roles. In 1921 he sang in Wagner's *Siegfried* at Covent Garden.

The Tilneys arrived at Cheam in 1909, and for the following three years lived in Red Lion Street in a house named Walden after Frederick's father. They then moved to Lumley Road, again naming their house Walden. Here they remained until first John died in 1942 and then Frederick on 4 May 1951. Una continued to live there alone until she entered a nursing home, where she died, aged ninety-seven, in 1961.

The family became an integral part of the scene and ethos of Cheam Village. In those days Cheam, with a population of just over six thousand, was still a village, still showing signs of the feudal system through the gentry who occupied the remaining large houses. Frederick Tilney, a man of short stature – in fact almost dwarfish – was eccentric, brusque and of uncertain temper. Regarded by many as a 'strange little man', he held dogmatic, traditional views and was always quick to rise to the defence of what he called 'True Art'. He is said to have quarrelled with many of his Cheam neighbours and he certainly quarrelled with the local tradesmen. He was fortunate enough to be able to rent his home for a nominal sum that scarcely increased over the years.

Yet he was a man of amazing talents and energies. In his younger days he had enjoyed rowing and sculling. Pursuing his artistic and theatrical activities with a single-minded fervour, he was a 'Brother' of the Art Workers' Guild and exhibited at many galleries. Etchings, oil paintings and watercolours by Tilney were hung at the RA where, in 1909, an oil painting of local interest was shown. Entitled *Miss R* (alternative title *Shall I?*) it is of a lady reading a letter. She is sitting in an armchair which has been identified as one which formed part of the furnishings at the Tilneys' home in Lumley Road. One of his major works, *Diana and Actaeon* (illus. in *The Artist*, April 1932, p. 64) was exhibited at the RA in 1931. It subsequently crossed the Atlantic, having been bought by an American collector. Under the pseudonym 'Niloc', Tilney won the first prize in *The Studio* magazine competition for a 'monotint landscape drawing' (illus. in *The Studio*, October 1909, p. i).

Two watercolours of *Lohengrin* – shades of his operatic career – were exhibited at the Walker Art Gallery, Liverpool in 1907, and two exhibitions of his work were held at Walker's Galleries in Bond Street, London. The first, a one-man show, took place in June 1934 when sixty or so watercolours of England, France and Switzerland were shown. The second, which Tilney shared with two other artists, was in May-June 1947 and included views of Cheam, and the painting *Peace*, which is now in Sutton Hospital.

Although his output was considerable, most of his paintings have remained in private hands; only occasionally does one turn up for sale. This writer was fortunate enough to be apprised of a folder of Tilney's work – mostly watercolours and sketches – for sale at Derek James's Antiquarian Bookshop in Sutton, and purchased them shortly before the shop closed down in the 1970s. After Frederick Tilney's death, his widow had offered a stack of the artist's paintings to Mr James, who had known the Tilney family well. He had to refuse most of them at the time, but with hindsight much regretted this decision. Subsequently, many of Tilney's paintings were dispersed through Parkin's Salerooms at Cheam.

Still selling well are Tilney's packs of Shakespearian Playing Cards, first patented in 1900 and reissued in 1920, 1968 and 1975 by Waddingtons; the early sets now sell at a premium. His Kings, Queens and Jacks are appropriate characters from Shakespeare's plays, with Touchstone as the Joker.

Tilney wrote two books on art, and countless articles on the subject for periodicals like the *Artist* and the *Art Chronicle*. He was the Editor, Founder and Proprietor of a monthly magazine called *Art and Reason* which ran from 1934 until 1948. The bulk of the copy was collated and written at no. 1 Lumley Road, Cheam. Many well-known personalities of the day contributed articles, including Sir Alfred Munnings, R.A. and Sir George Clausen, R.A. Tilney's writings, however one might agree or disagree with his sentiments, are remarkable for their lucidity, insight, classical learning and allusion. In lighter vein, he edited a series of children's books for J. M. Dent & Co., illustrating some of them himself, and employing distinguished artists, including Arthur Rackham, for the others.

One of his major interests was photography, his sympathies lying with the Linked Ring Brotherhood, whose aims were to use cameras 'to create a medium for individual expression, making beautiful pictures'. In addition to writing articles on photography, Tilney was often called upon to judge competitions, and during the 1920s was retained by the Sydney Camera Club, Australia, to comment on and criticise members' photographs. In 1932 he gave the club his valuable collection of sixty-four rare photographs by leading British, Continental and American photographers. So anyone visiting the Art Gallery of New South Wales should ask to see the 'F.C. Tilney Gift Collection of Photographs'. Nearer home, an exhibition on his life and work was held in the Europa Gallery of Sutton Library in 1979.

Edward G. Hallam

Exhib: L; LS; RA; RI; WG
Coll: Sutton LC
Published: TILNEY, F.C. *The Appeal of the Picture.* Dent, 1915; *The Lure of The Fine Arts.* Chapman & Hall, 1931; *Principles of Photographic Pictorialism.* Chapman & Hall, 1930; *Art and Reason: for sane and competent art.* [Periodical edited by F. C. Tilney, 1934–1948] Editor of *Tales from Many Lands;* J. M. Dent, 1913–1918. 20 vols.
Illus: BROWNING, E. B. *Sonnets from the Portuguese.* Dent, 1894; CRAIK, D. M. *John Halifax Gentleman.* Dent, 1898.
Bibliog: DBA; GW; PEPPIN; V; WOOD; *Who's Who in Art,* 1950; HALLAM, E. G. *Frederick Colin Tilney 1864–1951; an Artist of Cheam.* Privately printed, 1979

TILT, Archibald Preston 1853–1888
Lovelands, Brighton Road, Sutton c.1870–c.1880
Archibald Preston Tilt, who died at the comparatively early age of thirty-five, was a little-known artist who

exhibited one painting, *Dutch Fishing Girl* (1875), with the Society of British Artists; and one with a far longer title at the Royal Academy: "*Oh, Solitude, if I must with thee dwell, Let it not be amongst the jumbled heap of murky buildings*" (1877). One only hopes that he was not referring to Sutton.

Christened at Walton-on-the-Hill, Surrey, on 27 March 1853, he was the son of a fashionable portrait painter, Frederick Clarke Arnaud Tilt, who had a studio in London as well as a house named Lovelands, at Walton. Tilt senior, patronised by the Royal Family, painted miniatures of Queen Victoria and her children, and exhibited them at the RA. One of his watercolours is in the National Portrait Gallery: *Judge Sir William Erle (1793–1880).* Archibald's brother, Edward Preston Tilt, exhibited a painting entitled *Ada* at the RA in 1868.

Archibald Tilt lived in Walton until his father died in 1869. Then, with his mother, Emma Margaret Tilt, the sixteen-year-old Archibald moved to Sutton. Their new home, which was in the Brighton Road, was named Lovelands after their old one at Walton. Members of the Tilt family continued to live in Sutton until at least 1925, when a Miss Blanche Preston Tilt of Redlands, Brighton Road, died in a Sutton nursing home.

Archibald Preston Tilt died at 8 Albermarle Street, London, on 18 June 1888, leaving a widow, Sarah Ann Tilt. A 'Mrs Tilt' who exhibited with the Society of Women Artists from 1884 until 1887 may have been related to him.

Exhib: RA; RBA
Bibliog: WOOD

TILY, Eugène James, F.R.S.A. 1870–1950
The Rowans, Elgin Road, Sutton, Surrey 1907–1950
With an artistic reputation based on his success as a mezzotint and aquatint artist, Eugène Tily is now chiefly remembered for his coloured engravings after the English artists Reynolds, Gainsborough, Lawrence, Morland, Wheatley and Hoppner, and the French artist Meissonier. Published by Henry Graves, James Connell, Frost and Reed, and Bell, many were artist's proofs and are now rather scarce. He was also a painter in oil and watercolour, and an etcher.

Born on 4 March 1870 at Walkern, Hertfordshire, Tily came from a family with strong medical traditions. His father, James Tily, was a doctor, and it was rather assumed that Eugène would follow in his footsteps. But instead he chose to study art, first at the Bedford Park School of Art and then privately under Arthur Stock, R.A. and Walter Williams.

Tily's first important success came in 1904 at the Louisiana Purchase Exhibition, U.S.A., where he gained the highest award, the Gold Medal, for three stipple engravings in colours: *Mrs Robinson, Mrs Sheridan* and *Lady Castlereagh.* His work was also well-received in France, where he exhibited at the Paris Salon.

His etchings, usually in limited editions of forty or so, are illustrated in the annual volumes of *Fine Prints*

SYDNEY R. TURNER   Coloured drawing 419×616mm
Palace of Nonsuch in the time of Queen Elizabeth [1st]. 1943.   Sutton's Local Collection

GIDEON YATES   Watercolour 159×241mm
Rye Farm, Hoare Esq. 1826.   Sutton's Local Collection

of the Year (1920s), edited by Malcolm C. Salaman. Titles include: *Old Houses, Bristol*; *Ightham Moat Courtyard* and *John Knox's House*.

Tily came to Sutton in 1907 and lived at The Rowans in Elgin Road for over forty years, his main recreations being fishing, shooting and motoring. He died at St Helier Hospital on 9 September 1950, leaving a widow, Betty (née Stephen) Tily.

Exhib: CON; GI; L; P; RA; U.S.A.
Bibliog: BEN; DBA; ENGEN(1); GW; LISTER; TB; *Who's Who in Art* – several editions; SCHUBART, H. Ed. *The Homelover's Book of Fine Pictures*. Bristol: Frost & Reed, Ltd., 1956

TOTTON, Margaret Ann 1836/7–1904
10 Cathcart Road (now Clarendon Road), Wallington –1882–
Miss Margaret Ann Totton, a landscape painter who exhibited at Manchester and with the Society of Women Artists, was the daughter of Elizabeth and William Totton of Wallington, the family living next door to the artist James G. Bingley (q.v.) and only a few doors away from where the 'Brighton Railway Murderer' lived (see Ayling, Amy (q.v.)).

By 1897 Margaret had moved to Ashtead in Surrey, during that year exhibiting a painting entitled *Streets in Whitby* at the SWA exhibition. She died at Oulton-with-Woodlesford, Yorkshire, on 27 December 1904.

Exhib: M; SWA
Bibliog: DBA

TRAVERS, Howard Martin Otho 1886–1948
Architect of the new *Church of the Good Shepherd*, Carshalton, Surrey, 1930
Martin Travers was born in Norwich, the son of a brewer and the grandson of Otho William Travers of Cheam. He studied at the Royal College of Art and worked for a while with Ninian Comper (q.v.). He was a notable exponent of ecclesiastical design in the twentieth century, and his statues, decorations and stained glass windows are numerous and appear in many churches, particularly in the South of England.

He received the commission to build the new *Church of the Good Shepherd*, Carshalton-on-the-Hill in 1928. This was to be part of Bishop Cyril Garbett's (then of Southwark but later Archbishop of York) 'Twenty-five Churches plan', which aimed to provide churches in the rapidly growing outer suburbs which were not adequately served by the ancient parish churches. No records exist of the brief Travers was given, or of any discussions about design and detail. Father Corbould, the Rector of Carshalton, in whose parish this 'daughter' church was to be erected, was extremely autocratic and made all the arrangements to his own satisfaction. Travers's *Church of the Good Shepherd*, standing by the gate of Queen Mary's Hospital for Children, was finished in 1930 and was entirely designed, inside and out, and furnished by the architect.

Many changes have been made over the years but the basic intention of Travers's design can still be appreciated. Set among low, pantiled houses, the church was originally whitewashed, and with its green copper roof and belfrey was intended to resemble a Spanish mission church. Within is a splendid crucifix in Italian trecento style on the East wall and two good decorated windows, one of St Nicholas and one of the Virgin Mary. The altar was originally in Comper's style – the English altar with four posts and side screens – but this was altered after a fire in 1967 and would now, in any case, be inappropriate for current liturgical uses, in which the celebrant at the Eucharist stands behind the altar, facing the congregation.

Travers himself seems to have been something of an eccentric, rather fastidious and aloof and not one given to joining artistic guilds and associations. Most of his work was for the High Church party of the Church of England, but he was also responsible for the *Church of the Holy Redeemer*, Streatham Vale, 1932, which was of a much more Evangelical persuasion. There are good examples of his furnishings at *St Magnus the Martyr*, London Bridge and at *St Mary's*, Bourne Street, SW1.

Jean M. Moore

Bibliog: ANSON, P. F. *Fashions in Church Furnishings 1840–1940*. Faith Press, 1960

*TRAVERS, Norah Kathleen 1858–1922
Church Farm, Cheam 1858
Ballydawley, Pond Hill, Cheam c.1890–1902
North Lodge (Cheam Park Lodge), Malden Road, Cheam 1902–1922
Norah Travers was born in Cheam in 1858, and she lived there all her life. Her father, Otho William Travers, and his sister Jane first came to this area shortly before 1851, staying with their aunt, Mary Anne Steele, in Sutton Village, as Sutton was then known. By 1871 Otho Travers, then aged fifty-four, was the owner of Church Farm, Cheam, employing five men and six boys to farm its 220 acres. He was a widower, his wife having died shortly after the birth of their youngest daughter, Lillian Ethel. Little happened at Cheam in those days without Otho Travers having some hand in it. He was a church-warden at St Dunstan's, on the management committee of the Parochial Rooms and a member of Cheam Cricket Club.

His sister Jane, assisted by three servants, saw to the day-to-day running of the lovely old farmhouse, which has survived to this present day. Situated close to St Dunstan's Church, it dates back in part to Tudor times, although it was altered and enlarged in the eighteenth century and again in the nineteenth.

Two of Otho's daughters and one of his grandsons were artistic. His daughter Florence (q.v.) married Admiral Sir Arthur Limpus but continued to paint in her spare time, whilst his grandson Howard Martin Otho Travers (q.v.) was a church architect of some importance. Norah Travers, who remained a spinster, devoted much of her life to painting. Her watercolours, depicting landscapes or flowers, appeared regularly at the exhibitions of the Society of Women Artists, although she exhibited only one work at the Royal Academy: *Syringa and campanulas* (1910). In 1907, her painting *Alley near St Gregory's Church, Norwich* was shown at the SWA exhibition, carried out during a visit to her brother Howard, a brewer; whilst in 1918 one of local interest was shown there: *Daisies in a Cottage Garden, Cheam*.

There are two watercolours of old Cheam by Norah Travers in Sutton's Local Collection, one showing cottages in Malden Road, the other Red Lion Street on the corner of the High Street. Her last years were spent at North Lodge in Malden Road, where she lived with her sister Marion Henrietta Eliza Travers; and she died at Cheam on 13 January 1922.

Exhib: RA; SWA
Coll: Sutton LC

*TURNER, Sydney Robert, F.R.I.B.A. 1880–1972
27 West Drive, Cheam, 1930s–1972
Architect, draughtsman, designer, artist, collector, historian, antiquarian – Sydney Robert Turner, born in Reigate on 17 November 1880, was all these and more; a man of multiple interests and enthusiasms.

Although Sydney Turner's family came from the Redhill area of Surrey, he had been a resident of Cheam for well over forty years at the time of his death in 1972. We know little about his early background apart from the fact that his father was a scientist (an entomologist); and that he had a brother who died from consumption at an early age. As a young man during the 1914–1918 war he was a conscientious objector, but we have no record as to whether he was penalised in any way for his beliefs.

For some time Turner worked for Hamptons, the well-known furniture designers and cabinet makers, and to the end of his life he was a lover and collector of good furniture. Indeed, he left many beautiful pieces, including a mahogany Chippendale bureau, bequeathed to the Victoria and Albert Museum.

First and foremost, though, Turner was an architect, and his superb draughtsmanship is apparent in the architectural drawings of the Palace of Nonsuch, in Sutton's Local Collection. He was involved in many aspects of the archaeological work at Nonsuch – not always amicably – and lectured on the subject. He also produced a beautifully designed and printed booklet, describing Nonsuch in the time of Elizabeth the First – its heyday. The illustrations and text bring the gardens and the interior rooms of the palace vividly to life.

In the public sector, he was the architect of the *Magnet* building in Harrow Road, London, now demolished. Some time in the late 1920s he set to designing a home for himself. The result was no. 27 West Drive, Cheam, then one of only a few scattered houses in that part of Cheam. The house, with its fixtures and fittings of a period character, was left to the National Trust in Turner's will, but was subsequently sold by them.

Turner married fairly late in life and there were no children of the marriage. Quite how he would have fitted them into his busy life if there had been children, is a problem. Of more than just a casual interest to him was his collection of postal history (post marks, covers, etc.) and his status as a collector and historian led to him becoming very well known in that particular field. He was especially pleased and proud when his name was inscribed on the Roll of Eminent Philatelists.

But locally, because of his drawings, the name of Sydney Turner will always be associated with Nonsuch.

Beryl Maggs

Published: TURNER, S. R. *The Palace of Nonsuch 1538–1670*. Published privately at Cheam, 1948

UNKNOWN ARTIST. 16th Century.
Miniature painting on vellum of *Sir Nicholas Carew* (see Holbein (q.v.)). Circular. 1" diameter.

Coll: Fitzwilliam Museum, Cambridge. Bought in 1943

WALKER, Frederick, A.R.A., O.W.S. 1840–1875
Frederick Walker was born at no. 90 Great Titchfield Street, Marylebone, on 26 May 1840 and he lived in London throughout his life. He and his twin sister Sarah were the seventh and eighth children of William Henry and Ann (née Powell). Their father was a jeweller, with a small business and 'a talent for painting'. Their grandfather, William Walker, was a painter who had exhibited at the Royal Academy and the British Institution between 1782 and 1808. Ten children in all were born to Walker's parents, eight of whom were still living when William Henry died in 1847. His death meant that Mrs Walker was obliged to take on the role of breadwinner, which she achieved by means of her embroidery needle.

From an early age Fred wanted to paint, and his mother encouraged him. He was educated at the North London Collegiate School, Camden Town; and at the age of sixteen was placed in the office of a Mr Baker, architect and surveyor, where he stayed for two years. In 1857 he became a student at the British Museum, spending his days at the museum drawing Greek statues and his evenings attending life classes at Leigh's Academy. At Leigh's he first met John George Marks who was to become his brother-in-law and biographer. Then in March 1858 Walker was admitted to the Royal Academy Schools. It appears, however,

FREDERICK WALKER Oil 831×1264mm
The Vagrants. 1868.   Tate Gallery

that 'In none of these schools . . . was he a very constant attendant' (DNB).

Towards the end of 1858 he was apprenticed to the wood-engraver Josiah Whymper, and for three years applied himself seriously to studying the technique of wood engraving, whilst in his spare time he taught himself to paint in oils and watercolours. In 1859 he joined the Artists' Society in Langham Chambers, and its offshoot, the Langham Sketching Club, where a fellow member was Henry Stacy Marks (q.v.), the brother of John George.

At the age of nineteen, Fred earned his first income as an artist by contributing a drawing to the magazine *Once a Week*. It appeared in the issue for 18 February 1860. He continued to provide illustrations for this magazine until 1861, when his work came to the attention of William Makepeace Thackeray, then the editor of the *Cornhill Magazine*, in which Thackeray was about to publish, in serial form, his own story *The Adventures of Philip*. Walker was employed by Thackeray to work up the latter's own illustrations but was later allowed to create his own woodcuts for the story. When 'Philip' ended, Fred, by then a close friend of Thackeray, illustrated stories by Thackeray's daughter and subsequently worked on Thackeray's own last, unfinished work *Denis Duval*.

Both in his magazine and book illustrations (which

he largely gave up after 1866) and in his paintings, Walker was, in his short life, prolific. The most obvious influences on his style and subject matter were the Pre-Raphaelites, especially Millais, who, like Thackeray, became a personal friend. Many of Walker's paintings are set outdoors, his carefully-painted grass, flowers and foliage forming the foreground and background to sentimental subjects. Another of his biographers, Clementina Black, at one time a neighbour of J. G. Marks in Croydon, wrote: 'We may fairly guess that any person going about to manufacture a spurious 'Walker' would put into it an old wall and a blossoming tree'.

His first Royal Academy painting, hung in 1863, was *The Lost Path*, showing a woman lost in the snow and clasping a small child. The model for the woman was his sister Mary (his own family appear frequently in his paintings); the trees in the background he sketched in Croydon and the snow he painted from salt in his studio; all in good Pre-Raphaelite tradition.

In February 1864 Walker was elected an associate of the Society of Painters in Water-Colours ('The Old Watercolour Society') becoming a member in 1866. In 1871 he became an associate of the Royal Academy and an honorary member of the Belgian Watercolour Society. In all, he exhibited seven paintings at the RA and twenty-two at the OWS.

JOHANN ZOFFANY, School of   Oil 737×813mm
Mr. and Mrs. Burke of Carshalton.
Photograph courtesy of Sotheby's.

FREDERICK C. TILNEY   Oil 241×191mm
Portrait of Violet Keast. c. 1916.   Private collection

Whilst Walker's topographical links with Cookham, where his mother had a cottage, are often cited, his connection with Beddington, and to a lesser extent Croydon, are usually overlooked or ignored. Yet they are, in fact, very considerable. The local connection in *The Lost Path* has already been mentioned. By 1860, Fred's twin sister Sarah was married to J. G. Marks and living in Croydon. Walker visited them often, and by 1861 was drawing in the area, in locations which included Beddington churchyard. In 1863 Marks and his family moved to Beddington, to a house referred to as 'The Cottage'. The exact location of this cottage is still uncertain, but it seems to have been near Beddington Lane, and may have been the building on the east side of the Lane which appears on nineteenth-century Ordnance Survey maps as 'Pimm's Cottage' or 'The Thatched House'.

Marks later wrote, in his *Life and Letters of Frederick Walker:* 'I also had, about a month before [midsummer 1863] moved from Croydon to a cottage at Beddington, standing by itself in the fields; and as the place was easy of access from town, and at the same time quite in the country, formed a convenient base of operations for Walker of which he availed himself for some time to come. The first work he did there was a little water-colour called *Refreshment . . .*'

In the catalogue of Walker's posthumous exhibition, 1876, a note to item no.14, 'Unfinished Sketch of Cottage at Beddington, Surrey', said: 'At or in the neighbourhood of this cottage the Artist completed several and painted the backgrounds of some other works here exhibited'. At least twenty of Walker's works are known to have been painted in the district, in whole or part. They include some of his best-known pictures: *The Vagrants* (1867) *The Violet Field* (1867) and *The Wayfarers* (1865).

In a preliminary drawing, Fred originally used the Addington Hills as the background of his painting *The Wayfarers*, which shows a blind man led by a young boy, but he later substituted a copse at Beddington, where he also painted *Spring. The Violet Field* was a field belonging to a Mr Steadman, with a view towards 'Marrage's' or 'Marriage's' Farm. In the 1881 census, Beddington Park Farm, to the west of Beddington Lane, was managed by a Mr Alexander Marriage.

The Vagrants shows a family of gipsies, pictured in an area of hummocky grass and scrub. Walker's sister discovered the gipsies, Fred writing to his mother in 1867 that 'Sarah knows of some gipsies who are evidently brought into this world to sit for my picture . . .' The setting was Beddington (perhaps near Mitcham Common?) 'not so far from the cottage as *The Wayfarers*'.

For an edition of *Jane Eyre* by Charlotte Brontë, never actually published, Walker painted Mr Rochester seated in front of a wall 'taken from that enclosing part of the old home of the Carews at Beddington, now the Female Orphan Asylum' (Marks). This was one of the three trial pieces by which he gained his associateship of the Old Watercolour Society in 1864; as was *Refreshment*, another local painting.

He sketched and painted Marks's cottage at Beddington more than once. A watercolour called *New Arrivals*, alternative title *The Poultry Farm* (1865) shows what is probably the south side of the cottage, with the Crystal Palace visible in the distance. Models for this were J. G. Marks and Sarah, with their sons Geoffrey and Gilbert; as well as their poultry. (J. G. Marks's sons attended Whitgift School at Croydon, where one of them was nicknamed 'Black Marks'.) James George Bingley (q.v.) painted a copy of this watercolour and it is in the Leggatt Collection at the British Museum.

Walker achieved fame in his lifetime and was particularly fortunate in gaining the friendship and patronage of Sir William Agnew, the art dealer. His other friends, apart from Thackeray and Millais, included the painter John William North and the writer George Du Maurier, the latter featuring Frederick Walker both as himself and, rather confusingly, as 'Little Billee' in his well-known novel *Trilby*. Du Maurier describes him/them thus: 'both were small and slight though beautifully made, with tiny hands and feet; always arrayed as the lilies of the field for all they spun and toiled so arduously; both had regularly featured faces of a noble cast and most winning character; both had the best and simplest manner in the world, and a way of getting themselves much and quickly and permanently liked'.

Walker had various hobbies and interests beyond his painting; he played the flute; rode, swam and fished. He was a cat-lover, owning a black kitten given to him by Millais. Eel-eye was often mentioned in Walker's letters, usually 'in connection with some deed of rapine or murder' (Black). Immortalised in Millais's painting *Flood*, Eel-eye survived Walker and died in the care of J. G. Marks. Stacy Marks once bet Walker that he, Fred, could not keep a certain cat on his knees for half an hour without holding it; but he lost the bet. A graphic description of how Walker first enticed the large tom cat to him and then kept it happy for the allotted time, is given in *Our River* by G. D. Leslie.

Cats were one thing; but Walker never married, and no attachments, whether romantic, sentimental or physical appear to have been attributed to him, with one exception. This was Maria Ansdell, a daughter of Richard Ansdell, R.A. Walker painted her a number of times. Against a sketch in the Leggatt Collection in the British Museum, called *Lady Holding a Fan*, Leggatt wrote: 'The artist was in love with this lady'. A cutting from the *Morning Post*, 21 December 1906, records a 'delightful story' about Walker and Maria, said to have been told by W. P. Frith, R.A.

'He was the most alert-minded creature. I remember him dining with us at Pembridge Villas and in the middle of dinner he suddenly broke out into whistling. He had no idea where he was. He was very much in love with a daughter of Ansdell. We were staying up in Scotland at the time, and he used to follow her about all day biting his nails and whistling . . .'

Was it for her that Walker, in November 1867, wrote to his sister at Beddington: '. . . I am afraid you'll think me in a sad way, but could you get Steadman to send me a bouquet of violets about the size of a dinner plate. I dare say you will not be much puzzled as to where it

FREDERICK WALKER   Watercolour
The Poultry Farm, 'New Arrivals'.   British Museum
Copy by James G. Bingley.

is to go afterwards . . . ?' 'Walker was never married', comments Marks coyly at this point, 'but in the above passage the breath of violets comes across the years, telling us he knew of love'. Violets or not, Miss Ansdell was by this time the wife of a Mr Morley whom she had married in 1864; but Walker went on painting her.

Fred, in fact, lived all his life with members of his family, all of whom, like himself, appear to have had delicate or weak constitutions. His adult life was spent with his brother John, who died in 1868, his sister Fanny, and his mother. By 1873 he had become consumptive, and he visited Algeria for his health's sake. There was a temporary improvement; but in 1874 he was ill again and went to Devon. In May 1875, whilst staying with a friend for a fishing holiday, he had a haemorrhage and died two weeks later. He was buried at Cookham on the 8th June, beside his mother (who had died in the previous November) and his brother. His sister Fanny joined them a year later. His last projected work, sketched but uncompleted, for which he was still seeking a final location, was called *The Unknown Land*.

A memorial in Cookham church, with a profile medallion in low relief by Henry Hugh Armstead, R.A., was commissioned by his friends and admirers who, at a meeting at the Arts Club in June 1875 started a 'Walker Fund' for the purpose, and issued a printed prospectus. The Executive Committee of the fund included H. S. Marks, Richard Ansdell and Sir William Agnew. Du Maurier, Millais, North, Alma-Tadema, Frederick Leighton and G. F. Watts were among the sixty-seven people listed as the General Committee. The preamble said: 'Walker's genius, acknowledged from the first by artists of all shades of opinion, can hardly be said to have been appreciated by the public at large as it deserved . . . but that his work will live – that his fame will steadily increase – there can be no question . . .' As with so many other predictions, this has not come to pass.

Douglas Cluett

Exhib: OWS; RA
Memorial exhibitions: Deschamps's Gallery, London. January 1876; Dunthorne's Gallery, London. 1885
Coll: Ashmolean Museum, Oxford; BM; City AG, Manchester; Courtauld Institute, London; Fitzwilliam Museum, Cambridge; Tate AG; Towneley Hall, Burnley; V&A; Whitworth AG, Manchester
Illus: See HOUFE
Bibliog: BEN; DNB; ENGEN(2); HARDIE; HOUFE; LAMBOURNE; LISTER; MALLALIEU; TB; WOOD; CARR, J. C. *Frederick Walker*; an essay. Robert Dunthorne's Gallery, London, 1885; PHILLIPS, C. *Frederick Walker*. Seeley & Co., 1894; MARKS, J. G. *Life and Letters of Frederick Walker*. Macmillan & Co., 1896; BLACK, C. *Frederick Walker*. Duckworth, N. D. (1900)
N.B. Much original research, generously made available by Miss Auralie Stanton, is gratefully acknowledged

WALLIS, Henry, R.W.S. 1830–1916
Claverton, 60 Cheam Road, Sutton 1911–1914

In 1911, when Henry Wallis came to live in Sutton he was over eighty years old and rather crotchety. Fifty years and more had passed since he had run off with the wife of the writer George Meredith, causing a Victorian scandal. Today Wallis is remembered for this one blot on his character and for his painting *Chatterton*, generally known as 'The Death of Chatterton', now in the Tate Gallery; the two are closely linked. Another highly regarded painting by Wallis is his 'social conscience' picture *The Stonebreaker* (1857), in Birmingham City Art Gallery.

Wallis was born in London on 21 February 1830, the son of a well-to-do architect. After attending Cary's Academy and then the Royal Academy Schools, he went to Paris to study at Charles Gleyre's Atelier – Whistler was there at about the same time – and at L'Academie des Beaux-Arts. Wallis's early paintings, mostly historical, were painted in the traditional manner of the time; however his first Royal Academy painting, *Dr. Johnson at Cave's the Publisher* (1854), owes more to the eighteenth than the nineteenth century. It appeared at Sotheby's Belgravia on 27 March 1973 when it was sold for £800.

He came under the influence of the Pre-Raphaelites in about 1855 and by 1856 he was painting in their style. In 1856 his oil painting *Chatterton* was exhibited at the RA where it met with critical acclaim, Ruskin (q.v.) proclaiming it 'faultless'. Thereafter the artist was known as 'Chatterton Wallis'. This painting has recently provided the inspiration for Peter Ackroyd's novel *Chatterton*, shortlisted for the Booker Prize in 1987; it is illustrated on the book jacket.

Ironically, George Meredith, seen here without his usual beard and looking suitably young, pale and vulnerable, was the model for the poet Thomas Chatterton, whose suicide by poison in 1770 is the subject matter of the painting. Wallis was able to carry out the painting in the actual attic room in Gray's Inn where the poet had died, since in 1856 Wallis's friend Peter Austin Daniel occupied this set of rooms. Meredith, who received a fee for sitting, seems to have been largely unaware of his wife's growing attachment to Wallis until about 1857, by which time Wallis and Mary Ellen Meredith were lovers. The cuckolded husband never forgave either of them.

Although Wallis was obviously in love with her (his pencil sketch of Mary Ellen, drawn in 1858, clearly conveys this), one has the impression that he pursued the affair somewhat half-heartedly. In 1858 a son was born of their liaison, Harold Felix Wallis (registered as Harold Felix Meredith), who grew up to be a successful businessman. In 1859 Wallis and Mary Ellen went to Capri together but Mary Ellen returned alone, although they continued to see each other

HENRY WALLIS   Oil 622×933mm
Chatterton. 1856.   Tate Gallery

afterwards. Two years later, at the age of forty, the ill-fated Mary Ellen died of kidney disease. The saddest thing about the whole affair was that she went to her grave with neither her husband, nor her lover – not even her children – attending her funeral.

The whole experience had a far-reaching effect on Wallis, who never married. He devoted the rest of his life to painting and scholarship; and eventually regained his respectability in the eyes of society, in 1880 being elected a member of the Royal Society of Painters in Water-Colours. With a keen eye for a bargain, and familiar with all the best junk shops and museums in this country and abroad, he was also an enthusiastic collector of early ceramics, in particular Persian wares and Italian Maiolicas. He became a world authority in this field, writing books on the subject, some of which are illustrated with his own delicately-painted watercolours. His sketchbooks can be seen at the Victoria and Albert Museum.

Although Wallis was not actually a member of the Pre-Raphaelite Brotherhood, his name will always be associated with them, and he remained on good terms with them throughout his life. In 1915, a year before his death, he received a rather pathetic letter from Arthur Hughes (q.v.) who was then seriously ill. Hughes, concerned for the future welfare of his family, asked his friend if he would care to buy one of the Old Masters from his collection. Wallis must have either bought one or offered some financial assistance, since he later received a grateful 'thank you' letter from Hughes (Johnson, D. *Lesser Lives*).

Wallis, never short of money, was able to travel abroad at will, visiting Sicily, Egypt and other places in the East. He left his valuable collection of antiques and books to his son, some of the prize items later finding their way to the Victoria and Albert and the British Museums. He died of a stroke, at no. 1 Walpole Road, Croydon, on 20 December 1916 and is buried at Highgate Cemetery. Claverton, his home at Sutton for three years, was later pulled down and there is now a block of flats on the site.

Exhib: BI; GI; L; M; NG; RA; RBA; RWS
Coll: Birmingham AG; Tate AG; V&A
Published: WALLIS, H. *Egyptian Ceramic Art.* Taylor & Francis, 1900; *Oriental Influences on Italian Ceramic Art.* Quaritch, 1900; *Italian Albarelli.* Quaritch, 1904; and others
Bibliog: BEN; DBA; GW; HOUFE; MALLALIEU; TB; WOOD; *Who Was Who 1916–1928*; JOHNSON, D. *Lesser Lives.* Heinemann, 1973; WILLIAMS, D. *George Meredith; his life and lost love.* H. Hamilton, 1977

WALPOLE, Mrs S. C. Exhib: 1886–1905
Halstow, Park Hill, Carshalton 1887–1888
Mrs Walpole, a landscape painter, lived in Carshalton for just over a year, her address prior to that being Hampton Court Palace. She exhibited a total of eleven works at the Society of Women Artists' exhibitions, including one entitled *Near Esher, Surrey*, submitted from Carshalton. In 1888 she left Carshalton and returned to London, living in Kensington.

Exhib: SWA
Bibliog: DBA

*WARDALE, J. J. Exhib: 1887
15 Station Road, Carshalton 1897–1914
J. J. Wardale, a landscape painter in oil, lived in Carshalton for about eighteen years. He painted a view of Carshalton Church and two views of Wrythe Green which are all now in Sutton's Local Collection. Earlier, he had lived in Barrow-on-Trent, Derbyshire, and during this period had exhibited two paintings at Nottingham Art Gallery.

In Pile's local directories of Carshalton, J. J. Wardale is listed as the householder at the above address from 1897 until 1914. From 1915 onwards, however, a Mrs S. Wardale is listed as the householder.

Exhib: N
Bibliog: DBA

WARREN, Sophy S., S.W.A. 1837/8–1879
Millwood Lodge, Woodside Road, Sutton 1870–1876
Medmore Cottage, Sutton Common, Sutton 1876–1877
Ivy Bank, Carshalton Road, Sutton 1877–1879
Sophy S. Warren has emerged as a woman of some mystery. Throughout her exhibiting life, which began in 1864 when her small watercolour *On the Thames* was shown at the Society of Women Artists' exhibition, she was known as 'Sophy Warren'. But there is now enough evidence to suggest that her real name was Sophia Elizabeth Slayter and that for some reason, as yet unknown, she chose to live out her later life as Sophy Warren.

She appears as 'Sophy Warren' in the 1871 census return for Sutton, her address then being Millwood Lodge, Woodside Road. The only other person living there was Charles H. Warren, aged forty-five, described as a 'landscape painter in oil'. From Sophy's entry we can see that she was unmarried, aged thirty-three, a 'landscape painter in water colours' and the sister of Charles Warren. Both their birthplaces are listed as 'Hackney in Middlesex'.

In 1876 Charles and Sophy moved to a cottage on Sutton Common but lived there for only a year. Their next address was Ivy Bank, Carshalton Road, Sutton, next door to Linn Villa, where the artist Edmund Gill (q.v.) lived. They had only been there for a matter of months when, on 30 September 1877, Charles Warren died of heart disease, in his will leaving everything to 'Sophia Elizabeth Slayter', without mentioning her relationship to him. Two years later, on 19 July 1879, this same Sophia Slayter died at Thornton Heath (the artist Sophy Warren had exhibited her work for the last time in 1878). Rather curiously, Sophia Slayter's death was not registered; but she left a will and this confirms that until shortly before her death she was living at Ivy Bank in Sutton, although Church's *Directory of Sutton* for 1878 lists a 'Miss Warren' as the householder there. Sophia Slayter left everything to 'my friends Joseph Warren of Epping and Frederick Warren now residing with me at Ivy Bank . . .' and this rather implies that the Warrens were not related to her.

Ellen C. Clayton included Sophy S. Warren in her book *Female Artists*, where a rather vague account of

SOPHY S. WARREN   Watercolour 140×241mm
Boats on a calm river.   Photo courtesy Sotheby's

the latter's personal history is given – mainly that her family came from Fairford and that she had 'no instructor in art but constantly painted and studied with her brother'. It is possible that Charles Warren and Sophia Slayter *were* brother and sister; she may have been his half-sister and that would have accounted for the different surnames; but now that more than a century has passed since their deaths, the mystery has become almost impossible to solve.

The watercolourist Sophy S. Warren appears in several art dictionaries. As a member of the Society of Women Artists, she exhibited with them almost every year from 1864 until 1878; and also exhibited thirty-nine paintings at the Society of British Artists' exhibitions and six at the Royal Academy. Painting nearly always in pure watercolour, she would sometimes add touches of body colour to her work.

There are four of her watercolours in the National Collection at the Victoria and Albert Museum, including the delightfully nostalgic *Near Benhill Wood, Sutton, Surrey*, showing a horse-drawn cart and driver in a wooded landscape. Not a house is in sight; yet today nearly the whole of that area is built over, with only the name of a road, Benhill Wood Road, reminding us of the wood which was once there.

Most of her paintings were exhibited whilst she was living in Sutton; they included four views of this area – three of Benhill Wood and one entitled *A Cottage near Carshalton* – all exhibited with the SBA. When her paintings appear on the market today they are snapped up quickly, collectors realising that with their bright, fresh colours and attractive subject matter, they would enhance any home. Some of her paintings are in collections abroad. She is known to have sent work to the Continent, to America, to Australia and to New Zealand. *Early Morning-Exeter*, the last work she

exhibited at the RA (1878), is regarded as one of her finest works.

Exhib: B; RA; RBA; SWA
Coll: Dublin AG; V&A
Bibliog: BEN; FISHER; LAMBOURNE; MALLALIEU; TB; WOOD; CLAYTON, E. C. *English Female Artists.* Tinsley Bros., 1876, 2 vols.

*WATTS, William 1752–1851

William Watts, born in London in 1752, the son of a master silk weaver, was a professional line-engraver who studied under Paul Sandby and Edward Rooker. When the latter died, Watts took over his publication *Copper Plate Magazine* and printed a series of views after Sandby. Later, between 1779 and 1786, Watts's own series of engraved plates: *Seats of the Nobility and Gentry . . .* were published. Although some of the plates were engraved after other artists, Watts drew and engraved the plate *Carshalton House . . .* himself; two preliminary drawings for it are in his sketchbook, which can be seen at the Victoria and Albert Museum. His description of the house reads as follows:

> Carshalton House was built by the celebrated Dr. Radcliffe who, from its healthy and pleasant situation, styled it the Montpelier of England. It is a large and commodious Structure; the principal room which is the Library, is sixty-four feet in length. The Grounds are laid out with great Taste and are finely watered by a clear Spring, the Head rising a little Distance from the House, which, after running through the Village of Carshalton, falls into the River Wandell.

Watts, an ardent supporter of the French Revolution, went to Paris, where some French versions of his plates, engraved in colours by Laurent Guyot, were published in 1793. Interesting differences occur

131

between the English and French versions of the *Carshalton House . . .* plate. The English one shows an aristocratic lady, accompanied by an equally aristocratic gentleman, strolling through the grounds; but in the French version they have been transformed into a serving wench and gardener. In the Paris of 1793 aristocrats were most definitely 'out' and peasants 'in'.

Foolishly, Watts invested most of his money in French funds and had it confiscated. He had to wait until 1815 before he got some of it back. In the meantime he returned to England virtually penniless. To recoup his losses he had to set to work to produce more engravings. By 1814 he had made enough to retire to a cottage at Cobham in Surrey, where he died on 7 December 1851, aged ninety-nine, having been blind for his last few years.

Coll: BM; Sutton LC; V&A; Victoria AG, Bath
Bibliog: BEN; DNB; HOUFE; LISTER; MACKENZIE; MALLALIEU; TB

WEBB, Philip 1831–1915
Architect of no. 19 Park Hill, Carshalton (1867–8)
Philip Webb was a major architect of the Arts and Crafts movement and an associate of William Morris (q.v.). No.19 Park Hill is a good example of his smaller domestic buildings. By the time he designed this house, built in 1867–8, Webb had had his own architectural practice for eight years and was a leading member of Morris & Co., having met William Morris in the offices of the Gothic Revival architect G.E. Street in the 1850s. Webb's designs are typical of the Morris attitude towards vernacular architecture: use of traditional materials, use of asymmetry, particularly in the placement of windows, and a general lack of pretension.

The house was designed for William Hale White, the novelist 'Mark Rutherford', who was introduced to Webb by Ruskin (q.v.). White had been looking for a house to meet his requirements for some time. He first came to Carshalton in 1862 but moved away to Epsom three years later. In 1865 he read a letter from Ruskin in the *Daily Telegraph* which summed up his own views of 'houses' and 'homes'. Most people were forced to live in 'mean dwellings' of bad design, both aesthetically and practically. The *Telegraph* printed White's reply describing his fruitless search for a house of plain, unpretentious design, built honestly and sturdily. This led to a correspondence with Ruskin, who realised that White's views coincided with Philip Webb's.

Having found his architect, White bought a plot of land in Park Hill, which then had few houses built along it. The house Webb designed had many typical Arts and Crafts movement features – white-painted sash windows, a wide variety of building materials; including brick, hung tiles and pargetting, and an unostentatious honesty of purpose. Webb thought that a house was only a successful design if it was hardly noticable in its surroundings. No. 19 Park Hill does not assault the eye, but once acknowledged, has great charm which deepens with familiarity.

The house as built has a few alterations from the original design. Red bricks were to be used but were replaced by yellow stock bricks, presumably for economic reasons. The roof was to be tiled, but slates were used, and there are no external shutters, as had been planned. This is surprising as White had specifically mentioned shutters as a desirable feature, to shut out noise, of which he had an obsessive dislike. The original plan was amended as well. The cellar is much smaller and the staircase is in a quite different place from on the original plans. Webb insisted on overseeing all aspects of the design and construction of his houses and often fell out with his clients.

However, in spite of these alterations, he and White formed a lasting friendship. The latter wrote to the *Telegraph* describing his success in finding a house that was truly a 'home', but said it could be improved by an enlarged cellar, bread ovens and earth closets. The interior was panelled, and papered with William Morris wallpapers.

Whilst living in this house White took an active part in the life of Carshalton and was visited by such luminaries of the art world as Arthur Hughes (q.v.) and William Morris.

The house was divided into two flats for a while, but is now again a single private residence.

Cynthia Bradley

Exhib: RA
Bibliog: TB; WOOD

WESTMACOTT, Henry 1784–1861
Local works: *Memorial to Elizabeth Tchitchagoff*, 1811.
Memorial to Sir Nicholas Carew, c.1800.
Both in St. Mary's Church, Beddington.
Memorial to Philip Antrobus [in the neo-Greek style], 1816.
Lumley Chapel, Cheam.
Henry Westmacott was the thirteenth child of Richard Westmacott and a younger brother of Sir Richard Westmacott (q.v.). He was a competent general mason who could turn his hand to anything from plinths and chimney-pieces to monuments and architecture: eg. part of the Royal Mews, Pimlico, and also work at Buckingham Palace.

In 1830 he moved to Edinburgh where he became a frequent exhibitor of portrait sculpture at the Royal Scottish Academy.

Jean M. Moore

Exhib: RSA
Bibliog: BEN; GUNNIS; TB

WESTMACOTT, Sir Richard, R.A. 1775–1856
Local works: *Memorial to Sir Benjamin Hallowell-Carew*, 1834; in St Mary's Church, Beddington.
Memorials to *John Antrobus* and to *The Rev. Henry Peach*, both dated 1813; in the Lumley Chapel, Cheam.
Richard Westmacott, the brother of Henry Westmacott (q.v.), studied in Rome in 1793 under the distinguished sculptor Canova. He was very

successful in Italy and received the first Gold Medal of the Academy of St Luke (awarded by the Pope) for his bas-relief of *Joseph and His Brethren*. He returned to England in 1797 after an eventful journey and started up his own business in London.

He soon attracted a great deal of business in competition with Francis Chantrey (see Chantrey Bequest (q.v.)) and acquired decorative work at Windsor, at Kensington Palace and at the Royal Pavilion in Brighton, where he was responsible for the elaborate chimney-piece in the Music Room. He exhibited at the Royal Academy from 1797–1839, was made an associate in 1805 and a full member in 1811, finally becoming the Professor of Sculpture in 1827. Two years before his death, a knighthood was conferred upon him. Examples of his work abound in Westminster Abbey and St Paul's Cathedral, and locally in the parish churches of Mitcham and Streatham.

Jean M. Moore

Exhib: RA
Bibliog: BEN; GUNNIS; TB; *Art Journal*, 1856, p. 316

WHEELER, Frederick Exhib: 1902–3
Customers hurrying through the doors of the *National Westminster Bank* at the top of Sutton High Street usually fail to notice the distinctive Art Nouveau carvings above the door and windows. The bank, built in 1902, is Sutton's best example of Art Nouveau architecture. It was designed by Frederick Wheeler, who was also the architect of *Sutton Adult School* in Benhill Avenue, opened in January 1910, although this is in his more usual Queen Anne style.

Wheeler designed many commercial buildings in South London, including shops in Streatham High Road, and houses on the Manor Park and Woodlands Estates at Streatham. In the 1930s, the firm Frederick Wheeler & Son had an architectural practice at no. 43 High Street, Sutton and designed a new vicarage for St Paul's Church, Nork, Surrey, exhibiting the design at the Royal Academy in 1936.

Exhib: RA
Bibliog: CHERRY; DBA

FREDERICK WHEELER
Art Nouveau carvings on the National Westminster Bank, Sutton, designed in 1902.

WHITEHEAD, Elsie Exhib: 1923
Huntingdon Lodge, Benhill Road, Sutton 1919–1927
Elsie Whitehead, a sculptor, exhibited one work, a glazed earthenware figure of *Peter Pan*, at the Royal Academy (1923). She lived at Huntingdon Lodge, Sutton, where the householder at the time was T. L. Whitehead (Pile)

Exhib: RA
Bibliog: DBA

WIENS, Siegfried (Stephen) Makepeace 1871–1956
Hillcrest, Eaton Road, Sutton c.1885–1895
Siegfried Wiens, who early on in his career gained fame as a sculptor, later concentrated more on landscape and portrait painting. Born in London in 1871, he was the son of Henry Wiens, a merchant, and the grandson of the German poet Ferdinand Freiligrath, a political refugee who sought asylum in England in the nineteenth century. Siegfried, educated partly in Germany, entered the Royal Academy Schools in 1890, winning the Landseer Scholarship, the Creswick Prize and a British Institute Scholarship. He married J. Alicia Lambert Smith, by whom he had a daughter, and changed his first name to Stephen in about 1920.

He spent about ten years in Sutton; the Wiens family took up residence in Hillcrest House shortly before 1885 and remained there until 1895. During this period, Siegfried exhibited his first two paintings at the Royal Academy: *A Trout-stream* in 1893 and *Mrs. Freiligrath Kroeker* in 1894. By 1907, however, when his bronze, *Girl and Lizard*, was bought for the nation under the terms of the Chantrey Bequest (q.v.), he was no longer living in Sutton.

Shortly before the start of the First World War he was engaged on a design for a monument to his grandfather, Ferdinand Freiligrath (then back in favour in Germany), which was to be erected at Rolandseck-on-the-Rhine, the model for it being mentioned in *The Studio* (August 1913, pp. 222–3). Throughout the war, however, Wiens remained in this country and exhibited at the RA in 1915 and 1916.

He spent much of his life in Sussex, living by the coast where he was able to do plenty of walking and swimming – next to painting his favourite forms of relaxation. He visited Yorkshire, capturing in soft pastel colours the wildness and loneliness of its vast stretches of moorland, and was interested in the theatre, painting portraits of actors and actresses. Five of Wiens's paintings are in the Worthing Art Gallery, including his large, impressive portrait of *Edward John Trelawney, 1792–1881* (the English author and adventurer who was at Leghorn when Shelley died, performing the last services to the poet's body). Wiens died at Worthing on 25 June 1956, aged eighty-five.

Exhib: B; G; I; P; RA
Coll: Brighton AG; Tate AG; Worthing AG
Bibliog: BEN; DBA; GW; V; WOOD; *Who's Who in Art*, 1934; *The Studio*, vol. lix, no. 245, pp. 222–3, Aug. 1913; CHAMOT, M and others. *The Modern Paintings, Drawings and Sculpture in the Tate Gallery.* Oldbourne Press, 1964, 2 vols.

WILKINSON, William Scott 1886–1975
Elm End, 18 Elm Road, Sutton 1931–1975
William Scott Wilkinson, a sculptor in bronze, marble, stone and plaster, was born in Yorkshire on 25 July 1886 and lived in Sutton for the last forty-five years of his life. Between 1919 and 1966 he exhibited, in total, thirty-four works – mostly statuettes – at the Royal Academy. These included portrait heads, single figures of dancers and bathers, and groups of figures bearing titles such as: *The Rescue* (1922) and *The Entombment* (1923). Wilkinson was also a modeller of plaques and cameos.

He died at Sutton on 5 November 1975.

Exhib: RA
Bibliog: DBA

WILSON, Richard, R.A. 1714–1782
Although Richard Wilson did not exactly put Cheam on the map, he has – inadvertently and posthumously – put Cheam into no. 10 Downing Street. His painting *The Cock Tavern, Cheam*, painted circa 1745–8, hangs in the official residence of the Prime Minister.

He obviously regarded this view as a best-seller, painting at least three other versions of it, one of which is in the Tate Gallery. They all date from Wilson's early period, before he went to Italy, and show the wide sweep of Cheam Common, with the Cock Tavern to the left of the picture. Wilson has placed some country folk outside the inn and – perhaps as a contrast – one or two gentlefolk taking a leisurely stroll on the Common. To the right of the picture – in the far distance behind some trees – a large, as yet unidentified house can be glimpsed. The suggested site for the Cock Tavern in Cheam is Park Lane; it may have been the building which is now no. 26, a private house; but there are topographical difficulties in reconciling this location with Wilson's painting. Richard Wilson, born in 1714 in Montgomeryshire, Wales, arrived in London when he was fifteen and studied under Thomas Wright, the portrait painter. He gained early recognition for himself as a portrait painter, but is mainly admired for his landscapes, which secure him his place as a major figure in the development of English landscape painting. In 1749, following the fashion of the time, he went to Italy, spending much of his time in Rome. After six years, he returned to England, bringing back with him many fine landscape paintings.

Wilson's palette was limited to few colours, but he was a master of colour tones, blending them with exquisite taste. His colour sense was superior to his composition, which could be stiff and mannered at times. He was a founder member of the Royal Academy, where he was the Librarian in 1776.

Unfortunately, towards the end of his life his popularity waned, possibly due to illness and alchoholism. Failing to gain enough commissions, he was forced to live in much reduced circumstances, his fortune only taking a turn for the better in 1781, when he inherited a property at Llanberis. He returned then to the country of his birth but was there for only a year,

RICHARD WILSON   Oil 419×527mm
The Cock Tavern, Cheam, Surrey. c. 1745.   Tate Gallery

dying in 1782. John Constable (q.v.) said of him: 'He was one of those appointed to show the world the hidden stores and beauties of nature'.

Exhib: RA
Bibliog: BEN; LAMBOURNE; MALLALIEU; TB; WATERHOUSE; WRIGHT, T. *Some Account of the Life of Richard Wilson.* 1821; SOLKIN, D. H. *Richard Wilson . . .* Tate Gallery, 1982

*WINTER, William Tatton, R.B.A. 1855–1928

3 North Street, Carshalton 1883–1886
Rackham Cottage, 4 Camden Road, Carshalton 1886–c.1894
1 Parkside, Little Wrythe Lane, Carshalton c.1894–1897
William Tatton Winter was born on 2 February 1855 at no. 58 Warrington Street (next door to the Boston Arms Inn), Ashton-under-Lyne, Lancashire, a small town near the Lancashire/Yorkshire border where the local industries were cotton spinning, weaving, brewing and the manufacture of hats and machinery. His surname was actually Winterbottom – he was one of the six children of Martha and William Winterbottom – but he later shortened it to 'Winter' to avoid confusion with another Northern artist. He had an early adventure at the age of three, when his nurse ran away with him to Liverpool, had him re-christened in the Catholic Church, and was only caught, with William in tow, as she was about to board a ship bound for Australia.

He was brought up mainly by his mother. His father, who had gone to America to seek his fortune, taking with him his eldest son, was killed in the American Civil War, fighting on the side of the North. William's mother, a courageous, hardworking Lancashire woman, was left to bring up her family alone. To make ends meet she took a stall on Ashton Market Place, where she sold second-hand clothes. William was educated privately and at a local elementary school.

According to James Winterbottom, one of William's brothers, William started to draw 'almost from the time he could hold a pencil'; but his mother needed every penny William could earn, so he was obliged, on leaving school, to take a job in a foundry, studying art in the evenings. Later, he worked as a lather-boy in a barber's – which may be why he afterwards sported a beard – and then in a draper's store, where he was caught drawing caricatures of the staff. Reports differ as to what happened then; some say that he got the sack, others that his employer recognised his talent and encouraged him towards a career in art. At about this time he came across Ruskin's *Modern Painters* in the Manchester Free Library and avidly read every word, copying Old Master drawings according to Ruskin's plan; Ruskin (q.v.) remained an important influence throughout his life.

In Manchester he met George Milner, J.P. who served on numerous committees concerned with art and education, and was the Treasurer and Manager of the Bennett Street Schools, where William studied in the evenings. From Milner, whose interests were the

135

same as his own – walking, sketching and the 'observation of natural phenomena', he received tremendous encouragement and friendship. Milner introduced him to the people who could advance his career. One was Mr Rowley of Rowley's Galleries, Manchester, who took him to see Ford Maddox Brown, an associate of the Pre-Raphaelites. Brown, then engaged in painting his famous murals in Manchester Town Hall, took an interest in the young artist and gave him some valuable advice.

During the 1870s, William Tatton Winter studied at the Manchester Academy of Fine Art and joined the Manchester Athenaeum Graphic Club. He also took up teaching, his sketching classes in the country proving most popular on account of his genial good nature and helpfulness to his students. By then he had moved away from Ashton to live at Harpurhey, near Manchester; soon he would leave the North of England for good, to live out the rest of his life near London, centre of the English art world. Tatton Winter's early years in the North, however, influenced his style for the rest of his life.

Ashton-under-Lyne in East Lancashire is bordered on one side by the suburbs of Manchester, on the other by the small mill towns and villages which spill out over the slopes of the Saddleworth Moors. We know that William was familiar with the moors. Indeed, two early studies of Greenfield, a village is that area, were found in his studio at his death. The Saddleworth Moors have many moods. When the sun is on them and the purple heather is in bloom there is no place more beautiful. But for much of the year they are lashed with rain, whipped by a wind in which one can barely stand and are haunted by murders half a century apart. In the nineteenth century, murders took place at a lonely inn known as 'Bill o'Jacks'. The landlord and his son were hacked to pieces, the murders never solved. In this century the victims of the 'Moors Murderers' were buried here.

Few of Tatton Winter's Lancashire paintings are known, but throughout his life – even when he lived in Surrey – he painted bleak, rain-swept landscapes and became known more for these than for his brighter paintings. F. E. Green was puzzled why such a 'cheerful optimist' should choose to paint 'wind-swept , ragged trees . . . a stagnant pool faintly glimmering under a mystic glow of twilight; grey clouds and a somnolent silence pervading the entire atmosphere' (*The Surrey Hills*, 1915). He should have visited the Saddleworth Moors in bad weather; there he would have found his answer. The artist is represented in Lancashire by his watercolour *Wind on the Heath*, in Manchester City Art Gallery, and his watercolour *The Wind in the Trees*, in Oldham Art Gallery.

Whilst he was living in Manchester, Tatton Winter paid his first visit to the Continent, accompanied by an architect friend. With only £3 between them they arrived in Antwerp and then set off on foot for Rotterdam, where Tatton Winter made a sketch of Rembrandt's *The Gold Weighers*, watched by an American tourist who offered to buy it. Taken by surprise, Tatton Winter mentioned the first sum that

came into his head – 'twelve shillings' – which the American gladly handed over. In this way, by living frugally and selling a drawing or two, the young men were able to stay on the Continent long enough to see something of Amsterdam, Leyden and Haarlem.

Before becoming known for his watercolours, Tatton Winter specialised in black-and-white work, his careful handling of detail suggesting the influence of Frederick Walker (q.v.) and J. W. North. His skilful rendering of scientific drawings came to the attention of Sidney B. Skertchley, a geologist who lived at no. 3 Loughborough Terrace, Wrythe Lane, Carshalton, Surrey. He asked Tatton Winter to do him some drawings and also invited the artist to stay with him at Carshalton, where he introduced him to Alfred Tylor, an eminent geologist who lived at Shepley House, Carshalton, a small Georgian mansion set within its own grounds. Skertchley, the editor of Tylor's works, arranged for Tatton Winter to do some illustrations for Tylor.

Alfred Tylor was the local Chairman of the Science and Art Committee, and he invited Tatton Winter to give some drawing lessons at Shepley House, where one of the latter's pupils was H.R.H. the Duchess of Albany. On Tylor's death in 1884, the classes ceased, but Tatton Winter soon organised some more at Mr Brougham's rooms at Carshalton-on-the-Hill, inviting his friend Alfred Stamford (q.v.) to run them. Tatton Winter himself started a 'drawing from the object' class, aimed at youths with no previous art training.

Tatton Winter liked this area of Surrey so much that he decided to settle in Carshalton, taking rooms in a centuries-old house, no. 3 North Street, where he kept on his studio even after he had moved elsewhere. This was in 1883; and during the same year he spent five months at the Antwerp Academy, studying art under Charles Verlat. Three years later, on 9 January 1886, he married his 'first and only love', Edith Constance Fox Hudson, a Yorkshire girl, the daughter of Thomas Hudson, a solicitor. Their first married home was Rackham Cottage in Camden Road, Carshalton; they later moved to no. 1 Parkside, Little Wrythe Lane (now no. 29 Wrythe Lane). In 1897 they left the borough for good to live in Reigate, Surrey.

The artist's fifteen years at Carshalton are very important ones to the historians of the borough. He painted at least sixty watercolours – possibly many more – showing what Carshalton and Beddington looked like during the 1880s and 1890s. He painted Carshalton's High Street, church, ponds, mills, farmhouses and cottages, and also many views of the River Wandle. His Carshalton-period sketchbook of 1890/1 (given to this borough by his grandson, John Tatton Winter) includes drawings of skaters on the ponds, studies of his pretty young wife with her baby, and sketches of the Tatton Winter family on holiday at Ramsgate in 1891. Adept as he was at making on-the-spot impressions, when the paper mill in Mill Lane caught fire on bonfire night, 1886, Tatton Winter seized a charred bit of paper, made a rapid sketch of the scene, signed it and gave it to the Chief of Carshalton Fire Brigade.

Amongst his many friends in the borough were his

WILLIAM TATTON WINTER in his garden at Ashford Villas, Church Road, Reigate, c. 1900.
Photo courtesy The Bourne Gallery, Reigate

studio partner John Burman (q.v.), and his pupil Winifred Madder (q.v.), who was responsible for the borough obtaining a collection of Tatton Winter's watercolours. Later, when he lived in Reigate, he still kept in touch with his Carshalton friends and remained a member of the Surrey Art Circle (q.v.) which he had helped to found in 1888. Some present-day residents of Carshalton own paintings by the artist, handed down by parents and grandparents. Dr A. V. Peatling, a physician and local historian, had in his collection a number of watercolours of Carshalton by Tatton Winter, which he left to his son; these are now in South Africa, but colour photographs of them are in Sutton's Local Collection.

Whilst he was living in Carshalton, Tatton Winter became firmly established as an artist; from 1885 onwards exhibiting with the Society of British Artists (later 'Royal'). He became a member of the RBA in 1896 and, in total, showed nearly three hundred works at their exhibitions. His first painting to be hung at the Royal Academy, *A Breezy Upland, Sussex*, was shown in 1889; he exhibited there regularly until 1925, showing thirty-two paintings, of which eight were submitted from Carshalton.

Camden Road, Carshalton, showing the former home of WILLIAM TATTON WINTER.

In 1897 he settled in Reigate, where he was a popular resident. He is remembered there still. Olive Holmes of Reigate Heath, who knew the family well, still owns a watercolour by Tatton Winter of the farm where she used to live. On 31 May 1913, along with the Tatton Winter family and many other citizens of Reigate, she took part in the famous Pilgrims' Pageant. This was when groups of people, dressed in the costumes of successive periods of history, from 1200–1536, wound their way along the Old Pilgrims' Path to Colley Hill, where Lord Curzon ceremoniously dedicated over sixty acres of open space to the people of Reigate. Dressed as a friar, William Tatton Winter was the captain of the 1400–1450 group, which included his wife as an abbess, his son Cecil as a bearer of the canopy, his daughter Dorothy as a servant and his other daughter Molly as a page. This group won the first prize. Tatton Winter edited the souvenir programme, his watercolour of Colley Hill forming the frontispiece.

The Tatton Winters had two other sons. Gerald, their eldest, who was born in Carshalton, later lived abroad. John Douglas died in infancy, a tragedy from which his parents never fully recovered. Their grandson John, speaking in 1981 of his childhood, revealed that he always felt he was expected to take the place of the other John. Margery (Molly) Tatton Winter married Vincent Hooper, an architect in partnership with her brother Cecil. After he died she married a Mr La Fontayne. Cecil Tatton Winter served in the army during the First World War, and considered making the army his career, but took his father's advice and became an architect instead. He designed the wrought iron gates leading to Reigate Grammar School's Garden of Remembrance in Chart Lane, and carried out several etchings and watercolours. Vincent Hooper's sister, Miriam Mabel Hooper, was one of Tatton Winter's favourite pupils; she painted watercolours in his style.

Tatton Winter was an outdoor painter who enjoyed hill-walking and climbing. A photograph, inscribed in his own hand 'The Gamekeeper', shows him with a gun in one hand, a pheasant in the other. He dressed comfortably in tweeds, wore a deerstalker hat and smoked a pipe. A convivial, approachable man with a sense of humour, he had a large circle of friends who included the artists Walter Tyndale, Henry Sylvester Stannard, David Muirhead and Lamorna Birch (with whom he often stayed in Cornwall); and he enjoyed the social evenings, which he seldom missed, at the London Sketch Club, where he was elected a member in 1902. Although he was always willing to give advice to young artists and to judge local competitions, he never allowed anything, or anyone, to interfere with his painting time.

He made frequent trips to the Continent, returning with innumerable sketches, and was a prolific artist: over two thousand paintings were found in his studio at his death. Many of these were later sold in the Windmill Galleries at Reigate and Epsom, run by his daughter Margery. But the rest remained locked away in a trunk until they were rediscovered in 1980.

Although Tatton Winter's style is distinctively his own, we are reminded of Corot in his swaying poplars and willows, of Constable in his rare seascapes and of David Cox in his landscapes with shepherds and sheep; he also shared David Cox's pre-occupation with wet weather. In 1921 he enjoyed an 'April Fool's' day joke against the avant-garde artists of the day by painting The Emotions of a Futurist having sold a picture, signing it 'Watton Tinter'. He himself said of his work that people who owned his pictures confessed to 'liking them better and better as they live longer with them . . . because there is more nature in them than the possessor first supposed'.

He was both proud and delighted when, at the gracious request of H.R.H. Princess Louise, Duchess of Argyle, he was chosen to paint a miniature for Queen Mary's Dolls' House, now at Windsor. He painted a windmill scene, one of his favourite subjects; this is now in a folder in one of the drawers in the house.

Although his reputation as an artist is based on his success as a watercolourist, he was also an oil painter, and carried out some etchings which were published by the Museum Galleries. He was successful commercially, selling to customers in this country and abroad. Various members of the Royal Family owned his paintings, including H.R.H. Princess Louise, Duchess of Argyle; H.R.H. Princess Arthur of Connaught; and Queen Victoria. However, in the years following his death his paintings attracted little attention, and only recently have they become collectable again.

To the town where he spent the last thirty years of his life, he left his finest watercolours of Reigate, which hang, appropriately enough, in the Mayor's Parlour in the Town Hall, seen and admired by hundreds of visitors each year. Sometimes, when photographs of civic occasions appear in the press, tantalising glimpses of the artist's paintings can be seen behind important heads.

William Tatton Winter died suddenly at his home, Winterfold, on 22 March 1928, having just returned there from a visit to his doctor. He had moved into Winterfold in Park Lane only a few years earlier, before that having lived in a house named Avondale, also in the South Park area of Reigate. He is buried, alongside his wife and his sons John Douglas and Cecil, in Reigate Cemetery, near St Mary's churchyard, in Chart Lane, Reigate. He is in good company. The remains of the artists John Linnell and Samuel Palmer also rest there. In June 1934 Walker's Galleries in London held a 'Tatton Winter Memorial Exhibition'.

Footnote:
In September 1981 John Tatton Winter, on behalf of his mother, Glenolva Tatton Winter (the widow of Cecil), gave sketchbooks, photographs and other items of personal interest relating to his grandfather, to Sutton's Local Collection, where they are available, on application, to anyone wishing to study the life and work of this artist.

Until 1980 they had been in the care of William's daughter-in-law, Glenolva. They were only 're-discovered' when her son John walked into the

Bourne Gallery, Reigate and asked if the gallery would be interested in a collection of paintings by his grandfather. For some years, John Robertson of the Bourne Gallery had been hoping to mount an exhibition of the artist's work but had not, until then, managed to gather together enough items. The discovery of a trunkful of 'unknown' Tatton Winters was like the answer to a prayer, and in March 1981 the gallery held an exhibition where over a hundred paintings, drawings and etchings by the artist were for sale. The 'Private View' was an unprecedented success, a queue forming an hour before the exhibition was due to open. Dealers competed with private buyers for, of course, there was considerable local interest.

John Tatton Winter wished the sketchbooks and personal items to remain in one collection. Knowing that Sutton already had a number of his grandfather's paintings, he gave them to this borough, the official presentation taking place in a ceremony at the Bourne Gallery in September 1981. A month later, some of these items were on view in an exhibition held in the Music and Arts Department of Sutton Library. In 1982, after a short illness, John Tatton Winter died, but he will always be remembered at Sutton because of his generous bequest, and for a further donation of two watercolours by his grandfather, which he gave to the borough shortly before he died.

Exhib: B; FIN; GI; I; L; N; NG; P; RA; RBA; RHA; RI; ROI; SAC; WG
Coll: Cartwright Hall, Bradford; Manchester City AG; Oldham AG; Reigate Town Hall; Royal Collection; Sutton LC; V&A
Bibliog: BEN; DBA; GW; LAMBOURNE; MALLALIEU; TB; WOOD; *Who Was Who 1916–1928*; Surrey Artists and their Homes. XIV.–Mr. W. Tatton Winter. *Sutton and Epsom Advertiser*, 28 January 1888; *William Tatton Winter, R.B.A. 1855–1928*. Catalogue of an exhibition held at the Bourne Gallery, Reigate, March 1981; Tatton Winter family archive

*WORKER, Frank 1890–1958

Sutton (address unknown) 1891–
Durweston, Manor Lane, Sutton 1916–1928
Kemble, 13 Salisbury Avenue, Cheam 1929–1958
Still remembered in this borough, where he lived throughout his life, is Frank Worker, a local builder, artist and photographer, who recorded with his camera and sketchbook the changing face of Sutton and Cheam. On hearing that a building was about to be demolished, he would rush to the scene to make sure that although it was going, it would not be forgotten. In this way he captured the death-throes of many famous local buildings – Cheam School, Cheam Park House and Lower Cheam House amongst them. In 1937 he took a photograph of Sutton Public Hall, little realising that this famous venue, built in 1878, would also end up as a pile of rubble a few years after celebrating its centenary.

Frank Worker was a student at Sutton Art School in Throwley Way, 'in its happy atmosphere of friendly refinement', and studied under W. H. Osmond (q.v.) and the visiting artist H. P. Clifford (q.v.). When Miss

Howard-Mercer (q.v.) took over as Principal, she encouraged Frank to enter the Tate Gallery, where he spent three years as a student in oil painting. He records his gratitude to her in his book *My Sketch Book . . .*

My Sketch Book . . ., published in 1952 and illustrated with Frank Worker's own drawings and photographs, contains Frank's recollections of Sutton and Cheam. Earlier, he had contributed to C. J. Marshall's (q.v.) *A History of Cheam and Sutton*, and he used some of the material from this in his own book. He died suddenly, at his home in Salisbury Avenue, on 12 June 1958, leaving a widow, Rose Worker.

Published: WORKER, F. *My Sketch Book of Cheam, Sutton, Etc., being Sketches, Photos and Prints of the Neighbourhood, from the Collection of the Author, with Notes.* Cheam: F. Worker, 1952

*YATES, Gideon fl.1803–1840

Although Gideon Yates's name is fairly well known because of his watercolours of London bridges, virtually nothing is known of his private life. His early works are views of Lancashire, giving rise to a theory that he originated there. He may have been the Gideon Yates who married Hannah Pitchforth, on 21 September 1815, at St Giles Church, Camberwell, the signature on the church register being similar to the artist's. Yates has been referred to as 'Major Yates'. The *Local Historian* (vol. 10, no. 7, p. 358) mentions a Major Yates carrying out some 'lively drawings of London Bridge', but a search through old army records has failed to locate him.

However, there is a certain military precision about his drawings which could indicate that he received some tuition in art at one of the military academies. His fences are straight, his trees and buildings stand firmly upright, everything is neat and orderly. Yet despite a certain stiffness, Yates's views of London bridges are full of interest and detail. They show not only the bridges themselves, but also the foot passengers and horse-drawn vehicles on the bridges, the traffic on the river, and the buildings along the river banks.

During the 1820s, he may have lived in or near what is now the London Borough of Sutton, since he painted at least nineteen views of the area: two of Beddington, six of Carshalton, nine of Cheam and two of Sutton. They provide a valuable record of what some of the borough's buildings looked like during the nineteenth century, especially since only a few of the ones in Yates's paintings are still standing. There may be some significance in the fact that he painted six watercolours of the old St Dunstan's Church at Cheam (the one prior to the present one) – three interior and three exterior views. This church had a monument to Sir Joseph Yates, Judge of the King's Bench, who, like Gideon, came from Lancashire and may even have been related to the artist. Sir Joseph lived in Cheam towards the end of his life, and died there, of a neglected cold, in June 1770. When the old church was pulled down, some of its monuments were transferred to the Lumley Chapel, but Sir Joseph's was not amongst them; however, there is a monument in this chapel to his daughter-in-law, Charlotte Yates.

Gideon Yates's paintings occasionally turn up for sale. In 1977 a view by Yates of London Bridge was sold at auction for £460, and in 1978, £90 was paid for a set of four views of Lancaster.

Coll: Bishopsgate Institute, London; BM; Guildhall Library, London; Sutton LC
Bibliog: BEN; MALLALIEU

YOUNG, Frances Eleanor, R.M.S. 1871–1938
The Beeches, 7 Burnell Road, Sutton 1896–1905
Frances Young, a painter of portrait miniatures, lived in Sutton for nine years, and during this period was elected a member of the Royal Miniature Society, exhibiting a total of fifty-nine works at their exhibitions. Her work was also shown at the Royal Academy and at Liverpool.

She was married to Walter William Young, a stationer. The Youngs left Sutton in 1905 to live in Richmond, Surrey, later moving to Thornton Heath, where Frances Young died, aged sixty-seven, in November 1938.

Exhib: L; RA; RMS
Bibliog: DBA; GW

YOUNGHUSBAND, Richard
Bassa, 3 Parkhurst Road, Sutton 1908–1911
Rosemorran, Woodside Road, Sutton 1912–1920
Richard Younghusband, a sculptor, lived at Sutton for twelve years. He exhibited a design entitled *Mosiac frieze* at the Royal Academy in 1912.

Exhib: RA
Bibliog: DBA

ZOFFANY, Johann 1733–1810
An interesting gem from Carshalton's past is an oil painting entitled *Mr. and Mrs. Burke of Carshalton*. In recent years it has been the subject of artistic controversy. Until at least 1970 this group portrait, now in private hands, was thought to be by the German artist Johann Zoffany, who settled in London during the second half of the eighteenth century and gained fame as a portrayer of London society and theatrical personalities.

Indeed, the gentleman on the left of the group was thought to be Zoffany himself, with his god-daughter Elizabeth, the youngest daughter of the Burke family, leaning against his knee. The picture has a freshness of style and composition that could easily be Zoffany's;

and when the painting was offered for sale at Sotheby's in 1970, then still the property of descendants of the Burke family, it was catalogued as by Zoffany but failed to reach the expected Zoffany price. It appeared again at Sotheby's in 1977, this time as 'style of Zoffany'; so it seems that academic opinion has decided that the painting is not a genuine Zoffany.

Still, whoever painted it, it remains a charming portrait of a very interesting local family. John Burke, a distant relative of the famous Edmund Burke, originally came from Ireland. Although he has been described as a 'Recorder of Carshalton', Carshalton was never a borough, so would not have had a Recorder. In the group portrait, John Burke (Bourke, in local records) looks much older than his wife; in fact Mary Burke continued to live at Carshalton, in a house which is now part of the building called Honeywood (see Edwards, Mrs L. M. (q.v.)), for ten more years after her husband's death in 1805/6. Elizabeth Burke, the child in the painting, married General Sir Richard Bourke, K.C.B., the son of John Bourke of Limerick. General Bourke was the Governor of New South Wales, Australia, in the 1830s.

Gillian Mortimer

Bibliog: BEN; LAMBOURNE; TB; WATERHOUSE; MANNERS, Lady V. and WILLIAMSON, G. C. *John Zoffany, R.A.* John Lane, 1920; Sotheby's Catalogues: 17 June, 1970; 23 November 1977; Peatling Papers, Sutton's Local Collection; *Carshalton Society Newsletter*, June 1977

CONCISE CATALOGUE OF THE WORKS IN SUTTON'S LOCAL COLLECTION BY THE ARTISTS LISTED IN THIS BOOK

Abbreviations: A=artist's own title; C=coloured; c=circa; D=drawing (pencil, pen-and-ink, crayon); d=dated; E=engraving; L=lithograph; O=oil painting; W=watercolour. Measurements; in millimetres, height before width.

ANDERSON, John Corbet 1827–1907
Carshalton Church   CL A 235×356

BARENGER, James, junior 1780–1831
Earl of Derby's Stag Hounds (d. 1823)   CE A 749×838

BENNETT, Frank Moss 1874–1953
Mount Pleasant, Beddington   O 387×286

BOOT, William Henry James
1848–1918
Carshalton Ponds   W 140×203
Wallington Green (c. 1883)   CE A 102×140

BURMAN, John 1848–1935
Sutton Common (c. 1865)   O 349×248

COWIE, Richard Kenneth 1877–1956
Norman H. Michell, Civil Defence
Controller, Borough of Sutton and
Cheam (d. 1942)   W A 343×254
Sutton and Cheam Civil Defence Chief
Warden, Lt.Col. Bunker, with his staff,
1943   W A 356×559

DIBDIN, Thomas Robert Colman
1810–1893
Beddington, Surrey (d. 1858)   W A 349×495
Our cottage at Banstead   D A 241×324
Our lane and cottage, Banstead (d.
1857)   D A 368×254

DICKINSON, Frank Reginald
1874–1961
Borth   W A 254×381
Child's head   W 292×292
Cleave Abbey   W A 267×381
Copy of Botticelli's 'Primavera'   O A 527×819
Dovey Valley from Lilys Einion   W A 267×381
Dunster   W A 254×362
Escape from the tower   D 343×165
Eynsham   W A 254×406
French 15th and 16th century
decoration   W 552×387
High Street, Carshalton (d. 1906)   W A 260×184
Houses of Parliament across the
Thames (d. 1922)   W 305×597
In Memoriam   O A 762×432
Leith Hill   W A 229×394
Little Holland House, 40 Beeches
Avenue   W A 318×425
Mrs. Davis, The Rose and Crown, The
Quay, Wivenhoe   W A 343×241

The new order: a proposed
reconstruction scheme creating a civic
centre at High Street, Carshalton   W A 381×660
The painted house: designed by FRD   W A 387×559
Proposed civic centre at the High
Street, Carshalton   W A 737×533
River Ashop at 'Snake Inn' (d. 1937)   W A 318×457
Steep Hill Cove, Isle of Wight   W A 241×318
Thames above Oxford   W A 279×445
Nineteen miscellaneous watercolours,
comprising five river views; two views
of an unnamed house and grounds (d.
1937); two seascapes; two landscapes
with sheep; and eight various rural
scenes
NB: Well over a hundred works by
Frank Dickinson in various media are
held in Sutton's Local Collection. Many
of them are on view at Little Holland
House, Carshalton, the former home of
the artist (see Little Holland House,
published by the London Borough of
Sutton, 1974)

DRAGE, John Henry 1856–1914
Carshalton Upper Pond with horses
and carts in the ford (pre-1884)   W 660×956

GILPIN, William 1724–1804
Landscape view of mountains, river
and bridge   W 267×362

GOLDTHWAIT, Harold 1869–1932
Orchard Hill Cottages   W 273×368

GRIFFITHS, Tom 1887–1986
Anne Boleyn's Well (d. 1971)   W 229×381
Butter Hill (d. 1968)   W 273×381
Carshalton Church and Pond   W A 292×381
Carshalton Church and Pond 1887 (d.
1970)   W A 279×394
Carshalton Church and Pond (d. 1971)   W A 292×387
Carshalton Church and Pond with
black-headed gull, South African grey-
headed duck, a pair of mallard and a
coot (d. 1971)   W A 292×387
Carshalton Church, south side (d.
1972)   W A 292×387
Carshalton Church, south side (d.
1972)   W A 254×356
Carshalton High Street, looking east   W 273×381
Carshalton High Street, looking west   W 254×356
Carshalton Park gates   W 254×365
Carshalton Park grotto and water (d.
1972)   W A 273×368
Carshalton Pond (d. 1972)   W A 292×394
Cheam Park Barn   W A 292×394
Cock Hotel and High Street, Sutton   W 273×381
Cock Inn, Sutton (d. 1971)   W A 273×368
Crowd scene at The Cock Inn   W 267×356
Daisy bank on railway near Albert
Road, Sutton (d. 1961)   W A 254×356

141

Dame Duffin's 16th century cottage (d. 1973) W A 292×381

Flint cottage next to Sutton Station, 1875 (d. 1963) W A 184×235

The Greyhound Inn, Sutton W 279×337

Harwood's butcher's shop, Carshalton High Street W 267×368

High Street, Sutton, by West Street W 273×368

Margaret's Pool, with fanciful wildlife (d. 1969) W 286×394

Mr Bill Wood's lavender fields, near Oaks Park W 267×356

The old pump, Pound Street, Carshalton W 254×356

A scene in The Grove W A 375×241

The site of Croydon Aerodrome c. 1910 (d. 1968) W A 356×533

Wallington Green (d. 1970) W A 260×356

Wandle Lodge, Pound Street, Carshalton W 470×292

Whitehall [Cheam] (d. 1971) W A 292×394

Willows, Carshalton Place (d. 1971) W A 292×394

HARDEN, John 1772–1847

Lower Town Pond, Carshalton (d. 1842) (1905 autotype) D A 171×229

Upper Town Pond, Carshalton (d. 1835) (1905 autotype) D A 171×229

HASSELL, John 1767–1825

Cheam Church from the west (d. 1823) W 152×197

[Lower Cheam House] Sir Edward Antrobus (d. 1823) W A 159×203

New Parsonage [Cheam Rectory] (d. 1823) W A 159×203

Tower entrance to [Cheam] church (d. 1824) W A 152×197

Whitehall, Cheam (c. 1823/4) W 152×197

HILLS, Robert 1769–1844

The Fords, Beddington W A 222×191

HOWARD, Margaret Maitland 1898–1983

Adam and Eve in the Garden of Eden O 635×762

George Medallist from the rescue squad (1) O A 610×508

George Medallist from the rescue squad (2) O A 616×508

JARVIS, Henry Charles 1867–1955

Cheam from near Banstead W A 159×254

LEONI, Giacomo c.1686–1746

Engravings by B. Picart of Leoni's proposed designs for a mansion in Carshalton Park

The Elevation of the East Front of Carshalton House . . . (d. 1723) E A 432×838

The Elevation of the Greenhouse [Orangery] in Carshalton House . . . (d. 1723) E A 432×838

The Elevation of the West Front of Carshalton House . . . (d. 1723) E A 432×838

LIVENS, Horace Mann 1862–1936

Study of fowls E 140×305

MADDER, E. Winifred 1883–1972

The Baking Oven, Strawberry Cottage, Station Road (d. 1915) W A 197×152

Beach's Mill near Hackbridge (c. 1920) W A 184×286

Beevers Cottages [Wrythe Lane] (early 20th century) W A 197×292

Carshalton Church looking West from Lady Chapel (d. 1914) W A 241×165

Carshalton High Street (d. 1914) W A 318×241

Carshalton [High Street] (d. 1920) W A 229×311

Carshalton Parish Church; interior view (c. 1920) D 305×229

Carshalton Park Grotto (d. 1920) W A 165×241

Church Hill, Carshalton W 178×184

Cottages belonging to Hill Farm, top of Green Wrythe Lane (c. 1920) W A 191×260

End of Garden at Westcroft (c. 1920) W A 254×203

Green Wrythe Lane (c. 1910–20) W A 292×216

Green Wrythe Lane from The Culvers Avenue, looking north (d. 1911) W 298×210

The Greyhound Inn, Carshalton, from the Upper Pond (d. 1918) W 178×254

Meadows by Robert's [Mill] W A 241×343

Mill Lane, Carshalton, 1888 (after H. Romer) W A 178×260

A Mill on the Wandle, 1888 (after H. Romer) W A 298×210

Mill Wheel, Butter Hill (c. 1920) W A 254×356

North Street, Carshalton (d. 1913) W 191×146

Old Rectory, now college of St. Saviours (c. 1920) W A 184×279

The Paper Mill, Mill Lane, 1888 (after H. Romer) W A 254×178

Pound Street (d. 1919) W A 146×197

The Processional Way, Carshalton Church, looking North (c. 1920) W A 248×165

The Processional Way, Carshalton Church, looking South (c. 1920) W A 273×178

Robert's Mill, Beddington Corner (c. 1931) O A 343×445

Site of Windborough Road, off Stanley Park Road (d. 1913) W 229×330

South aisle of Carshalton Church (d. 1917) W A 191×279

Strawberry Cottage, North St. (d. 1912) W A 165×248

Strawberry Lane, leading to Butter Hill (c. 1920) W A 171×248

Unidentified view (note on back says 'Mill Green') (c. 1920) W 235×343

Unveiling of War Memorial at Carshalton, Sunday, March 13 1921 W 146×197

West Street, Carshalton, looking south from the corner of West Street Lane (c. 1920) W A 191×216

Westcroft Farmhouse, Carshalton (d. 1920) W A 203×311

Woodman's shop (d. 1920) W 197×235

142

Woodman's shop from the South (d. 1920) W A 235×229

Wrythe Lane above Prince of Wales Road W 298×197

Wrythe Lane, looking over Carshalton (c. 1920) W A 165×248

Group of four unframed watercolours of Carshalton Church, two interior, two exterior views, various sizes

MAISEY, Thomas 1787–1840
Cheam School (c. 1835) engraved after a drawing by Maisey CE A 165×241

MARSHALL, John Fitz 1859–1932
Mills at Butter Hill from Butter Hill Bridge (d. 1890) O 445×381

MOORE, Dorothy Winifred 1897–1973
At Sunset, Berwickshire Coast (d. 1922) W A 241×368
Eglwys Rocks, Llangollen (d. 1956) W A 267×470
In Gosford Park, East Lothian (d. 1930) W A 235×152
Quai du Miroir, Bruges (d. 1930) W A 248×356
River view with bridge (d. 1922) W 267×368
Self-portrait (oval) O 368×457

NASH, Joseph 1803–1878
Beddington, Surrey: The Hall CL A 375×305
View of Beddington Manor House, Surrey L A 197×406
East view of Beddington House L A 197×406

POLLARD, James 1792–1867
'Scenes on the Road, or A Trip to Epsom and Back'
Plate One: Hyde Park Corner CE A 394×508
Plate Two: Lord Nelson Inn, Cheam CE A 394×508
Plate Three: The Cock, Sutton CE A 394×508
Plate Four: Kennington Gate CE A 394×508
Published by Ackermann, 1838.
Engraved by J. Harris

PORDEN, William, attrib. c. 1755–1822
Cheam School (c. 1810–25) W A 140×203

POWELL, Joseph c. 1780–c. 1834
Dame Duffin's Cottage (c. 1792) D 114×159
The Grotto in Carshalton Park (c. 1792) D 108×152
A pair of sketches of a Carshalton mill, mounted together (identified as the snuff mill, later the Grove Iron Works) D 159×159 each
A pair of sketches of a farm at Carshalton D 108×152 each

ROWLANDSON, Thomas 1756–1827
Sutton [a view of the Old Cock Hotel] (d. 1790) CE A 222×292

SKELSEY, Maud
House on the site of the present Rectory (c. 1920) W A 178×267

STACEY, Doris Marion
Camouflage [making camouflage nets in St Philomena's Convent] W A 616×972

STARLING, Albert 1858–1947
View of the Barrow Hedges or Banstead Downs area (c. 1900) O 248×495
View of Westmead farmland, at the bottom of Highfield Road (c. 1900) O 241×495

STARLING, Matthew James 1805–1889
The Hall, Beddington House (after T. Allom) (d. 1850) E A 159×108

SWAN, Laura
Carshalton Mill (c. 1890) W A 254×356

TRAVERS, Norah Kathleen 1858–1922
Cottages in Malden Road, Cheam W 171×248
Red Lion Street at the corner of the High Street, Cheam W 171×248

TURNER, Sydney Robert 1880–1972
Nonsuch House on old London Bridge 1577–1757 (d. 1956) CD A 521×749
The Palace of Nonsuch: approximate plan (d. 1946) CD A 724×457
The Palace of Nonsuch at Cuddington in Surrey, built by King Henry VIII (looking NW) CD A 616×464
The Palace of Nonsuch at Cuddington in Surrey, built by King Henry VIII (looking SE) CD A 622×457
The Palace of Nonsuch in the time of Queen Elizabeth (d. 1943) CD A 419×616
The Palace of Nonsuch: Inner court from the Privy Gallery CD A 438×692
The Palace of Nonsuch: the Inner court, Privy Gallery elevation CD A 438×692
The Palace of Nonsuch: Inner court, south facing elevation (d. 1945) CD A 438×699
The Palace of Nonsuch: Inner court, west elevation CD A 445×699
The Palace of Nonsuch: the south front and Privy Garden CD A 610×438
The Palace of Nonsuch: the west turret from the Inner court CD A 616×394

WARDALE, J. J.
Carshalton; Recreation Ground, the Wrythe (d. 1904) O A 356×533
View of Carshalton Church from across the ponds (c. 1900) O 356×457
Recreation Ground, the Wrythe (d. 1902) O A 343×521

WATTS, William 1752–1851
Carshalton House. In Surrey (d. 1783) E A 191×203
Carshalton, Chateau de Theodore Henri Broadhead, Ecuyer (engraved in colours by Laurent Guyot, after Watts) (d. 1793) CE A 191×203

WINTER, William Tatton 1855–1928
All Saints' Church, Carshalton, and
Harwood's butcher's shop | W 349×248
Bridge and Ford, The Wandle near
Mitcham (c. 1890) | W A 235×330
The Blue House, Mitcham Common (c.
1890) | W A 292×445
Butter Hill, Carshalton | W 273×419
Carshalton Church from across the
ponds | W 133×229
Carshalton Church from across the
Upper Pond (d. 1890) | W 267×222
Carshalton Church: interior view
showing the choir stalls (d. 1917) | W 318×178
Carshalton Downs (c. 1880) | W A 235×324
Carshalton High Street, looking west
(d. 1880) | W 406×686
Carshalton Lawn Tennis and Cricket
Club, Prince of Wales Road (d. 1893) | W 171×292
Carshalton Village in the '80s | W A 483×813
The Fords, Beddington | W 248×165
Girl with geese, Mitcham (d. 1895) | W A 235×324
Goose girl in Park Road, Banstead | W 286×381
Green Wrythe Lane (c. 1910) | W A 292×216
Grove Ferry, Carshalton | W A 229×279
Landscape with man, dog and sheep
(d. 1884) | W 146×222
Landscape with sheep and trees | W 578×451
The Old Hack Bridge, view from the
north-east | W 165×311
Old Mill, Beddington | W 241×171
Simms Farm (d. 1918) | W A 216×273
Snuff Mill, Carshalton (c. 1900) | W A 241×489
The Strid [near Bolton Abbey,
Yorkshire] | W A 445×292
The Wandle at Mitcham (d. 1885) | W 235×165
Watercress Beds, Mill Lane
[Carshalton]. On East Side of The
Grove, about 1888 | W A 267×140
Watercress study | W 267×140
West Street Lane | W 171×133

*The following are unsigned, but are
attributed to William Tatton Winter*
Bridge over a river | W 203×260
Carshalton High Street (d. 1894) | D 273×216
Carshalton Village, view from the east | W 235×330
Carshalton; Winter scene | W 260×470

Footpath beside Carshalton Church | D 229×171
Honeywood, Carshalton | W 197×254
Mill at Butter Hill, latterly known as the
Grove Ironworks (c. 1880) | W 686×457
Snuff Mill, Carshalton (d. 1884) | W 178×254
The Wandle near Beddington Corner | W 241×305
West Street Lane | W 121×159

WORKER, Frank 1890–1958
Cheam House from Malden Road,
Surrey, from Mr. Sergeant's
photograph | D A 133×210
Cheam House from Park Lane, Surrey,
from Mr. Sergeant's photograph | D A 152×203
Lower Cheam House (d. 1932) | O A 292×432

YATES, Gideon
Barrow Hedges, Carshalton. –
Quinton, Esq. (d. 1825) | W A 165×248
Barrow Hedges, Carshalton. –
Quinton, Esq. (d. 1825) | W A 133×222
Beddington, Old Farm House, Mrs.
Gee's (d. 1825) | W A 159×260
Beddington, Old Farm House, reputed
to be the original Manor House, Mrs.
Gee (d. 1825) | W A 159×260
Carshalton National Schools (d. 1826) | W A 140×248
Carshalton, North West view of the
Waterhouse (c. 1820) | W A 146×229
Chancel, Cheam Church (d. 1826) | W A 165×267
Cheam Church (d. 1826) | W 267×191
Cheam Church from the sout-east | W A 140×200
Cheam Church, N.E. view (d. 1826) | W A 165×267
[Font] Cheam Church (d. 1826) | W A 229×159
Monument to Phillip Antrobus, Esq.,
Cheam Church (d. 1826) | W A 241×152
National Schools, Cheam (d. 1826) | W A 152×248
North view of the Waterhouse.
Carshalton, Surrey (d. 1825) | W A 146×229
The Rectory House, Sutton (d. 1826) | W A 152×235
Rye Farm, Hoare Esq. (d. 1826) | W A 159×241
Sutton [church font] (d. 1826) | W A 210×152
View of the Manor House of East
Cheam | W A 140×210
Attributed to Yates
Ancient gateway to the Manor House
of East Cheam (c. 1810) | W A 210×140

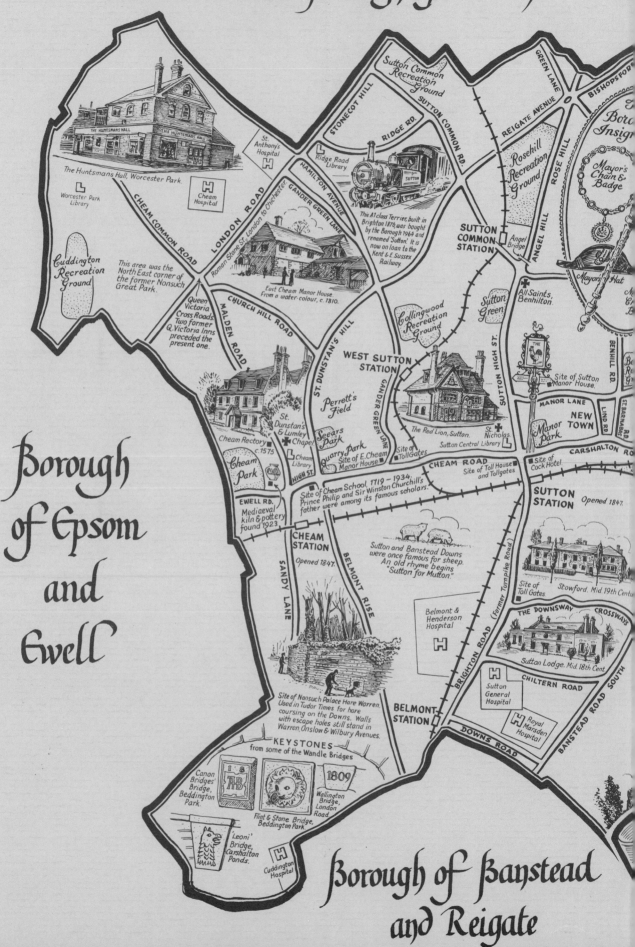

London Borough of Merton

Borough of Epsom and Ewell

Borough of Banstead and Reigate

The Huntsmans Hall, Worcester Park.

Worcester Park Library

Cuddington Recreation Ground

This area was the North East corner of the former Nonsuch Great Park.

CHEAM COMMON ROAD

LONDON ROAD

St. Anthony's Hospital

Ridge Road Library

Cheam Hospital

Queen Victoria Cross Roads. Two former Q.Victoria Inns preceded the present one.

Roman Stane St. London to Chichester

GANDER GREEN LANE

HAMILTON AVENUE

East Cheam Manor House. From a water-colour, c. 1810.

STONECOT HILL

RIDGE RD.

SUTTON COMMON RD.

Sutton Common Recreation Ground

This A1 class Terrier, built in Brighton 1876, was bought by the Borough 1964 and renamed 'Sutton'. It is now on loan to the Kent & E. Sussex Railway.

REIGATE AVENUE

ROSE HILL

Rosehill Recreation Ground

GREEN LANE

BISHOPSFORD

Borough Insignia

Mayor's Chain & Badge

Mayor's Hat

SUTTON COMMON STATION

Angel Bridge

ANGEL HILL

All Saints, Benhilton.

BENHILL RD.

Sutton Green

Site of Sutton Manor House.

THE

MALDEN ROAD

CHURCH HILL ROAD

ST. DUNSTAN'S HILL

Perrett's Field

WEST SUTTON STATION

GANDER GREEN LANE

SUTTON HIGH ST.

Collingwood Recreation Ground

Cheam Rectory c.1575

St. Dunstan's & Lumley Chapel

Cheam Library

Sears Park

Quarry Park

Site of E. Cheam Manor House

The Red Lion, Sutton.

St. Nicholas.

Sutton Central Library

MANOR LANE

NEW TOWN

LIND RD.

ST. BARNABAS

Manor Park

CARSHALTON RD.

Cheam Park

HIGH ST.

EWELL RD.

Mediaeval kiln & pottery found 1923.

Site of Cheam School, 1719 – 1934. Prince Philip and Sir Winston Churchill's father were among its famous scholars.

Site of Toll Gates

CHEAM ROAD

Site of Toll House and Tollgates

Site of Cock Hotel

Site of Sutton Manor House.

SUTTON STATION

Opened 1847.

CHEAM STATION

Opened 1847.

SANDY LANE

BELMONT RISE

Sutton and Banstead Downs were once famous for sheep. An old rhyme begins "Sutton for Mutton"

Belmont & Henderson Hospital

Site of Toll Gates

Stowford. Mid 19th Cent.

BRIGHTON ROAD (Former Turnpike Road)

THE DOWNSWAY

CROSSWAYS

Sutton Lodge. Mid 18th Cent.

CHILTERN ROAD

Sutton General Hospital

Royal Marsden Hospital

BANSTEAD ROAD SOUTH

Site of Nonsuch Palace Hare Warren. Used in Tudor Times for hare coursing on the Downs. Walls with escape holes still stand in Warren, Onslow & Wilbury Avenues.

BELMONT STATION

DOWNS ROAD

KEYSTONES from some of the Wandle Bridges

Canon Bridges' Bridge, Beddington Park.

A B

Flint & Stone Bridge, Beddington Park.

1809

Wallington Bridge, London Road.

'Leoni' Bridge, Carshalton Ponds.

Cuddington Hospital